Root, Throne, and Crown of Higher Education

ROOT, THRONE AND CROWN OF HIGHER EDUCATION

Editors

Dr. Preeti Oza

Dr. Gurudutta P. Japee

AUTHORSPRESS

Worldwide Circulation through Authorspress Global Network
First Published in 2019
by
Authorspress
Q-2A Hauz Khas Enclave, New Delhi-110 016 (India)
Phone: (0) 9818049852
E-mail: authorspressgroup@gmail.com
Website: www.authorspressbooks.com

Root, Throne, and Crown of Higher Education
ISBN 978-93-89110-18-0

Printed in India at Thomson Press (India) Ltd.

Introduction

Education is a process of facilitating learning or acquiring specific knowledge, values, habits beliefs or skills. Education has been the parameter of human development and there are many methods of education which are accepted by men as a part of the evolution process and also as a part of the acculturation process. Many methods are established for education; like discussion, training, oral imparting of instruction and knowledge, storytelling or the latest ones like the research and development. The methodology of teaching is called pedagogy.

In English, the term "Education" has been derived from two Latin words Educare (Educere) and Educatum. "Educare" means to train or mould. It also means to bring up or to lead out or to draw out, propulsion from inward to outward. The term "Educatum" denotes the act of teaching. It throws light on the principles and practice of teaching. The term Educare or Educere mainly indicates the development of the latent faculties of the learner.

As Dr. Radhakrishnan has rightly put it "education according to Indian tradition is not merely a means of earning a living, nor it is only a nursery of thought for school for citizenship. It is an initiation into the life of spirit and training of human souls in the pursuit of truth and practice of virtue."

As John Dewey puts it "education is not a preparation for life, rather it is the living. Education is the process of living through a continuous reconstruction of experiences. It is the development of all those capacities in the individual which will enable him to control his environment and fulfill his possibilities".

Education is different from Learning as Learning is a process of acquiring new knowledge or modifying or changing the existing knowledge which also includes a change in values, changes in reference, or change in behavior. Education can take place in a formal or informal setting whereas Learning usually takes place in a predefined or set environment. Education provides an experience which has a formative effect on a person's way of thinking, feeling or acting as a part of being educated. Whereas Learning is also known as an 'ability', which is possessed not only by humans but animals also, and of late, even machines. Some Learning is immediate and some are a gradual process of knowledge or skill accumulation, usually from the repeated experiences. So we can generalise that education which is a bit of formerly induced experience can have a limited time span whereas Learning is often a lifetime process and usually the changes induced by learning are often long-lasting. Educational learning to gain knowledge is a very systematic procedure adopted by mankind in various evolutionary phases.

Knowledge is defined as familiarity, awareness or understanding of someone or something such as facts, information, descriptions or skills which is acquired through experience or education by perceiving discovering or learning. Education is a gradual process which is targeted towards bringing in some positive changes for the betterment of human life and behavior. So with the reference to this, we can also define Education as a process of acquiring knowledge through study or imparting the knowledge by way of instructions or some other practical procedure. Education encourages us to distinguish between right and wrong and usually, it is the benchmarking of mental, emotional and social development. Education throughout life is based on four main pillars:

- learning to know
- learning to do
- learning to live together
- and learning to be.

The book *Root, Throne and Crown of Higher Education* is designed to understand this comprehensive and in-depth process, concept, theories and methodologies of higher education.

The idea of this book has been taken from the multi-dimensional concept of education, where education is utilised in three different senses – Knowledge, Subject and Process. To understand this multiplicity, this book will touch upon the following areas:

- Meaning and Concept of Education,
- Analysis of Education
- Aims and Scope of Education.

The editors of this book have planned all the chapters to influence the overall perception of education in India. The influences or modes of influences as discussed in this book are deliberately planned, chosen and analysed by the experienced faculty members for the welfare of the stakeholders of the rising generation the purpose of this book is to modify the perception and behavior of all the stakeholders of the higher education in such a way that it makes possible for a better adjustment of human nature in general and learners in particular consciously develop and cultivate the inert powers of Higher Education.

The Root, Throne, and Crown of education discussed here in this book form almost 360 degrees perspective. It is divided into three parts.

PART I – ROOT OF HIGHER EDUCATION

The base or the root of Higher Education always lies in the equity and equality for all. Some of the topics discussed in this part are:

- Role of spirituality in higher education
- Importance and aspects of spirituality in higher education
- Role of Vedas in higher education
- Creativity in higher education
- Learning achievements in higher education through the application of scientific methods.

PART II – THRONE OF HIGHER EDUCATION

Throne makes the strongest part and that is the most visible part of the higher education which is also keeping it connected to the rot and keeps it grounded through the strongest base. This part covers topics like:

- Skills and higher education
- Enlightenment in higher education
- Knowledge in higher education
- Academic freedom in higher education
- Skilled knowledge in higher education.

PART III – CROWN OF HIGHER EDUCATION

This is the part which is getting the maximum attraction and also shows the most visible as well as an attractive part of the higher education. This part includes topics like:

- Internationalisation of Higher Education
- Understanding psychology in higher education
- Major theoretical aspects in the sociology of Higher Education
- Politics of Higher Education
- Management of Higher Education
- Economics of Higher Education
- Role of finance in higher education
- History of higher education from ancient to the modern
- Language and literature of Higher Education
- Higher education statistics in India and
- Need for innovation in higher education.

The first two parts of the book deal with the first two pillars of learning to know is basically a combination of sufficiently broad general knowledge with the skill and ability to work on a small number of subjects or concepts. In general, this is known as *'learning to learn'* so as to benefit from the opportunities which education provides to us throughout life. The second pillar is called *'learning to do'* which is required in order to acquire not only survival and occupational skills but also the competence to deal with many life situations and practical knowledge. It implies to learning to do in the context of young learners in various socio-cultural experiences which are not very formal in nature but as a result of the local or national context involving different courses different pedagogy and a different set of the learning environment. The third pillar is called '*learning to live together*' or what we call a Social skill. This is imparted by the formal education from the very childhood and it is done through developing an understanding of other people other culture other environment and the general otherness and acceptance and appreciation of individuality and also interdependence. This is the most useful pillar of learning because it teaches us how to manage conflicts with respect to values mutual understanding and mutual living experience. The fourth pillar is known as '*learning to be*' and it is a highly individualistic development related personality aspect which helps us to act with higher and greater autonomy judgment and personal responsibility in various situations. This pillar is considered to be the most understated aspect of education but it also touches upon a complete personality of a person including memory reasoning aesthetic sense physical fitness personality and communication skills.

We are always indebted to our guru Shree Prashant Dave sir for keeping our spark of inquiry intact which makes us go for many such innovative academic ventures.

We hope and wish to make small but significant value addition in the field of Higher education with this book.

Dr. Preeti Oza
Dr. Gurudutta P. Japee

Contents

PART I
THE ROOT OF HIGHER EDUCATION

1

Equity and Equality in Higher Education

Dr. Preeti Oza

ABSTRACT

Higher education in India is always a socio-political way and a powerful engine of social mobility. It adds to the benefits to society as more people earning Higher Education credentials. It is proven that college graduates earn more. They are less likely to be unemployed. They are more likely to vote, more likely to volunteer, and more likely to maintain good health. India as a Globalised and developing nation has been little systematically progressing on the educational front since its independence. The government is making progress in reaching out to all the classes of its society. The improvement in the country's economic front has resulted in the upscaling of communication technology. The advent of the internet, have vastly leveraged the promotion of education across all verticals.

Keywords: Higher education, Equity, Equality, Socio-political barriers

According to UNESCO's Report of the International Commission on Education for the Twenty-first Century, education must be organised around four fundamental types of learning: the four pillars of knowledge – learning to know, i.e., acquiring the instruments of understanding; learning to do, so as to be able to act creatively in one's environment; learning to live together, so as to participate and cooperate with other people in all human activities; and learning to be, an essential progression which proceeds from the previous three (Delors,

1996). Formal education has traditionally been focused mainly, if not exclusively, on learning to know and to a lesser degree on learning to do. Learning to live together is an essential part of the socialization process of formal education. (Agarwal, 2006)

The multi-fold growth in all the sectors in India since the last ten years has been remarkable. The accelerated growth of the educational sector in the last decade is a sparkling testimony to this fact. These are some facts and figures showing an unprecedented improvement in higher education in India.

- The 'Right to Education Act' which stipulates compulsory and free education to all children within the age groups of 6-14 years, has brought about a revolution in the education system of the country.
- It has resulted in a staggering enrolment in schools over the last four years.
- The educational movement has been receiving tremendous government support through comprehensive planning in its various five-year plans.
- For the first time, we can see the active involvement of the private sector in the field of Education. The involvement of the private sector in higher education has seen drastic changes in the field. Today over 60% of higher education institutions in India are promoted by the private sector.
- This has supported the establishment of institutes which have originated over the last decade making India home to the largest number of Higher Education institutions in the world, with student enrolments at the second highest.

But even after such a huge leap and development, there is still no balance of Equity and Equality in Higher education. There are many problem areas where this imbalance is quite visible:

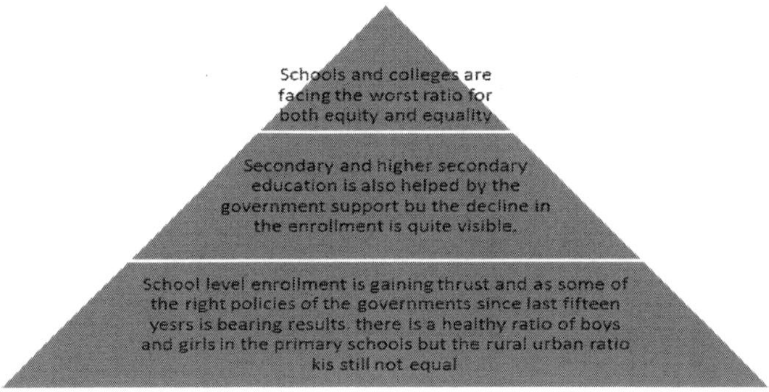

Hierarchy in the enrolment equity in the growth of education

As per the latest ASER report 2019 (http:// www.aser centre.org/):

> An Overview of Higher Education in India India's higher education system stands third in size in the world after the US and China with nearly 26 million students in over 45,000 institutions in the country. In the last decade, the country has witnessed a particularly high growth rate in student enrolment at a CAGR of 10.8% and institutions at 9%. The University Grants Commission (UGC) which enforces its standards is the main governing body at the tertiary level and advises the government, coordinating between the center and the state. Accreditation for higher learning is monitored by twelve autonomous bodies established by the UGC. Indian higher education has been progressing at a fast pace adding over 20,000 colleges and about 8 million students between the ten year periods 2001-2011. As of 2011, the Indian higher education system is spread over 42 central universities, 275 state universities, 130 deemed universities and 90 private universities.

Additionally, 5 institutions were established functioning under the State Act, along with 33 Institutes of National

Importance. Nearly 33,000 institutions function as Government and Private Degree Colleges which also include 1800 exclusive women's colleges. Today the number of private higher education institutions stands at 64% and enrolments at 59% of the total number of institutions and enrolments in the country. This is a significant jump from the statistics of the decade before where private institutions stood at 43% enrolments at 33% and is an obvious index to an improving educational system through private participation. The current emphasis in Indian higher education has been mostly on science and technology. Distance learning and open education also is an essential feature of the Indian higher education system. Indira Gandhi National Open University run by the Indian government is attributed to be the largest university in the world by a number of students with over 3.5 million students from across the globe.

Premium institutions of India, such as the Indian Institutes of Technology (IITs), Indian Institutes of Management (IIMs), National Institute of Technology (NITs) and Jawaharlal Nehru University have attained global acclamation for their high standard of education. About 8000 students are enrolled annually by the IITs and the alumni have made significant contributions to both the growth of the private sector and the public sectors of India. While figures convey a positive picture of the growth of higher education, in terms of Gross Enrolment Ration – GER, India remains at a dismal 16% against the global average of 26%. Though the government has undertaken several initiatives for the inclusion of all communities in its educational front its success has largely been questionable. Delivery of quality higher education has become a severe shortcoming in governance with several issues posing an overwhelming challenge.

At the end of the eleventh five-year plan 2007-2012, India has achieved a Gross Enrolment Ration – GER 17.9% upward from 12.3% from the beginning of the plan period. The twelfth five-year plan of the Indian government for 2012-1217 envisages several revolutionary initiatives to exponentially improve the quality and reach of higher education across the length and breadth of the country. (Courtesy- http://www.asercentre.org/)

EQUITY OR EQUALITY?

Sometimes we use these terms 'equity' and 'equality' in an interchangeable agreement. There is a common misconception that equity and equality mean the same thing and that they can be used interchangeably, especially when talking about education. But the truth is they do not – and cannot. Yes, the two words are similar, but the difference between them is crucial. If the government is funding education of all the students in every college, this is a matter of Equality. But the admission in the college on the basis of merit and aptitude is a matter of Equity.

(Credit: United Way of the Columbia-Willamette)

It is an important goal to make sure that all students have *equal* access to resources. Especially in a country like India which has a very strong history of Socialism, all students should have the resources necessary for high-quality education. But the truth remains that some students need *more* to get there.

India's multicultural; multi-ethnic and multilingual socio-culture milieu requires a great deal of equity for learners in various education frameworks. Students from poor economic class or the lower social class need a bigger push to come to a common ground to even start the competition. Here's where equity comes in. The students who are furthest behind because of the difference in socio-economic status require more resources to catch-up, succeed and eventually reach the same level as others. Many government schemes and policy decisions have helped to bridge this gap in the last many years but there is much left to be done still. Equality has become synonymous with "leveling the playing field." So let's make equity synonymous with "more for those who need it."

Equity in Higher Education

Equity in Higher Education is a measure of achievement, fairness, and opportunity in education. We cannot discuss education equity without studying equality and equal opportunity. For school level education, there are different challenges to getting equity. OECD, in its policy document, has provided some guidelines for it.

The OECD has recommended ten steps which would reduce school failure and dropout rates, make society fairer and avoid the large social costs of marginalised adults with few basic skills. Design

1. Limit early tracking and streaming and postpone academic selection.
2. Manage school choice so as to contain the risks to equity.
3. In upper secondary education, provide attractive alternatives, remove dead ends and prevent dropout.
4. Offer second chances to gain from education. Practices
5. Identify and provide systematic help to those who fall behind at school and reduce year repetition.
6. Strengthen the links between school and home to help disadvantaged parents help their children to learn.
7. Respond to diversity and provide for the successful inclusion of migrants and minorities within mainstream education. Resourcing
8. Provide strong education for all, giving priority to early childhood provision and basic schooling.
9. Direct resources to the students with the greatest needs.
10. Set concrete targets for more equity, particularly related to low school attainment and dropouts. (https://www.oecd.org/education/school/39989494.pdf)

But when it comes to Higher Education, India faces many challenges as far as the idea of Equity is concerned. First is there is no Fairness and the second is, there is no Inclusion. There are many factors which interfere with the academic profile and success of a student. Economic, social, political and many other factors directly or indirectly affect the decision and process of higher education. The growing importance of education equity is based on the premise that an individual's level of education directly correlates to the future quality of life. Therefore, an academic system that practices educational equity is a strong foundation of a society that is fair and thriving. However, inequity in education is challenging to avoid and can be broken down into inequity due to socioeconomic standing, race, gender or disability. Educational equity is also based in the historical context of the location, people and structure. History shapes the outcome of individuals within the education system

Factors Affecting Equity in Higher Education

Equity recognises that some are at a larger disadvantage than others and aims at compensating for these peoples misfortunes and disabilities to ensure that everyone can attain the same type of healthy lifestyle. Examples of this are:

- When government and NGOs offer literacy programs
- When schools/ Colleges offer courses in English or Communication Skills as a second language,
- When NGOs, Trusts, Philanthropists, and foundations target scholarships to students from poor families
- They operationalise a belief in the equity of access as fairness and as justice.

Equity recognises this uneven playing field and aims to take extra measures by giving those who are in need more than others who are not. Equity aims at making sure that everyone's lifestyle is equal even if it may come at the cost of unequal distribution of access and goods. Social justice leaders in education strive to ensure equitable outcomes for their students.

Equity can be accessed from the context of the position of the learner in the state/ society. Some students coming from the lower socio-political background need more hand-holding to come to the level of similarity to compete with the other mainstream students.

Equality

The American Library Association defines equality as: "access to channels of communication and sources of information that is made available on even terms to all – a level playing field – is derived from the concept of fairness as uniform distribution, where everyone is entitled to the same level of access and can avail themselves if they so choose."

In this definition of equality, no one person has an unfair advantage. Everyone is given equal opportunities and accessibility and are then free to do what they please with it. However, this is not to say that everyone is then inherently equal. Some people may choose to seize these open and equal opportunities while others let them pass by. In India, the deep-rooted social class structure and the newly developed economic disparities are the biggest challenges for any norm of Equality in higher education.

Challenges for Equity and Equality in Higher education in India:

- *Social Equity and Equality:* India is facing a multi-faceted challenge for social equilibrium. Multi-culture, multi-castes, multi-languages, multi-regionality, and multi-religion are making India a very dynamic milieu to propose and provide any Equity and equality for education.
- Gender equity and equality
- Economic Equity and Equality
- Low-income students today are just now enrolling at the same rate high-income students did 40 years ago.
- Low-income students and students of lower castes are far less likely than other students to enroll in institutions

where most students graduate and far more likely to enroll in institutions that graduate few of their students and saddle them with excessive expenditure on education.

- Even after accounting for all grant aid, low-income students must finance an amount equivalent to 76 percent of their family's annual income to attend a public university for one year – a far higher burden than the 17 percent required for higher income students.
- The bachelor's degree attainment rate among Black adults is just over half that of White adults, and the rate among Latino adults is even lower – just over one-third that of White adults.
- Students from high-income families are approximately five times as likely as students from low-income families to obtain a bachelor's degree.
- These disparities result in far too many low-income people and people of lower castes being denied the dream of economic opportunity and upward mobility. And communities and states being denied the talented and diverse workforce so desperately needed to compete in this economy.

Left unchallenged, these disparities will be even more devastating as our nation's population grows ever more diverse. People of lower castes already make up the majority of our nation's young people. And by 2030, the population of Dalits and other marginal groups will increase by 20% more. The implications are clear: For these students' sake and for our nation's collective sake, more students of lower socio-economic strata and students from low-income families must get to college and graduate.

REFERENCES

1. (https://www.econstor.eu/bitstream/10419/176564/1/WP180-Higher-Education-in-India.pdf)
2. Agarwal, Pawan. *Higher education in India: The need for change.* No. 180. Working paper, 2006.
3. Balarajan, Yarlini, Selvaraj Selvaraj, and S. V. Subramanian. "Health care and equity in India." *The Lancet* 377.9764 (2011): 505-515.
4. Jayaram, N. "Higher Education in India." *Asian universities: Historical perspectives and contemporary challenges* 85 (2004).

2

Role of Spirituality in Higher Education

Dr. Rupal S. Patel

ABSTRACT

'A healthy mind in a healthy body'.

– Swami Vivekananda

A human being is a combination of body, intellectuality, and soul. The body can be fulfilled by food, intellectuality can be fulfilled by day to day informative and knowledge providing education whereas soul can be fulfilled by the education of spirituality. In order to be an ideal human being and responsible citizen of the nation, one should be spiritually strong along with knowledge and information. Spirituality in education can convince the younger generation to acquire high ideals of perfect mastery over their senses, the idea of truth, liberty, equality and fraternity, peace and unity. One can also develop self-sufficiency, habits of helping others, respect for women, elders and teachers, gentleness, respect for one's culture and civilisation. They can control anger, lust, greed, vanity, conceit and over-ambitious nature. Such good habits make them good citizens. They should not criticize others but learn how to get rid of evils. Materialism should not be the only aim of their life, they would learn how to become a man of values than only success.

So the real purpose of education is not only physical development but also, intellectuality and soul with beauty. Spirituality molds the modern generation and makes them capable of living a perfect life. In short, spirituality offers students renewed life, energy, and enthusiasm towards life and nation. So the role of spirituality in education is essential.

A human being is a combination of body, intellectuality, and soul. The body can be fulfilled by food, intellectuality can be fulfilled by day to day information and knowledge providing education whereas soul can be fulfilled through spirituality. Life is incomplete without any one of them. So we need all three. Food enhances our physical development; knowledge enhances intellectuality while spirituality enhances our mental strength.

> A great soul will be strong to live as well as strong to think.
>
> – Emerson

Spirituality in general means a dynamic construct which includes genuineness, internal process to find out personal authenticity and openness of exploring the strong connection with a higher power. Spirituality is the acquisition of principles to guide our day to day living. It should not only be derived from religion but also from a personal philosophy and from personal beliefs which are concerned with morality, relationship with others and increased awareness of life and the world. It implies students' freedom to search for and decide the principles of life which they will adopt. It ultimately leads them to make an ideal human being. As Laura defines spirituality:

> Spirituality is our state of being which drives all our behaviors, decisions and relationships. Spirituality is our most authentic relationships to self, others, the universe and the transcendent – influence our personal health on all levels and domino-like, the health of our communities, our nations, and the world, as we interact with others and with the planet (Laura: 2005,1).

There is a great similarity between religion and morality. Both are emotionally charged words presenting the public as well as private practices. Spirituality is transcendent teaching. Transcendence means moving beyond and crossing our own psychological barriers and experience more clearly and minutely the true nature of things.

Now the question is how to establish and develop mental strength. For mental strength, spiritual education plays a key role as through such education one can develop the qualities of tolerance, patience, and sense of responsibility.

The qualities of tolerance, patience, and responsibility are essential for self-determination. We should cultivate them in both the classroom and outside the classroom. These qualities lead the students to self-determination. Students who are self-determining assume responsibility for their learning.

To develop spirituality, the classroom is the centre. The classroom becomes more unexplored area. Group discussion, reading, service projects, studying autobiographies and biographies who have a strong spiritual background, the inspiration for creative work, activities like elocution, extempore to build up a high level of confidence, participation in sports for physical and mental fitness, various co-curricular activities are such activities which can enhance spirituality in students. For that, we should introduce Vedic literature in education which is the core foundation of Indian culture and rich heritage. It is supposed to be part of daily life too.

In the modern education system, it is essential to maintain the discipline and to establish a cordial relationship between students and teachers. Such education can convince the younger generation how to acquire high ideals of perfect mastery over all senses, the ideals of truth, liberty, equality and fraternity, peace and unity. If we have to acquire these qualities, we will have to accept the ideals of Vedic education. In fact, Vedic education is the solution to many of the problems of our daily life. The aim of Vedic education is the formation of character by moral development through which we can make the students a proper member of society. It controls the animal side of human beings. Man is a social animal and spirituality emphasizes not only social duties and responsibilities but also promotes social happiness.

Education is not only earning a living. Education is for self-sufficiency. Students can develop the habits of helping others, respect to elders and teachers, gentleness. Such good habits make them good citizens. Students should not criticize others as they should learn that by criticizing others, they should harm themselves. They should understand how to respect women, how to get rid of social evils. Materialism should not be the only aim of their life, as they would learn how to become a man of values than only success. In the words of Dr. Radhakrishnan –

> "A civilisation is not built of bricks, steel and machinery, it is built with men, their quality and character."

The true aim of education is the development of body and soul with beauty. In the current situation, we have almost lost everything which was inherited to us. We have lost the cordial relationship between students and teachers, moral and social values, we need to re-remember our duties and responsibilities towards family, community, nation and the world. All things are possible only when spirituality will enter in education. Spirituality molds the modern generation. It makes an individual capable of living a perfect life. Students should learn the discipline – discipline means strict obedience of rules and regulations of life which are rooted in morality. Students should learn to give up anger, lust, greed, vanity, conceit and over ambition.

Teenage is the time period of students during which they are stuck between lots of workload and pressure. During this period, they have to attend college lectures, prepare for different types of exams, have to score excellent marks, perform better at their workplace, improve their performance and so on. In such circumstances, they have to be stable and perform well. Spiritual education like yoga provides mental stability to cope up with all these works. Yoga helps one's body to relax and soothe the mind. It makes the body flexible and enhances concentration power. So one can complete one's work perfectly.

Meditation and yoga bring positive vibes among the students. It renders self-education brings self-awareness and teaches how to live with wisdom. It brings physical, mental and spiritual enfoldment in an individual. It is a lifelong pursuit in the development of human psyche. If students engage themselves in "inner work" through activities like yoga, meditation and self-reflection and their professors actively encourage them to explore questions of meaning and purpose, spiritual enhancement in them should be possible.

Spirituality offers renewed life, energy and enthusiasm in teachers and students. Nowadays, students have lost their sense of curiosity, zeal, wonder, and enthusiasm for knowledge, learning, and creativity. Spirituality in education would bring energy and enthusiasm. It would seek to restore life and spark students' curiosity.

Students can develop the quality of acceptance of self and compassion for others. A student can also find meaning as well as excitement in their curriculum. Along with it, they also learn to accept their being and feel compassion for others. Spirituality in the classroom means inviting students to encounter their "inner selves". Such experiences make them think about the wellbeing of others outside as well as inside educational institutions. Spirituality in education promotes all dimensions of human development like physical, mental, social, emotional, aesthetic, moral and spiritual potential and intellectual abilities among students.

Besides, the problems experienced by teachers and students in education are indications of wider social crisis which is a demonstration of the alienation of mankind. The degradation and rottenness of the environment, the oppression of minorities, the exploitation of women, difference between rich and poor and various other human sufferings are the evidence of our current condition.

From college education, Spirituality has been declining. Their spirituality shows substantial growth. The larger questions of meaning, responsibility, and identity have been becoming more urgent at this time. If these questions are not taken into consideration, they can be inward, become toxic and explosive. Through spiritual education, students become more connected with others easily. The positive approach should come among students by spiritual education which definitely enhances their academic performance, psychological well-being, quality of leadership and the level of inner satisfaction.

Spiritually grown-up students can study abroad, cope up with interdisciplinary studies as they are able to connect themselves to new, varied and diverse students, people, cultures, and ideas. So exposing students to diverse people, culture, and ideas through study abroad, interracial interaction, interdisciplinary course work may lead them towards spiritual growth. Spiritual qualities like equanimity, ecumenical world view, ethics of caring would enhance students' academic achievements and individual development. It would provide students more opportunities to connect with their outer world which leads them to identify their own "inner selves" and inner strength and if positive direction would be given to them, they can rock the world and acquire highest achievements in their life. But it is a matter of concern that many educational institutions pay little attention to students' inner selves and inner strength.

Students can be more self-aware and enlightened by spiritual quest and they become able to find out answers of mysteries of life. They should be able to cope up with the world and find meanings in the time of hardship, acquire mental peace and serenity. They see each day as a gift and feel good about the direction of life. Ethics of caring should also be developed among the students and their commitment to values of life like helping others in a difficult time, reducing pain, suffering, and agony from the world and promoting racial understand would also be increased among them. Charitable involvement should be developed through participation in community services, helping them to solve various problems, doing the charitable task and developing the capacity to maintain their sereneness, calmness, quietness, and centeredness especially at the time of stress. Students can also take interest in different religious traditions. They understand various cultures and civilisations of different countries develop strong bondage with all humanity and believe that all lives are interconnected. Spirituality, thus, is a multifaceted quality and active quest for answers to life's tremendous issues would be properly fulfilled. Students can develop a global worldview.

In order to develop spirituality religious engagement of students is required and activities like prayer, attendance at religious services, reading sacred texts, a celebration of religious festivals, etc. should be performed through which students can develop personal strength and hesitate to do anti-social, anti-religious or evil tasks.

During college life, students exhibit the greatest spiritual growth if they are really engaged in "inner work" through contemplation, meditation, and self-reflection. Self-reflection and meditation strengthen their social, educational and religious commitment. For this, the faculty have to encourage the students to explore religious and spiritual questions. When faculty encourages students to explore religious and spiritual questions, the questions regarding meaning and purpose of their existence, they will become more actively involved in spiritual questing which would strengthen students' religious engagement and religious commitment.

Institute should take care of students' not only of their cognitive capacities but also of their mental and emotional development which includes their moral development, ethical development, and character development. Besides, the institution needs to provide students with opportunities to develop their understanding and appreciation for various forms of spiritual, moral and ethical engagement. They should also help them to develop the habit of inquiry regarding evidence-based and the analysis that is fundamental to high-quality learning.

Leadership training, participation in various students' organisations, community services and students' governance, etc. have been expanded to develop their demonstrated values. These values can be viewed as ways to facilitate students' spiritual development. I think the most direct way to strengthen the students and institutions' capacity is to enhance students" spiritual development. Those existing programs and practices would be extended which are already in practice of students" spiritual development.

In order to strengthen spirituality, a positive campus culture should be maintained. Campus climate, generally, has been focusing on race and sex and largely been neglected important aspects of students' identities. College campuses have become a centre of discrimination and violence. In such circumstances, how students can experience spiritual climate. A positive campus climate leads to learning.

The motive is another important aspect of Spirituality in education. The motive is a driving force for teaching and learning. It raises curiosity and control among students. Spirituality also means compassion in the classroom which brings interconnectedness of students, faculty and the subject. In "Nourishing Students in Secular Schools", Kessler described that the arc of adolescence bends towards connection. Students are always eager for a deep connection to themselves, to others, and also to nature or a supreme power (51-52). In Kessler's words:

> Students who feel deeply connected don't need danger to feel fully alive. They don't need guns to feel powerful. They don't want to hurt others or themselves. Out of connection grows compassion and passion – passion for people, for student's goals and dreams, for life itself (Kessler: 1998, 52).

In the modern age, we should feel proud of the culture and civilisation of our ancestors. Instead of materialism, we should prefer character, spiritualism, philosophy. Instead of wealth, power, violence and diplomacy, we should emphasize idealism and moral education which is enough for the success of every individual. The aim of true education is to impart a humanitarian approach and the spirit of service. It transcends individuality in conscious social participation. Instead of being jealous, clashing with each other or pulling each other down, we should develop the capacity to cooperate, to live and work together as a team.

So, the time has come to refocus and rethink about the disquisition on spirituality in higher education syllabus. For this educationists should take more efforts which would more emphasis on the spiritual development of the students. Students may re-evaluate their abilities, capacities, values, and beliefs and allow students the freedom to represent their views, thoughts, feelings, and choices during the development process and also allow them to make their own decisions perfectly.

REFERENCES

Flake, C.L. ed. *Holistic education: Principles, Perspectives, and Practices*. Brandon: VT: Holistic Education Press. 1993.

Glazer, S. ed. *The Heart of Learning: Spirituality in Education*. New York: Tracher /Puntam, 1999.

Jones, Laura. "What does Spirituality in Education Mean? Stumbling Toward Wholeness". *Journal of College and Character*. Vol. VI, No.7, October, Southern Oregon University, 2005.

Kessler, R. *Nourishing Students in Secular Schools*. Educational Leadership, 1998.

Palmer, P. *The Courage to Teach: Exploring the Inner Landscape of a Teacher's Life*. San Francisco: Jossey – Bass, 1998.

3

Importance and Aspects of Spirituality in Higher Education

Dr. Manish B. Raval & Dr. Ashish B. Gorvadiya

ABSTRACT

Spirituality involves exploring certain aspects such as love, compassion, generosity, selflessness, life after death, wisdom, truth, etc. that the saints or enlightened people have achieved and have manifested a higher level of development than the ordinary people. The role of spirituality is recognised in several wakes of life. The patients expect that the doctors fulfill their spiritual need, the professional bodies give more attention to the spiritual care of the clients. Thus spirituality is required in every woke of life. Here, we have tried to unveil the role of spirituality in Higher Education. Spirituality involves the humans' search for the true meaning of life whereas religion is related to the organised institution with the rituals and practices for the supreme power or the god. If the spirituality is added to the higher education, the real meaning of the education will be served and there will be true development of the students and nobility of the teaching profession would come back. In this article, our aim is to understand what spirituality is and what role does it play in higher education.

Keywords: Spirituality, Higher Education, Religion, Nobility, Teaching Profession.

INTRODUCTION

The development of spirituality is recognised as the requirement of some discipline in order to make progress. Spiritual development requires certain practices such as everyday prayer and meditation. The spiritual journey begins with healing and affirming the ego so that the positive state of mind is experienced. Secured self-esteem, belief in the self-worth, capacity for the love and generosity are the essential elements for the true spirituality. Spirituality involves exploring certain aspects such as love, compassion, generosity, selflessness, life after death, wisdom, truth, etc. that the saints or enlightened people have achieved and have manifested a higher level of development than the ordinary people. In this article, our aim is to understand what spirituality is and what role does it play in higher education.

Clarifying the Concept of Spirituality

The words 'religion' and 'spirituality' are used interchangeably, but there is a great distinction between the two. In order to understand the meaning of spirituality, we first need to understand what is a religion? Religion involves an organised entity such as an institution with some rituals, values, practices, and beliefs about God or some highest power. Religions have some definable boundaries and provide a framework within which the individual has to live. It sometimes happens that man's search for meaning and purpose of life is lost somewhere because of adherence to religious practices and beliefs. It is concluded that belonging to some religion does not mean a person is with spirituality or is spiritual.

Spirituality involves an individual's search for the meaning of life, peace, individuality, love, compassion, harmony, etc. The following dictionary meanings will be helpful to understand the underlying concepts of Spirituality:

Spirit:[1]
Spirit (Way of Feeling) **A particular way of thinking, feeling or behaving, especially a way that is typical of a particular group of people, an activity, a time, or a place…..**
Spirit (Not Body) **The characteristic of a person that is considered as being separate from the body, and that many religions believe continue to exist after the body dies…..** **The form of a dead person, similar to a ghost, or the feeling that a dead person is present although you cannot see them….**
Spirit (State of Mind) **A state of mind or attitude**
Spirit (Inner Character) **The character of a person thought of as different from the material person we can see and touch……**
Spiritual:[2]
Relating to deep feelings and beliefs especially religious beliefs…..
A type of religious song, originally developed by African Americans in the USA…
Of or relating to the inner character of a person…..
Spirituality:[3]
The quality that involves deep feelings and beliefs of a religious nature, rather than the physical part of the life….
Spirituality:[4]
The quality of being concerned with the human spirit or soul as opposed to material or physical things……

ROLE OF SPIRITUALITY IN HIGHER EDUCATION

The role of spirituality is recognised in several wakes of life. The patients expect that the doctors fulfill their spiritual need, the professional bodies give more attention to the spiritual care

1 https://dictionary.cambridge.org/dictionary/english/spirit
2 https://dictionary.cambridge.org/dictionary/english/spiritual
3 https://dictionary.cambridge.org/dictionary/english/spirituality
4 https://en.oxforddictionaries.com/definition/spirituality

of the clients. Thus spirituality is required in every woke of life. Here, we have tried to unveil the role of spirituality in Higher Education.

For Positive Youth Development

The Spirituality in Higher Education is very much important for the positive development of youth. Positive youth development includes the features such as bonding, flexibility, social competence, emotional competence, cognitive competence, cognitive competence, moral competence, behavioural competence, self-determination, self-efficacy, beliefs in the future, clear and positive identity, recognition of positive behaviour, etc. All these aspects help a student to be deterministic in learning and faster learning is possible.

For Removing Psychological Problems

Generally, it can be seen that the youth in higher education, nowadays are suffering from some psychological issues such as anxiety, depression, hopelessness, negativity and so on. These psychological issues give several ill effects on the learning ability of the student. Spirituality is the strongest weapon to fight with such ill effects. Once the students catch the spiritual path all such issues will not affect them or even they are caught in such issues, they will be able to find solutions to such issues.

For Removing Anti-social Behaviour

In many cases, it has been seen that the students during the age of learning are caught into some dangerous anti-social activities such as smoking, taking drugs, kidnapping, abusing and many more. If the students are turned to the spirituality, they will be away from all such anti-social activities and ultimately, the positive social behaviour will come out.

For Helping the Youth to Face Adversities

Life is not always on the full bloom; it sometimes gives adversities also. It has been seen in the recent days that the students have taken any small adversity in the biggest form and they feel helpless to sort out even the smaller issues. Consider the cases of suicide at the time of board results. One negative result is considered as the end of life and they feel death is the final solution. Spirituality is the panacea to cure such behaviour of the students. If the students are turned to spirituality, they will be rock strong to fight any adversity in life.

Providing the Motive of Life

The true meaning of spirituality is to find out the true meaning of life. "What is the purpose of existence?" is at the core of spirituality. When the students are trained for spirituality, they will learn the deep-rooted meaning of their life and will be able to serve the society selflessly.

Providing the Motive of Education

What is the actual purpose of education? It is nothing but to unveil the hidden self. Education must enlighten the mind of the learners. The true purpose of education is not only the self-development but the development of the others also. Spirituality gives this view-point to the students and students.

For Making Students Accountable

Spirituality makes the students accountable. The students take accountability of the decisions taken by them. This will be helpful to make them good citizens when they grow up and become professionals, businessman or employees. With spiritual minds, they will take the decisions that will give pervasive benefits.

For Improving Student-Teacher Relationship

Nowadays, the relationship of the teacher with the student has become a professional relationship rather than the actual *'Guru-Shishya Parampara'.* Spirituality will be a definite solution to this problem. Because of the lack of spirituality, education has become the business and the teachers have become the service providers and the students are the mere clients. The true meaning of education is lost somewhere. Spirituality is the only solution to this problem.

CONCLUSION

Spirituality is the inherent element of the human being. It is a subjective concept. For some, spirituality is connected with the religion and for the others, it is not. Some use spirituality and religion interchangeably, but in reality, they mean different. Spirituality involves the humans' search for the true meaning of life whereas religion is related to the organised institution with the rituals and practices for the supreme power or the god. If the spirituality is added to the higher education, the real meaning of the education will be served and there will be true development of the students and nobility of the teaching profession would come back.

REFERENCES

https://dictionary.cambridge.org/dictionary/english/spirit

https://dictionary.cambridge.org/dictionary/english/spiritual

https://dictionary.cambridge.org/dictionary/english/spirituality

https://en.oxforddictionaries.com/definition/spirituality

Bellingham R., Cohen B., Jones T. & Spaniol L. (1989) "Connectedness: some skills for spiritual health." *American Journal of Health Promotion* 4, 18–31

Burkhardt M.A. (1989) *Spirituality: An analysis of the concept.* Holistic Nursing Practice 3, 69-77

Ellison C.W. (1983) "Spiritual well-being: conceptualisation and measurement." *Journal of Psychology and Theology* 11, 330-340

Furrow, J. L., King, P. E., & White, K. (2004). "Religion and positive youth development: Identity, meaning, and prosocial concerns." *Applied Developmental Science,* 8(1), 17-26

Higher Education Research Institute. (2005). *The spiritual life of college students: A national study of college students' search for meaning and purpose.* Los Angeles, CA: University of California, Los Angeles. Retrieved from

http://spirituality.ucla.edu/docs/reports/Spiritual_Life_College_Students_Full_Report.pdf

4

Role of Vedas in Higher Education

Dr. Swati Saxena

ABSTRACT

Higher education is about developing a thought process which leads to analytical thinking. Ancient Vedas depicts a situation that can be related to modern day thinking algorithms. Deducing the learning from Vedas and applying it to the current higher education learning pedagogy. The write up is an attempt to bring out unbiased learning from the ocean of knowledge in different Vedas, religious books, & Upanishads.

Keywords: Vedic learnings, Business learning, Character building, Decision Dilemmas.

Science has taught us to swim beneath the fish in oceans and to fly above the birds in the sky, but how to live life on earth is described by Vedas. The objective of higher education is to create industry ready freshers.

India mythology is based on four Vedas:

1. *Rig-Veda* "Knowledge of the Hymns of Praise", for recitation.
2. *Sama-Veda* "Knowledge of the Melodies", for chanting.
3. *Yajur-Veda* "Knowledge of the Sacrificial formulas", forthe liturgy.

4. *Atharva-Veda* "Knowledge of the Magic formulas", named after a kind of group of priests.

There are four Vedas: the Rigveda, the Yajurveda, the Samaveda, and the Atharvaveda. Each Veda has been subclassified into four major text types – the Samhitas, the Aranyakas, the Brahmanas, and the Upanishads philosophy and spiritual knowledge. Some scholars add a fifth category – the Upasanas.

The objective of higher education is to create industry ready fresher's. Decision makers look for individuals with problem-solving capabilities. Higher Education is a platform that generates students that can investigate the matter and find the root cause of the underlying situation. Ramayana a 5000-year-old epic gives a direct resemblance to the situations that arise in today's world. Various depictions of the character of Ram is a subject of detailed study. The first and foremost question is what is the objective behind writing Ramayana? A written document is a treasure for generations to come. In a situation of flux, it can be referred for guidance in the higher education system has to some extent inculcated topics like ethics & value system.

A various instance in Vedas resembles present corporate life situations that need to be learned by learners in higher education. Building character of an individual is the prime responsibility of educator at this level of learning. Learners are like small saplings that are now a full-fledged tree in higher education that can be sculpted to imbibe a certain amount of knowledge. Ramayana, Mahabharat, Quran, Bible, Gurugranthsaheb all are an ocean of learning that can be implemented in our day to day personal as well as corporate life to fine tune our decisions.

When Ram (The protagonist) killed Ravana (antagonist) and Ravana was on his death bed, Lord Ram asked his younger brother to go to the antagonist and take some knowledge from his skills of music, his strength of worship of Lord Shiva, battlefield strategies, etc. The younger one went to the antagonist and stood near his head and waited for the antagonist to speak but, he did not.

LEARNING

Drawing direct analogy from the situation, it should be learned that even our worst competitor or enemy is also knowledgeable, and we need to learn from their skills & knowledge. Even after defeating them one needs to value them for the knowledge that they have and learn.

Continuing the situation above the younger one came back and stood silently beside Lord Ram. Lord Ram knew the situation and taught him that even if he (Ravan) was our enemy who has been defeated & punished by me for his deeds. In spite of all the ill feelings towards him, I still respect him for being very learned, full of wisdom, Musician, Expert in playing Veena, Knows Vedas by heart, a great shiv bhakta. etc. He is full of a man all should respect. He asked his younger brother to stand at Ravana feet and get learning.

LEARNING

Competitors are also teachers that a good source of learning. An individual can be viewed separately from his role. A person can have different abilities, which could be channelised in various activities' role of a younger brother here represents ego of being the winner /achiever, who looks down upon the loser, which is why he stood on his head. Learners should always be humble and indifferent to imbibe knowledge incorrect manner.

Obeying Lord Ram is equivalent to trusting the leader without any question. This is the leader's responsibility to develop complete trust in people who are in their team to achieve the desired result.

Another great Epic Mahabharata is also a bundle of instances that makes a person think towards causes and effects of behaviour's Krishna is the epicentre of all the activities in the epic. He directs, manipulates, skills, guides all the characters, but does not act himself.

LEARNING

Leadership is all about being visionary, they may not be at the forefront. Leaders inculcate skills that make the follower on the same thinking pattern as the leader. Even in the absence of the leader the follower can assume the duty of leader and be equally successful. Life situations will change forever as Heraclitus, a Greek philosopher, has been quoted as saying "change is the only constant in life." situations change but the basic premise of thinking, as well as decision making, will remain the same. Changing from door to door marketing to digital marketing is a similar situation.

LEARNINGS

Quran also encourages concepts of equal opportunity, waste reduction, teamwork, etc." No soul shall have a burden laid on it greater than it can bear." Is the principle in the Quran that is related to the delegation principle wherein it is the leader's responsibility to understand everyone's capability to work and then allocate task accordingly. This will further percolate to establishing working standards and performance criteria which will further create transparency in the organisation.

Duryodhana was one of the most learned people but his company made him fall prey to ill thinking. His knowledge was tremendous he studied under the same guru as Arjun, but both the students of Dronacharya were poles apart in their thinking, implementation of skills, ethics, etc.

LEARNING

Teachers impart the same knowledge but imbibing knowledge and filtering it through the personality changes implementation aspect of the same skill set. Higher education is about imparting the skill of differentiating between good and not good people.

Entire Mahabharat, Shri Krishna is the preacher and the epic continues. He does not act, but just directs the character something that resembles a true visionary transformational leader. He guides the action in the desired manner for achieving a predetermined outcome. But the key learning is to impart equal opportunity to all and develop a skill set in disciples that is as good as of the leader himself/herself.

The current generation of millennial does not have the privilege of learning's from these treasured books. Academicians across the world are referring to our Ancient Indian writings for establishing guidelines for all kinds of ethical systems. When Karan acquired knowledge from immortal Lord Parshuram by lying that he is Brahmin. When Karan needed the war skills desperately against Arjun on the battlefield, he forgot all his knowledge imparted by his guru. *Truth is of prime importance.* Anybody who lies once can lie anytime and this can become a habit. Corporates experience a lot of situations which are an outcome of false statements.

Ethical practices are enlisted and preached but the ultimate responsibility of practicing them rests with individuals. When such instances are cited through curricula it may have a lasting impact on learners.

Whistleblowing is a law introduced by corporates across the globe. Different scams and scandals that run into millions of rupees make it very difficult for umbrella brands and even individual businesses to sustain in the competitive era. Ethical and unethical practices are very well defined in Vedas. Draupadi Chirharan was an outcome when all the members of the parliament of Dhrithrashtra remained silent. None of the learned names in the court intervened to the mishap. Dhritarashtra had never ever paid heed to his son's wrongdoing, which made him lose his entire family in the battlefield. On the other side Shakuni (maternal Uncle of Yudhsitir) under the impression of being cheated. He was under the impression that his sister had been forcibly married to a blind man (Dhritarashtra). In order to take revenge, he plots all the ill thoughts in the mind of his nephew. It finally culminated to the great war of Mahabharat between brothers. Anyone who can stand up against wrong is a whistle-blower in modern terminology. The courage to stand up and speak for wrongdoings is missing since the ancient times and that is visible in the 21st Century even. Building the psychological character is of prime importance at a higher level of education. The concept behind higher education is to understand the root cause of a situation and try and eliminate the negative effect of the same.

5

Creativity in Higher Education – Reality and Ideals!

Dr. Vani Ramesh & Dr. Vishal C. Jaunky

ABSTRACT

Creativity in Higher Education is gaining more importance in recent times, both for the individuals, institutions, and society to a larger extent. Intensive research activities are exploring in generating new dimension of creativity higher education. Professionals with different disciplines with diverse cultural backgrounds work together and it is quite complex to arrive at a common understanding of the term 'creativity in higher education'. The present chapter analyses the influence of culture on the creative thinking of learners and teachers in higher education. How do professionals from different cultural backgrounds cope with the chunks of creative thinking? To understand and test empirically, Hofstede's Cultural Dimensions are swotted with the help of a well-structured questionnaire, 132 academicians from teaching, non-teaching and pursuers of higher education. Drop-off survey was conducted. The results are summarised in a framework that outlines the criteria and the respective cultural dimensions. The findings of this study would be a good contribution to the existing literature and also might help practitioners, learners, and pursuers of Higher Education to adopt and implement.

Keywords: Creativity, Higher Education, Hofstede, Cultural dimensions, CFA, Teacher, Learner.

1. INTRODUCTION

Creativity in Higher Education is scattering across the globe and solving many glitches of higher education (Buchanan, 1992).

Many countries such as the US, EU, Australia, China, Malaysia, Russia including India are able to adopt innovative solutions for impending encounters of higher education. Creativity relies on a set of criteria, such as team, environment, the way of the creative thinking process, and typical mindset (Kelley and Littman, 2001, Plattner, Meinel and Weinberg, 2009, Mueller and Thoring, 2012, Thoring and Muller, 2011). But the challenge is how these facets are perceived and valued in different cultures? This study focuses on different requirements regarding educational settings for creativity in higher education in different cultures. The study is intended to understand the cultural dimensions by Hofstede (1994, 1980) for selected professionals and pursuers of higher education in India.

Education and creativity should go hand in hand, but do they currently? Do the way education systems operate to inspire creative thinking across a range of disciples? Does it allow us to innovate for a sustainable global future?

To answer this, the chapter is structured as follows: The first section provides a brief introduction to creative thinking. In the second section, we specify cultural differences based on Hofstede's (1994, 1980) cultural dimensions for selected professionals. The next section deals with the mapping of cultural differences in creative thinking and summarises the outcomes in a framework. Finally, we discuss the results, as well as the limitations of the work, and presented an outlook for further research.

Creativity in Higher-education has diverse meanings and there is no simple definition. It can be articulated as an evolution of learning, utilising the previous skills or previous knowledge to enhance the knowledge of a particular domain. As 'Higher Education' is a relative term expressing the logical development of skill and knowledge based on the logical development of previous theories referring to historical background.

The international definition of tertiary education has divided into two parts:

a) Higher Education (HE), and

b) Further Education (FE).

Higher Education (HE) qualification at degree level, having theoretical underpinning, which would qualify someone to work in a professional field and usually taught at the environment which also includes advanced research activity. *Further Education (FE)* includes any added degrees after secondary education, which is not a part of higher education and not take part in an undergraduate or graduate degree. There is a wide range of courses available, such as basic English courses, maths to higher national diplomas, etc.

Developing student's creativity in higher education is a combination of thinking, knowledge, capabilities, ethics, values, skills and qualities to work with convolutions.

Figure 1: Developing Student Creativity

Source: Jackson N.J. (2014) Developing student's creativity through higher education.

Educational institutions are also playing an equal role in creating interactable social environments by designing creative modes to tackle societal problems. The products of creative higher learners are capable and more willing to support the system to be more complex, creating wealth and prosperity. Creativity in Higher Education has taken shape in every stage of learning and teaching. It is the student-centric approach and encourages the students to be more proactive in influencing the content, activities, materials, and pace of learning (Balchin, T. 2006). The students are provided with opportunities to learn independently and from one another and coach them in the skills they need to do so effectively. It is more student-centric learning, where every learner is a clean slate and tries to learn creatively and change themselves to be more effectively and efficiently. Think-pair-share, Roundtable, Minute Papers, Bookend Lectures, Immediate feedback via classroom technology, student presentations, and projects, learning cycle instructional models, peer-led team learning (incorporating inquiry into courses and problem-based learning and case studies) are some of the approaches to expand the creativity knowledge among Higher Education pursuers.

Student development and learning must be ethically supported by leadership and teacher that values and supports creativity in student learning that likely to foster a climate where the development of learners is maximum possible. Therefore, a culture that values the professional creativity of teachers is more important, as the creative development of learners is largely facilitated and hindered by their teachers (Jackson N.J., 2014). These are some of the important practices that would be considered in developing creative thinking and development of pursuers of higher education (Jackson N.J., 2014).

a. Drawing Inspiration from the Discipline

Most of the academicians presume that creativity in higher education has only a meaning when it is contextualised in disciplinary problems.

What actually does it mean to be a creative engineer, doctor, historian, teacher or any other practitioner in a discipline???

Many studies conducted reveals that teachers share similar perceptions of what being creative means in their respective disciplines and sites for thinking creatively and that characteristic appear to be available in most aspects of disciplinary practices. Mounting and explicit understanding of what exactly the creativity is the first step in appealing the academy with all these challenges.

What does it mean to be creative in your discipline or professional area of practice?

b. Pedagogies for Creative Development

The teaching pedagogy has a high impact on cultivating creative thinking of students. Curricular and co-curricular should involve the learners in understanding the challenges that require them to replicate what they already know and they can do. Strategies that support metacognitive development by encouraging the learners to think about and articulate their own creativity and its effects. In general, the approached used by higher education teachers to promote student development can be categorised as:

- Sage on the stage (knowledge transmitter)
- Guide on the side (facilitator)
- Meddler-in-the-middle (an involved co-learner/co-producer in the learning process)

These are relevant and can be used to aid student learning and development where the teachers are playing the role of 'meddlers' and 'facilitators'.

The question that can be raised here, what are the teaching and learning contexts that are able to meddle or facilitate the students creative thinking? Are there more opportunities for meddling?

c. A Curriculum for Creative Development-importance of Personal Learning Ecologies

A curriculum that prepares the students for learning in the real world outside the 'comfortable', low-risk environments of higher education is inevitable for the learners to expose to risks and challenges of unfamiliar contexts and problems. The curriculum should encourage the learners to develop their own ecologies for learning rather than imposing own learning outcomes. This is an informal world of learning and problem solving which provide the learners with great opportunities, relationships, and resources for learning, development, and achievement. The question here is,

- To what extent does the curriculum engage with these perspectives?
- Is there scope for further development?

d. Recognising Learners Own Creative Lives

The learners, out of their university life, should be able to adopt a life wide concept of education (life wide curriculum) to embrace all the spaces and places for learning, personal development, and self-actualisation in a person life. The question here is, How does the curriculum accommodate students lifetime experiences and recognise their creativity in those experiences?

2. Creative Thinking

Creative thinking is an innovative way of generating a solution for complex issues (Buchanan, 1992; Rittel, 1972), by a user-cantered approach with multi-disciplinary resource persons. Creative thinking though introduced and shaped by the corporates and consultants (Kelley and Littman, 2001), is becoming more popular among higher educational institutions. The following are some of the main categories that are crucial for creative thinking (Plattner, Meinel and Weinberg, 2009):

- Specific creative thinking (process),
- A specific gathering of multidisciplinary teams,
- A flexible work environment,
- A specific creative thinking culture (mindset).

a. Stages in Creative Thinking

As creative thinking is a technique of tacking the issues and situations from a fresh outlook that advocates unconventional solutions. Creative thinking can be inspired both by a vague process such as brainstorming and also by a controlled process such as adjacent thinking. These are the 4 stages that are regulating the creative thinking process in general.

- *Preparation:* Articulate the problem and collect facts and materials necessary for finding new solutions.
- *Incubation:* The unconscious thought process of finding a solution to the problem.
- *Illumination:* The sudden flash of idea i.e. the 'eureka' experience.
- *Verification:* Evaluate the validity of the solution.

b. Keys to Creative Thinking Process

The creative thinking process has 3 keys,

1. *In-the-box:* This applies knowledge accumulation and critical thinking to the problem. Based on their expertise, innovators can generate many relevant ideas and make connections later.
2. *Out-of-the-box:* This is a wide-angle and unfocused thinking process. It allows the innovators to imagine an entire universe of possibilities.
3. *New-box:* Once ideas are evaluated, they need to be synthesized by rearranging and reconstructing through dot-connecting, then refined and put into place in a new context.

c. Creative Thinking Techniques

1. *Mind Mapping* – Brainstorming or spider diagram
2. *The Checklist* – why, where, when, who, what, how
3. *Thinking Hats* – facts, emotions, judgment, logic, creativity, control
4. *Lateral Thinking* – sidestepping
5. *Random Word* – imagine the association
6. *Picture Association* – imagine the association

   Change Perspective – in other people's shoes

   Get up and go outlet your mind wander

d. Creative Thinking Culture and Mindset

Creative thinking and mindset can be demarcated as below:

i. Be Open to Change

7. To meet the challenges of society and be aware of the way the world is transforming, and keep track of

change, one should have to be open to accept and adopt the possible consequences. This is justified with the help of Kubler-Ross Change Curve as below:

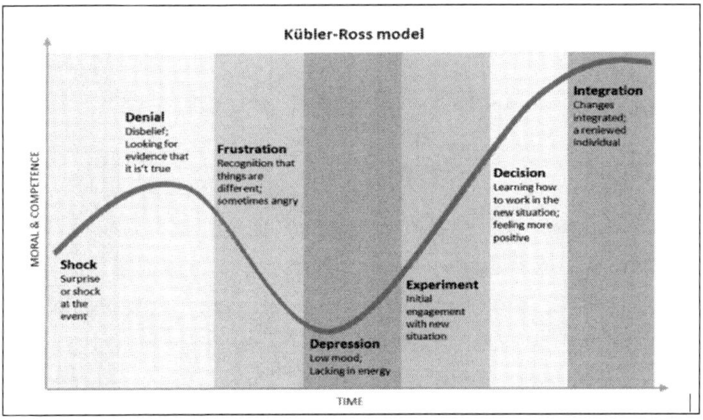

Figure 2: Kubler-Ross Model of Emotions

Source: The Change Curve (1960), Elisabeth Kubler-Ross

The *Kubler-Ross Change Curve* which is also known as the 5 stages of grief is a model consisting of the various levels or stages of emotions which are experienced by a person who is soon going to approach death or is a survivor of an intimate death.

ii. Embrace Creativity

The creative mind-set should truly solve the problems, rather a traditional scientific method. From the concept of design thinking, innovation is an art and stresses that the starting point for creativity, rather implementation of management processes.

iii. Think Big

Creative thinking is an ability and courage to think bigger and beyond the current norms and truths. It is something stretching ordinary thinking.

iv. Show Courage

Creativity and innovation should really need the courage to constantly rethink how things can be done in a different way.

v. Think and Act Fast

Creative thinking and innovation must be fast and apply quickly.

3. CULTURAL DIMENSIONS

The important questions are, though more and more Higher Educational Institutions (HEI) are creative, whether particular cultures are appropriate and effective in supporting this creativity. The present study aims at identifying the relationship between Hofstede (1980) and Cultural Dimensions and Creative Thinking. According to Hofstede (1980) model, the predispositions of human to respond to a specific milieu, like educational context (universal, cultural and individual factors) (ref. Fig3). Culture is a wide-ranging term that covers professional culture, organisational culture and national culture (Hofstede, 1994).

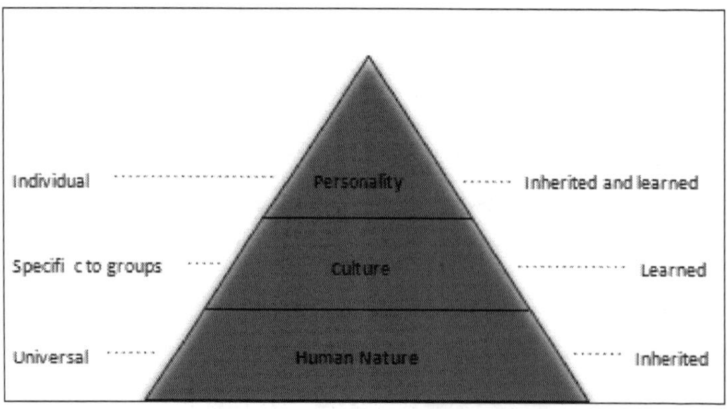

Figure 3: Three Levels that determine Human Action

Source: Hofstede (1994, p. 6)

Hofstede (1980) conducted a broad international analysis of work-related attitudes between 1967 and 1973 at IBM, in which he analysed about 117,000 survey questionnaires from 88,000 employees. Four dimensions of national culture were found by clustering answers about value orientation, and index scores for forty countries were developed. Index scores for the dimensions were normalised to the interval (0, 100). The four dimensions are individualism/collectivism, power distance, uncertainty avoidance and masculinity/femininity (G. Hofstede, 1980). Later, a fifth dimension was added: Long Term Orientation.

Table 1: Cultural Dimensions in different Countries (Hofstede, 1994)

Country	Power Distance (PDI)	Individualism (IDV)	Masculinity (MAS)	Uncertainty Avoidance (UAI)	Long Term Orientation (LTO)
Germany	35	67	66	65	31
UK	35	89	66	35	25
France	68	71	43	86	39
Hungary	46	80	88	82	50
Poland	68	60	64	93	32
Russia	93	39	36	95	–
Turkey	66	37	45	85	–
China	80	20	66	30	118
Malaysia	104	26	50	36	–
India	77	48	56	40	61
Australia	36	90	61	51	31
USA	40	91	62	46	29
Brazil	69	38	49	76	65
Argentina	49	46	56	86	–

Source: G. Hofstede, 1980

Table 1 shows an overview of the cultural dimensions indices for selected countries.

Those countries were selected based on the following criteria:

a) At least one country from each continent,

b) Countries that have established design thinking schools or Universities, and partly

c) Countries where we have access to those design thinking institutions, in order to conduct case studies in the future.

Note, that there exist countries with scores that are higher than 100. This is because Hofstede analysed these countries after he published the first scores and he didn't re-normalise the scores. For some countries, no Long Term orientation was calculated. In the following, the five cultural dimensions of Hofstede are described briefly. These dimensions are adopted and tested for the present study with the help of a Likert scale to understand the impact of culture on the creativity of higher education in India.

Table 2 shows a framework, mapping the identified creative thinking to the 5 cultural dimensions defined by Hofstede. The high value within the cultural dimension influences the respective creative thinking criterion in a positive (+) or negative (–) way.

4. THE IMPORTANCE OF DEVELOPING STUDENT CREATIVITY

According to Jackson, Oliver, Shaw and Wisdom (2006), it is very much essential and need of an hour to inspire and motivate the student (s), to be more creative, especially in Higher Education (HE), those keen on aspiring and updating their skills and knowledge to meet the global competition. Creativity in Higher Education is at times personal, economic and social reasons. At a personal level, improved creative capacity is likely to generate gains in satisfaction, wellbeing, happiness, and self-identity. This is a well-enhanced potential for professional development, by exploring their own potential and new possibilities for their self-growth and others. 'Personal creativity understood in terms of the 'performance ethic' and is a way of rational that tries to adjacent a huge gap in modern living, the gap between who we are and what we do (Kane, 2004).

Developing creative thinking skills among Higher Education students for social reasons are paramount (Brockling, 2006). The present-day world is ever-changing and "super complex", rather than complex: A *complex* world is one in which we are assailed by more facts, data evidence, tasks and influences that we can easily handle *within* the frameworks in which we have our being. By contrast, a *super complex* world is one in which the very frameworks by which we orient ourselves to the world are themselves contested (Barnett, 2000, p. 257). Developing new, different and creative thinking will allow students to respond to both the potentials and difficulties presented by this super complex world.

For example, we need creative thinking to tackle global problems including world poverty and global environmental issues, to "enrich the future instead of impoverishing it" (Csikszentmihalyi, 2006, p. xix). In turn, we need pedagogies that can support and nurture this kind of thinking: The challenge to humanity is to adopt new ways of *thinking,* new ways of *acting,* new ways of *organising* itself in society, in short, new ways of *living* (Wilson 1997, p.11)

5. Facilitating Student Creativity

How do we facilitate creativity among Higher Education Students?

These questions have been addressed by many researchers and academicians through extensive research and comprehensive reviews of the literature on creativity, teaching, and learning (Stein, 1988, Fryer, 2003). There has been a lack of critical engagement with the question of introducing creativity to the higher education system and most of the time it is neglected (Gardner, 1982). This gap has been addressed by Jackson, Oliver, Shaw, and Wisdom (2006), who focus on the role of creativity in Higher Education (HE). According to Csikszentmihalyi (2006), if young people become more involved with what they adore, the foundations for creativity will be in place. It follows therefore that teachers must model the joy of learning themselves and be able to spark it in their students.

To facilitate this, the pedagogy should be intensive on arousing student imagination and engagement. Since the late 1990s, several studies have identified common themes in what students and teachers say about how best to facilitate student creativity in Higher Education (HE). For example, Cropley (2001) recommends that surveys have shown that in theory at least, teachers prodigiously sustenance creativity as rather that should be nurtured in the classroom. Besides, teachers who successfully simplify creativity are likely to be those who inspire independent learning, yield student questions seriously, promote self-evaluation, reward courage as much as correctness, and who have a cooperative, socially integrative teaching style.

A study conducted by Oliver *et al* (2006) on students' 'experiences of creativity' in a broad banquet of subject chastisements points to precise teaching techniques that students contemplate to be creative. These include,

- Role-playing,
- Debates
- Posters for class
- Presentations.

Some quite foreseeable forms of teaching are also nominated as creative, precisely dialogic teaching with discussions that distillate on students' current understanding or beliefs. One-to-one tutorials are highlighted as especially accommodating students, as are providing inspiration, giving examples or offering feedback. Teachers should note that it is *how* these techniques are used, rather than the mere inclusion of them within our repertoire of techniques, that is the key to success. A study by Fryer (2006) identifies several teaching techniques for facilitating creativity: heuristic strategies i.e. problem-based learning (Barrett 2005); game-based learning that utilises challenging problems; real-life scenarios; practical exercises; and group work.

According to a study conducted by Oliver *et al* (2006), positive teacher attitudes and supportive factors such as the relationship between tutor and students are also significant in facilitating a creative learning environment. Teaching specific creative thinking tools in a way that is embedded in the discipline is important to provide the foundations for students to work creatively (Baille 2003). There are several thinking tools such as the six thinking hats technique that can be used to stimulate creativity among students (de Bono, 1999; Baille, 2003). These techniques have been proven to stimulate creativity in both education and work contexts.

Several initiatives are taking place in learning and teaching to foster student creativity.

For example, Diehm's (2004) research focuses on the use of 'electronic portfolio projects' to highlight the 'creative nature' of student learning. Through the use of 'efolis', students are reinvigorated to learn new skills and simultaneously are being tested to implement them. Certainly, in recent years, technology has been observed as having a hypothetically critical role to play in supportive and converting creative communities at all levels and stages in the Higher Educational (HE) process. The technology, whatever its nature, should support the pedagogical purpose sustaining creative learning by sharing goals, purposes, knowledge, multiple perspectives and experiences.

Figure 1 below depicts suggested approaches for fostering student creativity. Although none of the pathways must be followed in a linear manner, we do suggest a possible route towards the integration of creative learning strategies into teaching practice.

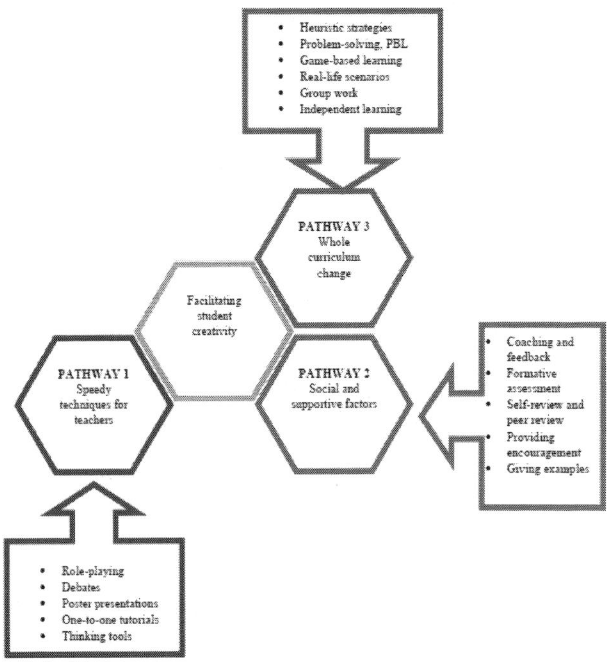

Figure 4: A Suggested Approach to Facilitating Student Creativity

Source: Fryer (2006)

Pathway 1

Participatory teaching techniques and pedagogical strategies that are an important tool in the teaching repertoire. These tactics include high group member participation while they enable meaningful and fun learning, through strategies such as role-playing, debates, poster presentations, one-to-one tutorials and the use of creative thinking techniques and tools. They all have their own complex structures and variations but are all also conducive to tapping into the creative potential of students.

For example,

- Role-plays are structured and have a defined set of participants with specific times, places, equipment, and rules.
- Debates are powerful models of teaching because they help student's master concepts and learn to be effective in pursuing goals.
- Presentations, the student must not only understand what is being presented, but also to whom it is being presented, and apply appropriate presentation strategies.

Each of these strategies helps foster creative potential as they are in contrast to the passive reception of knowledge of teacher-centered classrooms; this style of teaching promotes active, student-centered learning.

Pathway 2

Emphasizes the significance of feedback and support from someone who understands the creative process. More specifically, decisive feedback (including self-review and peer review) can be used to quick creative performance, develop creative talent, improve learning relationships, deal with creative "blocks" or "dry spells" and help students learn specific skills such as presentation, negotiation, coaching and influencing others.

It can also:

- Encourage students to reflect on their creative processes and working relationships
- Help students tap into powerful "creative flow" states
- Develop students' unique creative thinking and learning styles
- Help students explore strategies for more effective communication and collaboration.

Pathway 3

The focus of education should be not so much on what students learn as on what they can do with their learning (Torrance, 1974). Particularly concerned with addressing all aspects of cognitive development, especially students' capacity to think and to be happier.

Creativity involves forming ideas or hypotheses, testing them and communicating the results; adventurous thinking (stepping into the unknown); and invention, discovery, curiosity, experimentation, and exploration (Torrance, 1974). According to Torrance, (1974), creativity is relevant right across the curriculum. He focuses on,

- Teacher education and development,
- The classroom context,
- Teacher-student relationships and
- Students' learning needs at various levels.

Any programme that addresses creative education desires to shelter every aspect of being creative, including motivational and emotional factors, the expansion of knowledge and skills, the capacity to imagine (especially via the arts) and the capacity to solve fuzzy problems using heuristics and insight learning (in mathematics and other areas such as drama). It should be noted that in this pathway, the term "problem-solving" is used to mean "resolving anything puzzling or unclear". This is a key function of all thinking and active learning, equally applicable to creativity in the arts, sciences, and humanities. The negative connotations often associated with the term "problem" do not apply here.

6. Assessment that Stimulates Creativity

According to Biggs (1999, assessment is among the most important influences on learning, Dissatisfaction with assessment practices in Higher Education (HE) continues to the present day, and in recent years, there have been increasing calls for alternative assessment approaches that include performance-based, portfolio and authentic assessment (Anderson, 1998). Beghetto (2005) suggests that assessment practices can influence students' creativity. Studies have demonstrated that imagination and visualising had a positive effect on student performance on exams, and such studies have illustrated that creativity is tangled with reasoning (Claxton, 1999). Building on the work of Csikszentmihalyi (1997), Beattie (2000) concludes that creativity can and should be assessed although it is recognised that attempts to produce methods for the assessment of creativity that have not been straightforward.

Students feel that essay-based course-work is more effective than exams in supporting creativity through collaboration, with peer assessment offering the potential to improve students' work. The general consensus from the literature is that assessment should be varied in order to order to support the development of different aptitudes and encourage thinking in different ways. A diversity of assessment types can be an important stimulus to creative work, including more formative assessment and a balance of written and practical work. Particular examples are report-writing, article critique, group work and negotiated projects between students.

There are, however, well-recognised difficulties with integrating creativity in assessment practices. Cowan (2006) argues that of all the cognitive abilities, synthesis or creativity is the most difficult to assess. There is significant variation in the evidence teachers seek creativity: examples include originality, innovative thinking, entrepreneurship, problem-solving ability, initiative, inventiveness, the ability to generate ideas, and motivation. The core problem is that the creative process, for any learner, is unpredictable and difficult to capture. But moving from assessing the creative process to assessing a creative product does not necessarily offer an easier solution. Arguably, this is partly because the best person to judge the conception and development of an innovator product is the creative student him or herself.

7. Incorporating Creativity into the Professional Development of Teachers

Creativity among the teachers should not be considered as "Employability Skills" (Howard-Jones, 2008). Though there has been thriving of interest in the fostering of creativity among young people (Roberts, 2006, Downing *et al.*, 2007) and yet the provision of support for teachers and trainee teachers to achieve this remains a key task for education. It is important to consider how best to support teachers to teach creatively so that they can, in turn, transfer the benefits of creative learning strategies to their students.

Why should higher education teachers be interested in creativity?

Creatively as educators will, in turn, help our students endure and prosper in this world and help them to lead more satisfying and meaningful lives. It is vigorous that teachers have a respectable sympathetic understanding of creativity and creative education. Many teachers are already doing inspiring work that could be capitalised on, in collaboration with other providers, to put creative education resolutely on the teacher professional development agenda.

An integral part of teaching methodologies designed to foster creative reflection is the type of classroom environment which the teacher helps to create. What is needed are teachers who engage their students in meaningful activities:

- Ones which incorporate students' unique interests, abilities, backgrounds and community needs.
- Supporting the development of creative thinking is the need for cultural change in higher education so that the value of creativity is more accepted (Wisdom, 2006).

Many academicians and researcher argue that teachers need professional development opportunities to develop the knowledge and skills to nurture creativity in their students. Teachers need to understand and appreciate their own creativity and to recognise it as a fundamental part of their professional development. Each student has some innate creative potential, which can be enhanced by teachers who are aware of and knowledgeable about proven and effective ways to teach creative behaviour.

Table 2: Mapping Hofstede Cultural Dimensions with Creativity of respondents in Higher Education.

Respondents of Higher Education	Power Distance (PD)		Individualism (IDV)		Masculinity (MAS)		Uncertainty Avoidance (UAI)		Long term Orientation (LTO)	
	No.	%	No.	%	No.	%	No.	%	No.	%
Teaching	44	33	41	31	58	44	39	29	36	28
Non-teaching	32	24	15	11	12	9	15	12	20	15
Pursuers	56	43	76	58	62	47	78	59	76	57
Total	132	100	132	100	132	100	132	100	132	100

Source: Authors computation

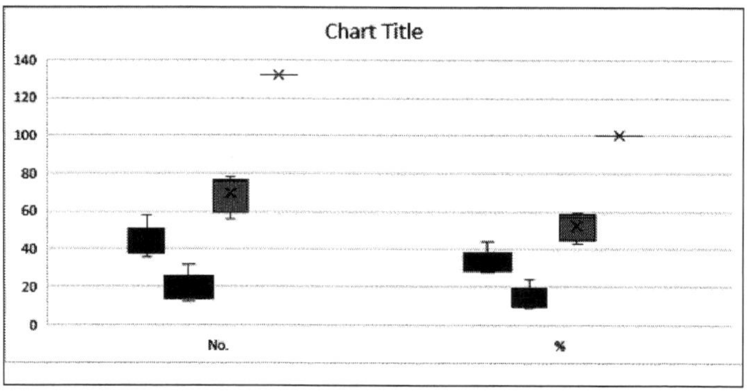

Figure 5: Mapping Hofstede Cultural Dimensions with Creativity of respondents in Higher Education.

Source: Authors computation

a. Power Distance Index (PDI) and Creativity

Power Distance is defined as "The extent to which less powerful members of organisations and institutions expect and accept that power is distributed unequally" (Hofstede, 1994). This index measures the perception concerning the decision-making style of superiors and the fear of disagreement with supervisors. Cultures with a high Power Distance Index (PDI) tolerates social inequality and the leadership style is benevolent autocratic and employees fear to disagree with their managers. In low PDI, high social equality is expected and the employees prefer a more democratic style of leadership with more independence in decision-making.

The table....shows the percentage of agreement of the respondents regarding PDI. Pursuers (43%) are more towards disagreeing with inequality followed by teaching (33%). It is evidenced very strongly the respondents are open towards innovation and creativity in higher education.

b. Individualism versus Collectivism (IDV) and Creativity

The individualism-collectivism dimension measures the "Relationship between the individual and the collection which prevails in a given society" (G. Hofstede, 1980, p. 148) and the degree to which individuals are integrated into groups. Cultures with high Individualism Index (IDV) have loose ties between individuals: "Everyone is expected to look after him/herself or his/herself immediate family" (Hofstede, 1994). Work environments that are challenging and allow individual achievements and working styles are preferred. Pursuers (58%) with high IDV are more independent in having creativity than in groups, it can be interpreted that the learners are more creative in contributing for the higher education from the point of view, research and innovative activities. This is followed by the teaching community (31%). Respondents with low IDV are integrated into strong, cohesive groups, which continue protecting them in exchange for unquestioning loyalty" (Hofstede, 1994). Groups goals and group harmony are more important than individual goals.

c. Masculinity versus Femininity (MAS) and Creativity

Masculinity describes the "preference in society for achievement, heroism, assertiveness and material reward for success" (G. Hofstede, 1980). Societies with high MAS index are more competitive. Femininity refers to "A preference for cooperation, modesty, caring for the weak and quality of life". Societies with low MAS index are consensus-oriented. Teachers (44%) and pursuers (47%) are shown very competitive and incline to the changes in the environment. Also, they are more towards modesty and materialistic.

d. Uncertainty Avoidance Index (UAI) and Creativity

Uncertainty Avoidance is the "Extent to which the members of a culture feel threatened by the uncertain or unknown situation" (Hofstede, 1994). Societies with high UAI try to manage uncertainty by following written and unwritten rules strictly and by establishing highly structured environments. Job tenure is expected to be very long. People appear busier and more restless. People with low UAI are more comfortable with ambiguous and unstructured circumstances and dislike formal rules. More towards "easy going" (Hofstede, 1994) and G. Hofstede, 1980). Pursuers with 59% are more towards UAI followed by 29% of teachers. Can be interpreted that, the learners of higher education are more determined to innovate to structure their environment to avoid any threat. They do not seem to be comfortable and prefer easy going since they are proactive in creating innovation activities.

e. Long-term versus short-term orientation (LTO) and Creativity

In societies with a long-term orientation, "people believe that truth depends very much on the situation, context and time"

(Hofstede, 1994). There is an ability to "adapt traditions to changed conditions, a strong propensity to save and invest, thriftiness and perseverance in achieving results". In societies with a short-term orientation, there is generally a "strong concern with establishing the absolute truth" normative thinking, "great respect for traditions, a relatively small propensity to save for the future, and a focus on achieving quick results" (Hofstede, 1994). Pursuers with high (57%) of LTO adopt more to the changed conditions and can be interpreted as highly creative.

8. Conclusion

However, we cannot provide precise guidelines about how to deal with the consequences of creativity and culture. One could either adapt the design thinking criteria to make people from a specific culture feel more comfortable (e.g. reduce the playfulness, change the space layout, establish more hierarchies with a determined team leader, etc.). However, the exact opposite might also be a promising strategy. Maybe, creating some kind of 'culture shock' and confronting people with inconvenient rituals is exactly what is needed to reach a creative leap.

Hofstede (1994) distinguished between professional, organisational, and national cultures, and he suggested the same five dimensions for organisations. Design thinking institutions (universities or companies that teach or apply design thinking) can be seen as organisations with a specific culture. Organisational culture can, to some extent, be different than the culture of the nation in which the organisation is located. Because Hofstede used his dimensions also for analysing organisational culture, we think our work might be helpful to understand also the effect of organisational culture on design thinking.

Summarising the aforementioned differences in cultural dimensions, we can say that there is not one 'perfect' culture for the design thinking method. Every cultural dimension has some positive and some negative effects on design thinking, and every culture has some characteristics that can cope well with the methodology. This leads to our conclusion, which suggests to always combine team members from different cultural backgrounds within a design thinking project, in order to gain from specific positive aspects of one culture and to balance possible negative aspects.

9. Limitations

Creative Thinking and Creativity in Higher Education is a broad term and can be perceived differently by different cultures. Also, we may be able to conclude on creative thinking criteria, steps, tools and team setup, mind-sets, since some cultures might be more predestined (Hofstede). Also, Hofstede study is old age and may not be appropriate for the present generation, since the dimensions might have changed. And these insights have to be handled with a lot of precaution.

Another limitation of the study is that Hofstede's data is almost 30 years old; it is more than likely that some countries (especially Asian countries) might have experienced some major development during the past decades, and some dimensions might have changed accordingly. However, since there is no alternative data of such comprehensibility available, we are limited to Hofstede's dataset. However, we believe that in fact, difficulties might occur, when taking creative thinking in Higher Education (HE) to other countries without considering the different cultural traditions and mindsets.

REFERENCES

Anderson, R.S. (1998) "Why talk about different ways to grade: the shift from traditional assessment to alternative assessment", in *Classroom Assessment and the New Learning Paradigm*, (Eds.) R.S. Anderson & B.W. Speck. San Francisco: Jossey-Bass. pp. 5–16.

Buchanan, R. (1992). "Wicked problems in design thinking." *Design Issues*, 8(2), 5-21.

Baille, C. (ed.) (2003) *The Travelling Case: Creativity in Art, Science, and Engineering. How to Foster Creative Thinking in Higher Education* [online]. York: The Higher Education Academy. Available from: http://www.heacademy.ac.uk/resources/detail/ourwork/tla/The_Travelling_CA SE [Accessed 26 June 2008].

Balchin, T. (2006) "Evaluating creativity through consensual assessment", in *Developing Creativity in Higher Education*, (Eds.) London: Routledge. pp. 173-183.

Barnett, R. (2000) "Supercomplexity and the curriculum", *Studies in Higher Education,* vol. 25, no. 3, pp.255–388.

Beattie, D.K. (2000) "Creativity in art: the feasibility of assessing current conceptions in the school context", *Assessment in Education: Principles and Practice*, vol. 7, no. 2, pp.175–192.

Brockling, U. (2006) "On creativity: A brainstorming session", *Education Philosophy and Theory*, vol. 38, no. 4, pp.513–521.

Claxton, G. (1999) *Wise Up*. New York: St Martin's Press.

Cowan, J. (2006) "How should I assess creativity?" in *Developing Creativity in Higher Education*, (Eds.) N. Jackson, M. Oliver, M. Shaw & J. Wisdom. London: Routledge. pp. 156-173.

Cropley, A.J. (2001) *Creativity in Education and Learning: A Guide for Teachers and Educators*. London: Kogan Page.

Csikszentmihalyi, M. (2006) Interview with *Wired Magazine* [online], no. 4, 9 September. Available from: http://www.wired.com/wired /archive /4.09/czik.html [Accessed 26 June 2008].

Csikszentmihalyi, M. (1997) *Creativity: Flow and the Psychology of Discovery and Invention*. London: Harper Collins.

de Bono, E. (1999) *Six Thinking Hats*. London: Penguin Books.

Diehm, C. (2004) "Classroom practice: from worn-out to web-based: better student portfolios", *Phi Delta Kappa*, vol. 85, no. 10, p.792.

Downing, D. and Lamont, E. with Newby, M. (2007) *HEARTS Higher Education, the Arts, and Schools: an experiment in educating teachers*. Slough: NFER.

Fryer, M. (2003) *Creativity across the Curriculum: A Review and Analysis of Programmes Designed to Develop Creativity*. London: Qualifications and Curriculum Authority.

Howard-Jones, P. (2008) *Fostering Creative Thinking: co-constructed insights from neuroscience and education.* Bristol: HEA Academic Subject Centre for Education. Available online from http://escalate.ac.uk/4389 [Accessed 16 July 2008].

Hofstede, G. (1980). *Culture's consequences: international differences in work-related values.* Beverly Hills: Sage Publications.

.... (1994). *Culture and organisations: Software of the Mind.* London: HarperCollins.

Jackson, N., Oliver, M., Shaw, M. & Wisdom, J. (eds.) (2014) *Developing Creativity in Higher Education.* London: Routledge.

Jackson, N. (2006) "Creativity in higher education: creating tipping points for cultural change", SCEPTrE Scholarly Paper 3. Available online from http://portal.surrey.ac.uk/pls/portal/docs/PAGE/SCEPTRE/RS/PAPER%202% 20PDP%20AND%20CREATIVITY%20JAN%2006.DOC[Accessed 26 June 2008].

Jackson N.J (2014) "Developing student's creativity through higher education." In A Xie and L Lei (Eds) International Symposium on ' *The Cultivation of Creativity in University students*' 8-28 Macao: Macao Polytechnic Institute.

Kane, P. (2004) *The Play Ethic: A Manifesto for a Different Way of Living.* London: Macmillan. Bristol: HEA Academic Subject Centre for Education. Available online from http://escalate.ac.uk/4389

Kelley, T., & Littman, J. (2001). *The art of innovation: lessons in creativity from IDEO, America's leading design firm.* New York: Currency/Doubleday.

Gardner, H. (1982) *Art, Mind, Brain: A Cognitive Approach to Creativity.* New York: Basic Books.

Oliver, M. Shaw & J. Wisdom. London: Routledge. pp.xviii-xx.

Oliver, M., Shah, B., McGoldrick, C. and Edwards, M. (2006) 'Students' experiences of creativity', in N.J. Jackson (eds.) *Developing Creativity in Higher Education: An Imaginative Curriculum*, London: Routledge-Falmer.

Plattner, H., Meinel, C., & Weinberg, U. (2009). *Design Thinking*. Munich: miwirtschaftsbuch. Stanford d.school. (2011). *Bootcamp Bootleg*, from http://dschool.stanford.edu/wpcontent/uploads/2011/03/Bootcamp Bootleg2010v2SLIM.pdf (last accessed 1.6.13).

Rittel, H. W. J. (1972). On the planning crisis: Systems analysis of the first and second generations. *Bedriftsokonomen*, 8, 390-396.

Roberts, P. (2006) *Nurturing Creativity in Young People*. London: Department for Culture, Media and Sport.

Stein, M. I. (1988) "Creativity: The process and its stimulation." In Flach, F. (Ed.), *The creative mind* (pp. 50-75). Buffalo, NY: Bearly Limited.

Torrance, E.P. (1974) *Torrance Tests of Creative Thinking: Norms and Technical Manual*. Bensenville IL: Scholastic Testing Service.

Wilson, Richard A., ed. (1997) World Commission on Culture and Development *(1995) Our Creative* Diversity. Paris: *UNESCO*. Wilson, Richard A., (Ed.)

Wisdom, J. (2006) "Developing higher education teachers to teach creatively", in *Developing Creativity in Higher Education*, (Eds.) N. Jackson, M. Oliver, M. Shaw & J. Wisdom. London: Routledge. pp.183-197.

6

Learning Achievement in Higher Education through the Application of Scientific Methods

Dr. Vani Ramesh & Dr. Vishal C. Jaunky

Abstract

Higher Education Learning will be meaningful if it links with the scientific approach and scientific concepts. The purpose of this chapter is to review the scientific approach of learning in higher education. The scientific approach in imparting skills and knowledge in higher education in creating knowledge is very much essential in recent days. It is an attitude towards acquiring and creating knowledge. It is the outcome of critical thinking which provides a solid foundation for higher education learners. This will help the students to learn life skills and critical thinking to have a solid foundation. If students are guided towards a critical approach to the observations they will be able to list a number of hypotheses. More they hypothesize, the eager they will be to inquire and reach the truth. It is always proved by many scientists and researchers; scientific literacy and a better understanding of the scientific methods is an added advantage for the higher education seekers. Lack of understanding of the scientific method is lusher than is commonly whispered, at least in part because many scientists and science educators do not understand all the components of the scientific method. Specifically, misuse of the term "hypothesis" obfuscates genuine understanding of the scientific method. The widespread use and teaching of the "scientific method" suggest and helps us organise our thoughts about the scientific process that generates reliable knowledge. The main objective of this contribution is to encourage consensus in teaching and learning higher education and contribution to the existing literature. The author intends to have empirical evidence of the same in due course for a better understanding of the theories which can be practiced in higher education learning and teaching process.

Keywords: Higher Education, Scientific Methods, Learning, Skills, Hypothesis.

1. INTRODUCTION

Developing quality education, especially in Higher Education is very important. The quality of Higher Education can be improved with the help of scientific approach, by adopting and applying more innovative, creative and good scientific reasoning. The quality education in India, particularly Higher Education still requires special attention. Though abundant resources are available, the quality of higher education in India to make it better is to apply scientific methods in teaching and learning, that has the right destination. The study conducted by Trends in International Mathematics and Science Study (TIMSS) in 2007, showed that Mathematical literacy learners in Indonesia occupy 36 of the 49 countries. According to the OECD (2006), when viewed from the study report Program for International Student Assessment (PISA) in 2003, the quality of education in Indonesia for Science and Mathematics Literacy is ranked in position 39 of the 40 participants, 50th out of Malaysia, 36 out of 40 in Thailand, Singapore 39 0ut of 40.

Science is one branch of science that is commonly known as the 'Natural Sciences' in which is divided into three sciences, such as,

- Chemistry,
- Physics and
- Biology.

Acquiring knowledge of these subjects will enable the students to possess the necessary skills and implement them in practical life. In Higher Education, acquiring these skills are more appropriate for their professional growth. Students typically receive theoretical knowledge in the classroom given by lecturers.

For Example**,** Students get the concepts of material physics chemistry algorithmically, but when applied to the concept that there should be learning more emphasis on hands-on activity.

Experimenting the theoretical learning is a tool for students in understanding science. Experiments activity is to do a proofing by smearing the theory in actual activity. Through the practicum students can conduct scientific activities in the laboratory. Scientific approachable to assist learners in mastering the material and laboratory skills with carrying out important five activities in a scientific approach. These are,

- Observe,
- Ask,
- Try,
- Associate (reasoning), and
- Communicate.

The Scientific method of teaching and learning was first introduced in the United States of science education in the 19th century, as the emphasis on formalistic laboratory methods that lead to scientific facts. The scientific method has the characteristics of "doing science". This method allows teachers or curriculum and pedagogical developers to improve the learning process, namely by breaking the process down into steps or stages in detail which contains instructions for the students to carry out learning activities. This has given inspiration for the Indian academics to have some guidelines for the curriculum and pedagogical development for teaching and learning activities both at undergraduate programmes, post-graduate and higher education. Though there is no standard difference between the scientific methods and scientific approach, the objective is to improve the skills, attitude, knowledge, and skills of the learners. This has been explained in detail as below:

Skills acquired through activity,

- Observing,
- Questioning,
- Experimenting,
- Associating and
- Communicating

Characteristic Features of competence along the path difference acquisition participate affect the characteristics of the standard process:

1. Observing

Observing is one of the most effective and were more prioritise of the meaningfulness learning process. This method can present the object media as real, this can make the students happy and were motivated to be challenged, and easy for implementation. Though the observing activity usually requires long preparation time and mature, relatively high cost and effort, it cannot do the best will obscure the meaning and purpose of learning.

2. Questioning

Effective teachers can inspire students to improve and develop the realm of attitudes, skills, and knowledge. The students will be acquiring good thinking skills which makes them deeply involved in the subject to think creatively and during the process to become more inquisitive to learn and understand the subject. This makes the task more and more questions deeply. By the time the teacher asked, at the same time in charge of guiding or guide the students to learn well. When the teacher answered student questions when it also served to encourage their students to be good listeners and learners.

3. Experimenting

Once the students are confident of the learning process and able to gain the necessary knowledge and skills, they would obtain real or reliable learning. Students should try to this knowledge practically, especially for materials or substances that are well-suited.

For example, Students who are pouring physics should understand the concepts of physics and its relationship to daily life. They should also have the skills to advance their knowledge in the particular environment, as well as being able to use the scientific method and scientific attitude to solve the glitches they aspect in the day to day life.

4. Associating

This is broadly understood as the "Student Centric" approach of learning and teaching, where the students take part actively and both teacher and student play an equal role in learning and teaching. Both teacher and student play an active role in active actors. The emphasis of course in many ways and situations students must be more dynamic than the teacher.

'Reasoning' is the process of thinking logically and systematically over-the word empirical facts that can be observed to obtain a conclusion in the form of knowledge.

'Reasoning' question is the 'scientific reasoning'. The experiences that have been stored in the memory of the brain relate and interact with prior experience are already available. That process is known as 'association' or 'reasoning'.

5. Communicating

Collective learning is personal of philosophy is more than learning techniques. Collaboration is a 'way of life' and 'lifestyle' of human interaction that locates and interpret cooperation as a structure interaction, elegant and proposed to enable 'cooperative efforts' in order to achieve a mutual goal. The success of implementing learning is often seen in the final assessment of learners. Whereas a learning process always influenced by factors that occur during the learning process takes place. If this is used for pennillion successful implementation of the learning process when there is a practical application in real life situations. This has been well illustrated in the below table1:

Table 1: The linkage scientific approach with the learning activities of Higher Education Learners.

An aspect of Scientific Approach in Higher Education	Learning Activity
Observing	Reading Hearing Listening View or Sensing (without or with tool)
Questioning	1. Asking questions about the information that is not understood from what is observed? 2. Asking questions to gain additional information about what is observed. 3. Asking questions that are from fact. 4. Asking questions that are from the concept 5. Asking the questions that are from hypothetical.

Experimenting	1. Conducting experiments 2. Reading of sources other than books 3. Observing objects/events 4. Activities (learner activity) 5. Interviews with resource persons
Associating	Finding links between the various information collected Finding patterns of relatedness of the various information collected Summing up of the sharing pattern found The information is processed to add breadth and depth of knowledge Processing of information collected for the search of solutions from a variety of sources that have a different opinion
Communicating	1. Deliver the result of observations orally, in writing or other media 2. Deliver the conclusion based on the analysis of oral, written or other media.

Source: D. Hudson (1996)

For the purpose of a better understanding of the process, the following diagram is introduced:

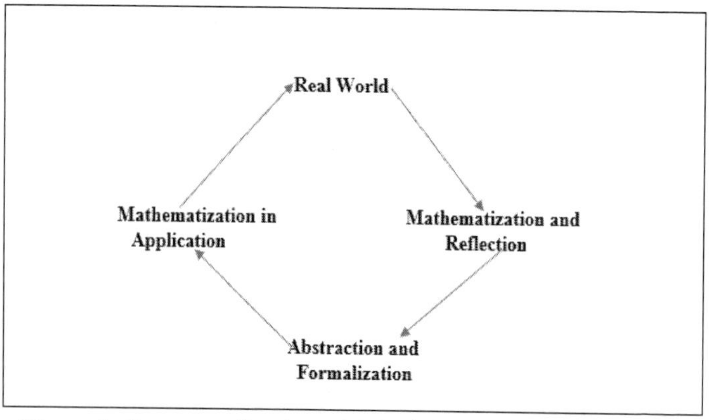

Figure 1: Conceptualisation of Scientific application in Higher Education.

Source: V. Maria and F. Michael (2016)

LEARNING THEORIES

There are many theories to explain how individuals acquire, organise and deploy skills and knowledge. For the purpose of this review and chapter, these are some of the learning theories reviewed and referred.

For a better understanding of the concept learning, the learning theories are grouped into three basic categories.

- Behaviourist Learning Theories,
- Cognitive-information processing learning theories
- Cognitive-constructivist Learning theories.

(Please note, a brief review is done for the readers understanding)

a. Behaviourist Learning Theories

The origins of behaviourist learning theories may be traced backed to the late 1800s and early 1900s with the formulation of "Associationistic" principles of learning. The general goal was to derive elementary laws of learning and behaviour that may then be extended to explain more complex situations. Inferences were tied closely to observed behaviour in "lower organisms" with the belief that the laws of learning were universal and that work with laboratory animals could be extrapolated to humans. It was believed that a fundamental set of principles derived from the study of learning in a basic or "pure" form could then be applied to the broader context of learning in schools.

Three experimental approaches are related to the study of 'Associationistic Learning' including:

1. The use of nonsense syllables and individual words to study the association of ideas

2. The use of animals to study the association between sensations and impulses
3. The use of animals to study association and reflexology

The Association of Ideas Following a tradition begun by Edwards, A.W.F. (1972).researchers studied learning in terms of memory for individual items, most commonly nonsense syllables and individual words. It was assumed that understanding simpler forms of learning would lead to an understanding of more complex phenomena (Hull (1934, 1952), Popper, K.R. (1981), Sober, E. (1984).

Behavioural learning theories have contributed to instruction and education in several significant ways. The three applications summarised here include:

1. Behaviour Modification
2. Classroom Management
3. The Management of Instruction

'Behavioural Modification' is also known as 'Behaviour Therapy' or 'Contingency Management. Behaviour modification is typically used to treat behaviour problems in social, personal, or school situations. Some clinical applications include treatments for phobias, obsessions or eating disorders (Koch. S. 1944) (Skinner, B.F., 1944).

b. Cognitive-Information Processing Theories

As psychologists became increasingly unsatisfied with the limitations of behavioural theory and methods, and persuasive arguments against radical behaviourist theories were being put forth by linguists studying language development, the "time was right" for the emergence of cognitivism. Another projecting factor was the development of computers (Koch. S. 1944), which provided both a credible metaphor for human information processing and a significant tool for modeling and exploring human cognitive processes.

One major group of cognitive theories may be classified as, Cognitive-information processing learning theories (CIP). The human learner is conceived to be a processor of information, in considering the same way a computer is. When learning occurs, information is input from the environment, processed and stored in memory, and output in the form of a learned capability. Proponents of the CIP model, like behaviourists, seek to explain how the environment modifies human behaviour. However, unlike behaviourists, they assume an intervening variable between the environment and behaviour. That variable is the information processing system of the learner (Atkinson and Shiffrin., 1968) memory in which information received by the processing system undergoes a series of transformations before it can be permanently stored in memory.

The degree to which an individual can spread their attention across two or more tasks (or sources of information) or focus on selected information within a single task depends on four factors:

1. The meaning of the task or information to the individual
2. The similarity between competing tasks or sources of information
3. Task complexity or difficulty
4. The individual's ability to control attention Pattern Recognition Just attending to information is not enough to ensure its further processing.

c. Cognitive-Constructivist Learning Theories

Constructivist approaches to teaching and learning are grounded in several research traditions (Perkins, 1991; Pappas, C.C., Kiefer, B. Z., and Levstik, L. S. (1990). The origins of constructivism may be traced back to a little known Latin treatise, De antiquissima Italorum sapientia, written in 1710 by Jacobs, H.H. (1989) (Glasersfeld, 1991). Vico suggested that knowledge is knowing what parts something is made of, as well as knowing how they are related.

"Objective, ontological reality, therefore, may be known to God, who constructed it but not to a human being who has access only to subjective experience" (Glasersfeld, 1991).

A second, related path to constructivism originates from 'Gestalt theories of perception' (Kohler, 1924) that focus on the ideas of closure, organisation and continuity (Resnick, L.B. (Ed.) (1989). Like Vico, Gestalt psychologists suggest that people do not interpret pieces of information separately and that cognition imposes organisation on the world. Theories of intellectual development provide a third research tradition contributing to the notion of cognitive construction (Piaget, 1952, 1969, 1971; Baldwin, 1902, 1906-1911; Bruner, 1974). Developmentalists believe that learning results from adaptations to the environment which are characterised by increasingly sophisticated methods of representing and organising information. Developmental scientists also forward the notion that children progress through different levels or stages which allow children to construct novel representations and rules.

The fourth line of research depicts learning as a socially mediated experience where individuals construct knowledge based on interactions with their social and cultural environment. Like Piaget and Bruner, Vygotsky (1962, 1978) believed that the formation of intellect could be understood by studying the developmental process.

According to Malcolm Knowles (1970), adult learners differ from children in the following six ways:

1. *Need for Knowledge:* Adults need to know "why" they should learn.
2. *Motivation:* Adults are driven by internal motives. They will learn if they want to learn. For instance, a compelling answer to the "what's-in-it-for-me" question is a powerful internal motivation.
3. *Willingness:* For adults, the willingness or readiness to learn comes from perceiving the relevance of the knowledge. They want to know how learning will help them better their lives, and they learn best when they know that knowledge has immediate value for them.
4. *Foundation or Experience:* Adults bring with them rich reserves of experiences that form the foundation of their learning. They analyse, rationalise, synthesise, and develop new ideas or tweak old ones through the filter of their experiences. As an instructional designer, you should tap into the well of experiences to help them make connections, perceive relevance, and derive inspiration.
5. *Self-Direction:* Adults are self-directed individuals who want to take charge of the learning journey. They are independent beings who want to feel in control.
6. *Orientation to Learning:* Adults learn best when they "do." They find relevance in task-oriented learning, which they can align with their workplace realities. Besides, task-oriented learning exercises their problem-solving

ability that in turn, gives them the confidence that they can conquer their challenges with their newly-acquired knowledge. David A. Kolb reveals the cyclical nature of experiential learning by explaining how it takes place in four stages:

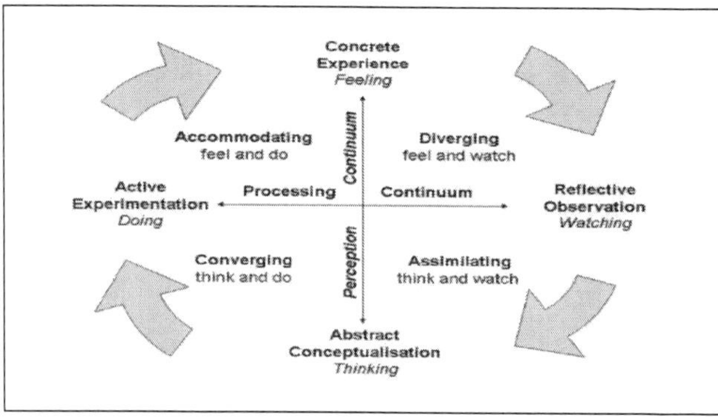

Figure 2 (a): David A. Kolb Cyclical Nature of Experiential Learning:

Source: David A. Kolb (1984)

1. Concrete Experience - (a new experience or situation is encountered, or a reinterpretation of existing experience).

2. Reflective Observation of the New Experience - (of particular importance are any inconsistencies between experience and understanding).

3. Abstract Conceptualization (reflection gives rise to a new idea, or a modification of an existing abstract concept The person has learned from their experience).

4. Active Experimentation (the learner applies their idea(s) to the world around them to see what happens).

Figure 2 (b): David A. Kolb Cyclical Nature of Experiential Learning:

Source: David A. Kolb (1984)

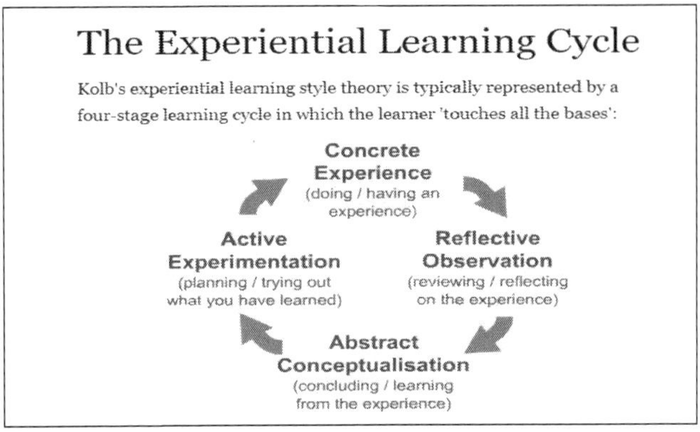

Figure 3: David A. Kolb Cyclical Nature of Experiential Learning: Matrix

Source: David A. Kolb (1984)

It's often easier to see the construction of Kolb's learning styles in terms of a two-by-two matrix. Each learning style represents a combination of two preferred styles. The matrix also highlights Kolb's terminology for the four learning styles; diverging, assimilating, and converging, accommodating:

	Active Experimentation (Doing)	**Reflective Observation (Watching)**
Concrete Experience (Feeling)	Accommodating (CE/AE)	Diverging (CE/RO)
Abstract Conceptualization (Thinking)	Converging (AC/AE)	Assimilating (AC/RO)

Figure 3 (a): David A. Kolb Cyclical Nature of Experiential Learning: Matrix

Source: David A. Kolb (1984)

1. *Concrete Experience (CE):* Adults learn best when the learning experience goes beyond the chalk-and-talk routine. Kinesthetic learning or learning by encouraging physical actions (simulations) and learning that evokes strong emotional responses (realistic scenarios that reveal cause-effect relationships) create powerful experiences that are not forgotten easily.
2. *Reflective Observation (RO):* Adults need to engage with and reflect on their experiences to glean insights and acquire knowledge. So it is critical to not only create opportunities for experience-based learning but also provide time and space to encourage reflection. Create opportunities for "watching" the action unfold before the eyes (demonstrations) and "analysing" processes and procedures (scenario-driven activities, case studies).
3. *Abstract Conceptualisation (AC):* The success of experiential learning lies in the learner being able to decode abstract concepts from their reflections, generalise these ideas, and realise the relevance to their reality. Designs assessments to encourage learners to exercise their "critical thinking" abilities, so they can formulate concepts and procedures.
4. *Active Experimentation (AE):* Role-playing activities, internships, and other hands-on tasks let learners apply the learning and thus truly "learn by doing." Active experimentation leads to concrete experiences, and the cycle of experiential learning resumes.

CONCLUSION

Application of scientific approach in Higher Education have high criteria and the highest scope for learning and acquiring good skills, knowledge, and qualities to sustain the professional competition. This review intends to be in some light on the theories and concepts that can support the application of scientific methods in learning and teaching of higher education pedagogy.

REFERENCES

(Please note for authors information, more references are included):

A. A Putrawan, "Pengembangan Perangkat Pembelajaran Matematika Dengan Pendekatan Scientific Berbantu Geogebra dalam Upaya Meningkatkan Keterampilan Komunikasi dan Aktivitas Belajar Matematika Siswa Kelas VII SMP," *Thesis*, Universitas Pendidikan Ganesha, 2014.

Ackerman, D.B. (1989). "Intellectual and practical criteria for successful curriculum integration." In H.H. Jacobs (Ed.), *Interdisciplinary curriculum: Design and implementation* (25-37). Alexandria, VA: ASCD.

Applebee, A.N., Langer, J.A., & Mullis, I.V. (1989). *Crossroads in American education: A summary of findings: Educational Testing Service.* Princeton, NJ.

Baldwin, J.M. (1902). *Development and evaluation.* London: Macmillian Baldwin, J.M. (1906-1911). Thought and things or genetic logic: A study of the development and meaning of thought, Vols. 1-3. New York: MacMillan.

Bruner, J. (1974). *Beyond the information given.* London: George Allen & Unwin.

Collins, A., Brown, J.S., & Newman, S.E. (1989). "Cognitive apprenticeship: Teaching the crafts of reading, writing, and mathematics." In L. Resnick (Ed.), *Knowledge, learning, and instruction: Essays in honour of Robert Glaser* (453-494). Hillsdale, NJ: Erlbaum.

D. Hudson, *Journal of Curriculum Studies* 28, 2, 115-135 (1996).

Edwards, A.W.F. (1972). *Likelihood.* Cambridge, MA: Cambridge University Press

Fogarty, R. (1991). *How to integrate the curricula: The mindful school.* Palatine, IL: Skylight Publishing, Inc.

Glasersfeld, Ernst von (1980a). "The concepts of adaptation and viability in a radical constructivist theory of knowledge" (Annual Meeting of the Jean Piaget Society, Philadelphia, 1977). In I. Sigel, R. Golinkoff, & D.

Brodzinski (eds.), *New directions in Piagetian theory and their application to education,* (87-95). Hillsdale, New Jersey: Erlbaum.

Hull, C (1952). *A behaviour system: An introduction to behaviour theory concerning the individual organism.* New Haven, CT., Yale University Press.

.... (1943). *Principles of behaviour.* New York: Appleton-Century-Crofts.

.... (1938). *The goal-gradient hypothesis applied to some "field-force" problems in the behaviour of young children.* Psy.Rev. 45,271-299.

.... (1951). *Essentials of behaviour.* New Haven ct: Yale University Press.

I. K. Gading, "Pengaruh Pelatihan Kendali Diri dan Jenis Kelamin Terhadap Prilaku, Prokrastinasi Akademik Siswa SMP", *Dissertation*, Universitas Negeri Malang, 2014.

I. Kurniasih and B. Sani, *Implementasi Kurikulum* 2013*: Konsep dan Penerapan* (Kata Pena, Surabaya, 2014).

In R.D. Tweney, M.E. Doherty & C.R. Mynatt (Eds.), *On Scientific Thinking* (pp. 92-99). New York: Columbia University Press.

J. L Rudolph, "Epistemology for the masses: The origins of the scientific method in American schools", in *History of Education, Quarterly*, 45, pp. 341-376 (2005).

Jacobs, H.H. (1989). "The growing need for interdisciplinary curriculum content." In H.H. Jacobs (Ed.), *Interdisciplinary curriculum: Design and implementation* (1-11). Alexandria, VA: ASCD.

Knowles, M. S. (1970). *The modern practice of adult education: Androgogy versus pedagogy.* New York: New York Association Press.

Koch, S. (1944). *Review of Hull's principles of behaviour.* Psy.Bull,.41. 269-286.

Kolb, D. A. (1976). *The Learning Style Inventory: Technical Manual.* McBer & Co, Boston, MA.

.........,. (1981). Learning styles and disciplinary differences. *The modern American college*, 232-255.

.........., (1984). *Experiential learning: Experience as the source of learning and development* (Vol. 1). Englewood Cliffs, NJ: Prentice-Hall.

........., & Fry, R. E. (1974). *Toward an applied theory of experiential learning.* MIT Alfred P. Sloan School of Management.

Kolb, D. A., Rubin, I. M., & McIntyre, J. M. (1984). *Organisational psychology: readings on human behaviour in organisations.* Prentice Hall.

M. O. Martin, I. V. Mullis, and S. J. Chrostowski, TIMSS 2007: *International science report* (Chestnut Hill, Boston College, 2008).

M. Purnader, A. A. Tabassi and P. Baloh, *International Journal of Project Management* 33, 419-434 (2015).

Marzano, R.J. (1991). "Fostering thinking across the curriculum through knowledge restructuring." *Journal of Reading*, 34(7), 518-525

N. Dantes, *Metodelogi Penelitian* (C.V Andi Offset, Yogyakarta, 2012).

OECD. PIRLS. OECD, (Paris, France, 2006).

Pappas, C.C., Kiefer, B. Z., & Levstik, L. S. (1990). *An integrated language perspective in elementary school: Theory into action*. New York: Longman.

Peraturan Menteri Pendidikan dan Kebudayaan Republik Indonesia No. 22 (2016) Tentang Standar Proses.

Peraturan Menteri Pendidikan dan Kebudayaan Republik Indonesia Nomor 81a (2013) Tentang Implementasi Kurikulum Pedoman Umum Belajar

Peraturan Menteri Pendidikan Nasional nomor 16 tahun 2007

Perkins, D.N. (1986). *Knowledge by design*. Hillsdale, NJ: Erlbaum.

.... (1991). *Educating for insight*. Educational Leadership, 49(2), 4-8.

Piaget, J. (1952). *The origins of intelligence in children*. New York: International Universities Press. Piaget, J. (1969). The mechanisms of perception. London: Routledge and Keger Paul.

.... (1971). *Genetic epistemology*. New York: W.W. Norton.

Popper, K.R. (1981). *Science, pseudo-science, and falsifiability*.

Resnick, L.B. (Ed.) (1989). *Introduction. Knowing, learning, and instruction: Essays* in honour of Robert Glaser (1-24). Hillsdale, NJ: Erlbaum.

Skinner, B.F. (1944). *Review of Hulls Principles of behaviour Amer*. J.Psy., 57, 276-282.

Sober, E. (1984). *The Nature of Selection: Evolutionary Theory in Philosophical Focus*. Cambridge, MA: MIT Press.

Sterner, R.T. (1998). *The scientific method: An instructor's flow chart*. The American Biology Teacher, 60, 374–378.

Tchudi, S. (1991). *Planning and assessing the curriculum in English language arts*. Alexandria, VA: ASCD.

Thagard, P. (1992). *Conceptual Revolutions*. Princeton, NJ: Princeton University Press.

Thaiss, C. (1986). *Language across the curriculum in the elementary grades.* Urbana, IL: ERIC Clearinghouse on Reading and Communication Skills and the National Council for the Teaching of English.

Tompkins, G.E., & Hoskisson, K. (1991). *Language arts: Content and teaching strategies.* New York: Merrill, an imprint of Macmillan Publishing Company.

V. Maria and F. Michael, The Scientific Method and Scientific Inquiry: Tensions" In *Teaching And Learning,* (Wiley InterSci., New York, 2008).

Vico, Gesalt, Reviewed by Paul Oskar Kristeller, *The Philosophical Review*, Vol. 54, No. 4 (Jul. 1945), pp. 428-431

Ward, G. (1988). *I've got a project on... Australia: Primary English Teaching Association*, distributed by Heinemann, Portsmouth, NH.

Y. Abidin, *Desain Sistem Pembelajaran dalam Konteks Kurikulum* 2013 (Refika Aditama, Bandung, 2014).

Y. S. Lincoln and E. G. Guba, *Naturalistic inquiry* (Sage, California, 1985).

Part II
Throne of Higher Education

7

Skills and Higher Education

Dr. Lila Simon

ABSTRACT

Your earning ability today is largely dependent upon your knowledge, skill and your ability to combine that knowledge and skill in such a way that you contribute value for which customers are going to pay –

Brian Tracy

The Indian Higher Education is Organised into 'General' and 'Professional 'streams, yet can definitely boost of itself for producing enough degree holders every year, but the world of business/industry experts thinks that 80% among this pass-outs does not possess any identifiable marketable skills and are not fit to be employable. They have regularly voiced their concern over the lack of skilled manpower ready to be absorbed in various sectors. In fact, the employability of major graduates of our educational system is becoming a matter of giant concern.

In general, it is perceived that with academic qualifications, it is easier for students to pursue Masters or go for research-oriented academic programs, but with vocational education, vertical growth of skill holders is at stake. Our system of education does not prepare for a life beyond classrooms and hence steps should be taken by the education policymakers that Universities and Colleges should now turn into Skill Development Hubs. The paper is divided into three parts: The Issue, The skills required in Higher Education and The Action.

Keywords: Skills, Higher Education, Education System, Adaptive, Communication, Technology

INTRODUCTION

India is a country which is witnessing a large dropout rate of children quitting school at a young age. Ideally after completing education, one should not hunt for the job, else the employers should come forward in search of this skilled manpower. It is perceived very clearly that the attention of education policymakers and the International Education Community is moving away from the skills required by the workforce to promote economic growth though universally, skill development has been talked with considerable seriousness.

The Gross Enrolment Ratio [GER], a statistical measure to regulate the number of students registered in various programs within the country expressed as a percentage of the population indicates that India is aiming to attain GER of 30% by the year 2020, which is still far behind like the US which is at 85.8%

THE ISSUE

Any school going student when asked about their desire in life has rarely revealed any curiosity in becoming a chef, cobbler, mechanic, plumber or driver. Same is the case with parents. It is the hyped insight of the parents that only a few professions can offer stable income. This outlook of the parents forces the child to be a 'Jack of a few trades and master of none'. Such children when bound to choose careers, out of compulsion, fails to excel in their careers as they are either interested or don't have an aptitude for the same resulting in failure on keeping up to expectations of their parents. Every parent sets up a very high benchmark for their children and wants to fulfill their childhood dreams through them. They never bother to accept the real capability of their children. Parents and students realise very late that vocational education would have helped them to stand in the highly professional world. Though the Higher education systems and institutions are under pressure to reform to provide adequate skills and knowledge for the evolving labour markets, they must realise that for many students the switch from education into employment is not just a straight forward matter

In the 1990s with the considerable expansion in graduate numbers, the fact is many students were ill-equipped for the transition from education to employment. Most students prefer to get into Higher Education institutions for a college degree as they presume that quality education is the key to a successful career.

Though the National Skills Education Qualification Framework (NVEQF) addresses a few of the existing challenges. As academicians, one must reflect on the diverse attributes that the student community needs to develop while at higher education Institutes. It's now time to stop practicing lower level skills and help students to develop higher-order thinking skills.

Furthermore, it should also be understood that the nature of employment is also changing even for those in work. It is against this background that national debate has arisen about what should be offered to the students in universities and other institutions.

GROWING DEMAND FOR THE HIGHLY SKILLED

Though the government is taking measures when it comes to eliminating or reducing the challenges, being faced in the vocational education domain, an extensive set of literacies, abilities and character potentials that is thought to be judgmentally significant to success in the current world.

There is a debate at the global – level on the specific skills that should constitute the '21st Century skills 'and how this can be executed in Higher Education Institutions.

With the changing times, the Higher Educational Institutions need to focus on developing the following skills: –

Adaptive Flexibility

Students need to be taught to adapt and learn from the challenges encountered and have the ability to respond flexibly to change. They must be made aware that students with a high degree of adaptive flexibility can adapt different styles of learnings.

Communication

Students to be taught to communicate with clarity and precision as it is one of the rudiments of generic skills that each one must possess at University Level. Healthy communication must be encouraged among the student community by facilitating provisions of group discussions/chats etc. Being an effective communicator helps people to make a positive contribution to the organisation.

Adaptive Thinking

Adaptive Thinking is all about learning how to think and be more responsive to the environment. It helps to learn better and allows to respond to changing situations. Researches have proved that Adaptive Thinkers can show Impulse Control and leave the ego at the door.

Managing Impulsivity

Impulsivity is very common among most of our students and they react on a whim without thought. It is important to learn the art of patience and apply discipline to one's thought.

Time Management

Managing time either to prepare the lessons or attempting exams is a matter of concern among most of the students, which needs to be addressed. Students should be made to practice, eliminating distractions and get into organised work. Most students foresee themselves as being successful in their studies but they fail to establish a routine to achieve academic success. They should be taught to prioritise their activities as part of Time Management Skills.

Developing Academic Writing

The present generation just doesn't want to spend quality time with academic texts as a result do not exert any effort in identifying texts that pertain to their curriculum. In fact, students should practice the habits of visiting the library and reading academic texts critically and effectively. This would help them in developing the habit of Academic Writing and improvement of spellings and grammar which is also becoming a matter of concern in the present Higher Education System

Collaboration

The collaboration will help the students to explore significant questions and create expressive projects. To create such a conducive environment, learning must happen in small groups thereby creating opportunities for students to engage in subject-specific discussions with peers and to learn how to work together with mutual support. Today's student community lacks such kind of collaborative attitude and prefers isolation. The collaboration will also enable in developing higher level thinking skills and even promote student-faculty interaction. Further, it will also increase student retention power and enhance satisfaction in the learning experience thereby fashioning an environment of active, involved exploratory learning.

CRITICAL THINKING AND PROBLEM-SOLVING

In the present system, employers need employees who are good at problem-solving and generating ideas. A manager with Critical Thinking Ability can always make better decisions. It is ironical that the present generation is least interested in the process of Critical Thinking and Problem – Solving.

Questioning and Problem Posing

The classroom should offer space for the students to Inquiry, which is not much encouraged by most of the faculties for various personal reasons. As an academician, we must cheer inquiry-based learning and use it widely as an advocated pedagogical approach at the Under Graduate and Post Graduate level.

Technology

As we know that the millennials are very techno-savvy, yet when it comes to the part of their learning, like curriculum, it is often challenging for Faculty as well as students. This is where the need for smart classroom arises. Faculty need to be updated with the technology to be used in the classroom and students must be encouraged for the same. This will definitely encourage Digital use in this Digital era when change is happening more rapidly. Students should be encouraged for preparing and delivering digital presentations

Creativity and Innovation

These are the two frequently heard rapports in Higher Education. Creativity and Innovations along with collaborative conversations can always encourage an atmosphere of providing interdisciplinary and cross-class projects. Students must be given the freedom to put forth their creative minds in the classroom thereby generating a culture of Creativity and Innovation.

Empathy and Perspective

The capacity to empathize is a revered trait in most societies across the Globe and is considered a motivating factor. Empathy can be refined by practicing role play methods and promoting Emotional Literacy. This can create a sense of community within the student.

Global Citizenship/Competency

The driving resolution behind Global Learning is to become a Globally Component. Globally competent students are curious and interested to know more about the world. The idea of global competence articulates the knowledge and skills that are needed by the students in the 21st century.

Entrepreneurial

Helping the students to attain entrepreneurial skills just doesn't necessarily mean that they need to opt it as their career, but they can be taught to think like an entrepreneur. This skill allows the students to push limitations, generate ideas and do things differently. An entrepreneurial mindset can always help students to lead projects that can brand with a difference in the world.

Sustainability Literacy

Sustainability Literacy is a significant skill required by a professional in all areas. It is the level of understanding which would permit a professional to identify issues and decisions which have implications, thus leading them to make relevant inquiries and studies. Students with Sustainability Literacy will be prepared with involvements and skills required to address local and global challenges.

THE ACTION

Indian Higher Education needs radical reforms after witnessing rapid and impulsive growth. The demand for decidedly skilled employees so as to meet the needs of the knowledge economy has continued to grow and hence the Indian Education system needs a deep-seated rethink on the following:

Changing Curriculum with time

The curriculum must keep changing with time. It must include all those skills and Knowledge necessary to produces product that is highly competitive and ready to be part of today's workforce. The present curriculum does not provide the opportunity to experience real-life work settings while being enrolled. Though few premier institutes design their curricula in a way that students get on-the-job training, yet when it comes to only vocational education then the students become bothered about their future. The program content should be delivered through workshop, seminars, tutorials, industrial and field visits in addition to the classroom lectures and the students should be guided to refer to a large number of reference books. Most of the courses/programs do not have internships and if at all they have, these internships are not undertaken seriously by the students. All courses to be designed to provide, high quality and enjoyable experience and should be able to deliver the skills needed by the labour market.

Providing Skill-Based Training

Presently most of the Higher Education institutions are focussing on knowledge and skills of students but fail to prepare them to live after graduation. Companies with requisite experience in Skills training should be roped in to expedite the process of enhancing the skill development of Youths in Colleges and Universities and ensure that young generation develops the skills that actually make a difference in much more effective way as required by the industry.

Guidance for Students whose First Language is not English

Special attention needs to be taken for students who come from rural background especially if their first language is not English. The institutions should provide them with remedial and tutorial classes. English labs should be set up in institutions as part of the basic infrastructure to improve the language.

Increasing Industry Linkages

The increasing role of knowledge suggests that the Higher Education Institutions and industry must interact not just to create but also to employ the skills for development. As Universities are known to be centres of Knowledge generation and training for community development, Strict Compulsory Internship Programs should be included in Curriculum and the industry must support to generate skills and abilities that cannot be taught and learned within the four walls of the Institution. Association with Sector Skills Council [SSSCs] will help a lot in creating industry linkages and massive awareness as they play a decisive role in the Skill Development Ecosystem. They also ensure that training is provided which is appropriate to industry needs as it is associated with the National Skilled Development Policy. Industry and Academe are the major players who can deal with skill shortages.

Improved Classrooms

Classrooms must be equipped with the latest technology required for training students so that they get acquainted themselves with the same. In India most of the government institutions do not have even elementary facilities and if at all they have, the faculty are not trained to operate them. Students are unique and the same is the way they learn, hence we as facilitators should use teaching tools that are student-centric.

Qualified Subject Experts

The faculty must be qualified in the subjects or skills they are about to teach. Most of the time, it is observed in many Indian Universities/Higher Educations Institutions that teachers are compelled to teach subjects not of their interest but by compulsion and hence don't teach effectively. Indian Institutions do not embrace the culture of hiring professors, known for their expertise.

Traditionally, Higher Educational Institutions stressed the accumulation of information and did not emphasize nurturing skills, but now that our society is moving with a fast pace in terms of Global Network & Technology updates, the products of Higher Education Institutes are expected to be problem solvers and critical thinkers. Our government is intervening by starting National Skills Development Council (NSDC) and numerous other skill development initiatives, but unless our Higher Education awakens up to respond proactively, the products of Higher Education would find it hard to claim a place in the world.

In today's world, particularly in India, the Higher Education is vaguely linked with Skill Development; the earlier Higher Education accepts and acts accordingly, the better it is for the country and its growth. The growth of the country remains under threat because without the requisite human resource the magic growth is impossible. Its time that the Higher Education, in India needs to reconsider its role in the growth and Development of the country and make it mandatory to establish Skill Development Centres at Universities and College campuses by providing specific funds. At the same time only, Government agencies and system cannot accomplish their task of upskilling the youth, the fact also remains that no one wants to take up the road less traversed.

REFERENCES

Oliver Schinkten, *10 skills all students need to be successful*, Jan 12, 2017, Linked in.com-The learning Blog

R Natarajan, *Industry-academe linkages in education*, R &D and Innovation Q Science proceedings, Engineering Leaders Conference,2014

8

Self-Reflexivity in Higher Education

Dr. Gurudutta P. Japee

Abstract

India is essentially a Land of Knowledge and it must rediscover itself. Once this rediscovery is done we can achieve the quality of life, strength, and sovereignty of a developed nation.

Maharshi Patanjali in the Yogsutra said "When you are inspired by some great purpose, some extraordinary project, all your thoughts break their bonds: your mind transcends limitations, your consciousness expands in every direction, and you find yourself in a new great wonderful world. Dormant forces faculties and talents become alive, and you discover yourself to be a greater person by far than you ever dreamed yourself to be". Higher Education should nurture the quality of knowledge through discipline and dedication, through growth and excellence, and also through inner and outer harmony, Let us nurture the mind of our nation a unique opportunity, a decisive moment has come to shape India. This article is divided into two part, the first part talks about the crisis and the requirement and later talks about the suggestions.

Keywords: Knowledge, Rationality, Legitimacy, self-reflexivity

Introduction

Every page of higher education must unfold and directly converge with knowledge development in its richest diversity. Higher education should be exulted with truth, knowledge, righteousness, and responsibility. We need unprompted and unassisted critical creativity for unrivaled wisdom. Such knowledge can be achieved while considering knowledge alone as the paramount of wealth. *Prasa□gābhar□*a rightly says "*Vidhyadhanam Sarvardhana Pradhanam*". Higher education demands a qualitative assertion about knowledge. Quality of knowledge is not about finding knowledge but about creating knowledge. Knowledge here is a performative act of imagination and representation of the past, present, and enactment of future possibilities. Knowledge is an abode of the dawn of the future civilisation.

Higher Education should nurture the quality of knowledge through discipline and dedication, through growth and excellence, and also through inner and outer harmony. It is a pre-requisite obligation of higher education to cultivate the capacity to inquire and to create the potential of self-reflexivity. For the march of quality in higher education, we must nurture discipline, growth, and excellence in knowledge and kindle care and love towards humanity. Self-reflexivity demands non-singular, multi-dimensional and comprehensive capacity to think. This capacity to think is not dispersion but organised thinking that leads to creativity and innovation. The kernel of self-reflexivity demands conviction that we must envy ignorance and to imitate is suicidal.

Self-search generates the courage to muse differently and can convert a signature into an autograph. Pedagogy, Pedagogues, students and academic institutions have to fight against self-constructed myopia and obsolescence. Quantum shift in higher education is mandatory from descriptive and prescriptive pedagogy; we must make a shift to critical, creative and self-reflexive pedagogy. Higher education is a continuously pulsative excitement to create something new. Students, teachers, curricula, classroom teaching, examination, academic writing, administration, academic institutions, policy makers and executors should be a volcano of quality education.

Students must aspire for critical creativity. Teachers must have a creative mind. Excellence is not an accident but a continuous process and academic institutions must nurture it with warmth. We must make thinking as our capital but this can be made by violating the schizophrenic monolithic foundationalist structure of disciplines. We must address to multidisciplinary and multidimensionality. This will ensure critical and creative capital. Knowledge must be made an open-ended enterprise. Education has to shine like a Sun, first, it has to burn like a sun. This is the time and opportunity to burn like a Sun so that the quality of higher education can shine like a sun.........

WHAT DO YOU MEAN BY SELF-REFLEXIVITY?

To reflect is to contemplate. "*Self-reflexivity is an activity wherein one thinks about the credibility of one's own premises*".

It involves no externality. It is not reproductive. It is within or even mimesis are not possible. It saves you from the rhetoric of judgment.

It is an activity which compels to inquire about an open-ended inquiry. Uncommitted inquiry regarding the premises wherein the truth of premises is under the scan. Self-reflexivity is opened to the correction that is to say it is an open-ended inquiry which generates the probability of truth where one is not asked for T but t.

It is a sphere of probable knowledge is to achieve self-consistency regarding the truth of the premises. Self-reflexivity will not allow any kind of bourgeois ideology

ROLE OF SELF-REFLEXIVITY IN HIGHER EDUCATION

Instead of a monolithic structure of governance, we require a non-singular structure of governance that can put stress on two academic values. Which in turn, would serve the global academic demand, at the same time; it will nurture Indian identity, which would serve for national unification. The backbone of National harmony can be integration and prejudice-free living.

The state can also excerpt their choices. The responsible partnership will be created in the form of accountability, which would voice the legitimate claim of the state, and this will, in turn, save us from three crises.

This will be a barrier for the erosion of academic vitality of Indian Universities. In education, we require only one skill and that is self-reflexivity is the hard-core of any higher academic institutions. Academic practices must aspire and inspire for self-reflexivity. Many institutions of the world who they practice this, are the world's best universities. Instead of imparting the knowledge we have to create knowledge for both teachers and students. Our institutes should go for higher education instead of further education. Responsive participation is required from all the stakeholders including state, which would shrink itself from the rhetoric of gay participation. Only political will is not required or not only criteria it has to be executed and asserted by action, by performance. Political will should be treated as a performative act and not as wishful thinking, it is not wishful thinking, it is a committed execution. The same is applicable to all institutions, universities colleges, teachers and students.

SKILL DEVELOPMENT

Prepositional and ability knowledge should be inculcated. One of the capabilities of skill development is self-reflexivity and second is through self-reflexivity we should indulge in creativity. So entire compass is on critical, creative, self-reflexive thinking.

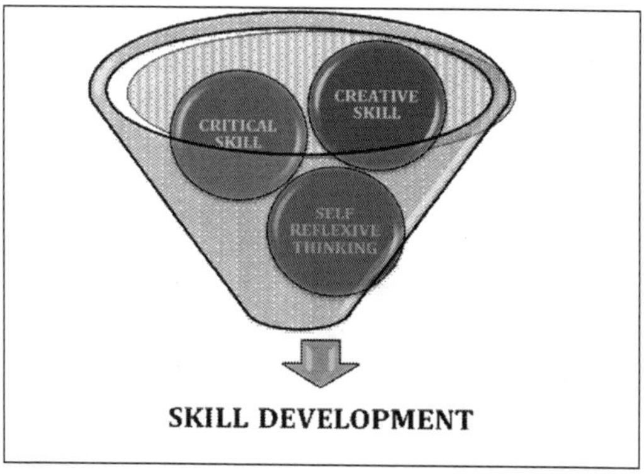

What is required the first authenticity of knowledge? Knowledge is a part of generative phenomena it is an activity, not a finished product. It demands knowledge by doing, by doing would save us from mimesis of higher education this demands not answering the question but questioning the answer because it is not dogma learning. Dogma learning will indulge in dogmatic learning. For the said purpose it is required the questioning Spirit. Questioning spirit is the pursuit of inquiry will take place that pursuit would enter into the domain of the self-learning process. This reflects one basic skill of self-reflexivity exemplified by the responses. This self-reflexivity is the hard-core of any academic enterprise. Education Policy is necessarily people's choice, care, and concern for education, which obviously needs Revision, Reformation and Refinement. This is possible if we assert quality education and potential for Knowledge creation. For that, we do require the thrust of creativity and innovation, which would serve as the backbone of Higher education in India. We need Global participation for quality enhancement in Knowledge. To make the enhancement of knowledge Higher education and education, in general, must anchor the capacity of 'Learning to Learn', which has been successfully executed by Japan and perhaps it is the only country who has exhibited the potential for learning to learn.

This self-learning process would be an instrument of creative learning. For that we require

- Less student teachers ratio so that communication can be possible on either side or this would save us from mass learning which is basically not learning but unlearning. A kind of dogmatic slumber from which academy must be saved.
- We must have ample space and time for negotiation class act must not reduce to speech act.
- Curriculum (it is the most serious activity) but almost taken in a rudimental way
- Imparting understanding should be the hardcore for teachers as well as students and it should be a participatory act (Participation skill should be involved)
- Student must not be treated as passive receiver. Teacher has to save and secure the authenticity of knowledge but it must be done in non-authoritative way.

We must have learning skill/imparting skill which would be nonauthoritative this would come through communication, our discourse must not have necessarily noncommunicative because very logic of imparting is to communicate the other. The communicative learning process should induce discursive learning. This discursive learning will imply a body of knowledge gained by a personal pursuit on the side of teacher and students, Karl Popper has rightly remarked that Ignorance is infinite, Knowledge is limited. Our quest must be necessary to erase ignorance and acquire knowledge.

Knowledge and Society

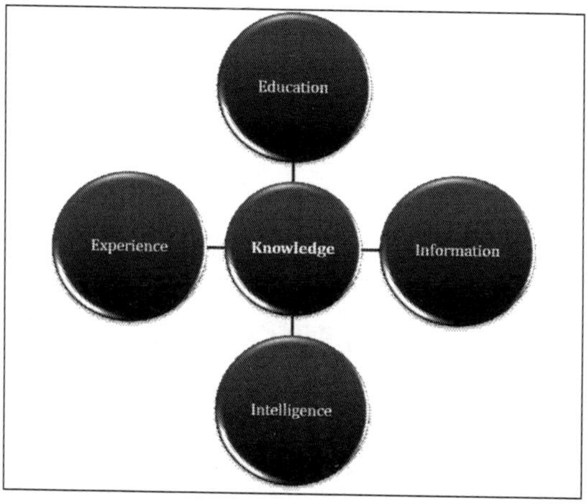

To me Knowledge has Plural forms and can be acquired through our heritage and history, the rituals, epics, and traditions which have created our consciousness is also a vast resource of knowledge as our libraries and universities. They are the hidden treasures of knowledge. Today knowledge is the prime mover of

- Prosperity
- Power

The acquisition of knowledge has been our thrust area. For Education Policy:

1. The ability to create and maintain the knowledge infrastructure

2. To enhance skills
3. Increase Productivity through the exploration of advances in various fields of Knowledge is the key to the knowledge society.

The Knowledge Society is Judged by two Things

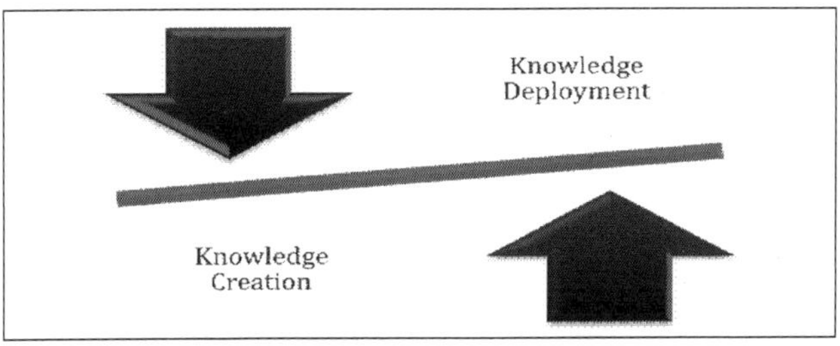

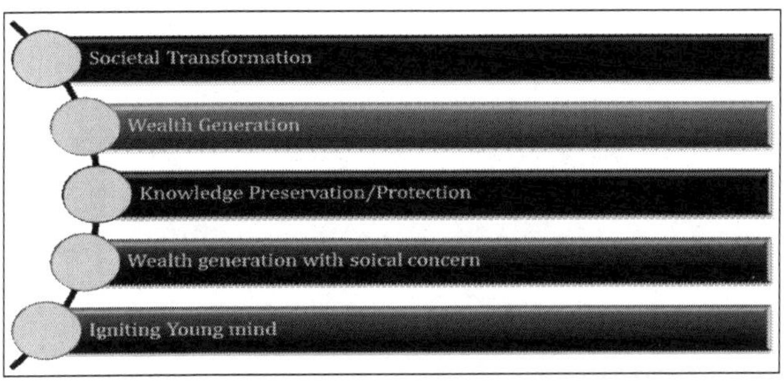

The knowledge society has five very important components

There should not be any alienation between knowledge and society. There is an implication or rather a bipolar relation between the two and this relation must be asserted by both knowledge and society.

Society must be responsive to the academic enterprise and knowledge also must ask an assert for the benefit of the society because knowledge in this exercise is a social good. So society must stand by the academic institutions and be responsive to cater to the needs of the institutions. Knowledge must negotiate with societal needs and society also in turn actively participates in the academic activity. Knowledge must care for the well-being of society and society, in turn, must care for the well-being of the academy. Then only Economic surplus must be invested for academic interest.

STATE

The state is the most viable institution to assert and execute academic excellence. The state has to be performative and this performance must be transparent or state must execute a democratic value of the capacity to negotiable. By ascertaining the code of self-reflexivity being executed by all its stakeholders.

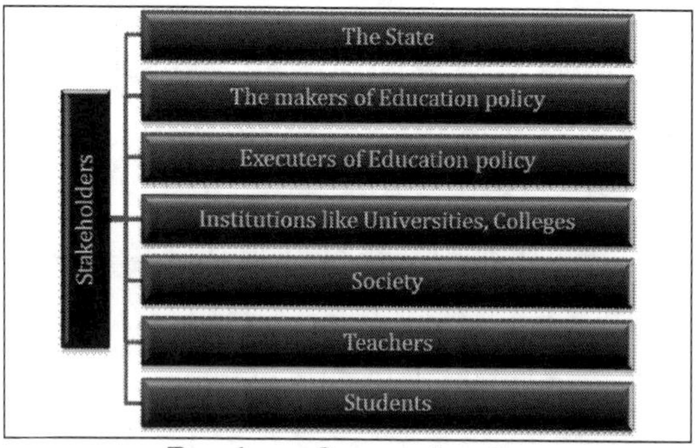

Post-haste Steps to be taken

An education ultimately should be an open-ended inquiry. In short MICRO level changes should be made as an essential component.

For the Present Situation in Indian Higher Education, we make Some Specific Suggestions.

Quality improvement in higher education should be focused on "Expansion of enrolment in higher education with inclusiveness, quality, and relevant education and supported by necessary Academic reforms in the University and College system.

There is a need to adopt the strategic "4E" approach of education to be Explicit, Experiential, Embedded and Evaluative for the concrete enhancement of quality in higher education.

Institutional leadership and decision making bodies should play their part in shaping the institutional quality culture. They can be the initiators of quality initiatives in higher education. Adequate time, human resources, funding, and facilities must be dedicated to achieving the desired level of excellence.

It is sought to the reform the governance structure of higher education institutions, so better establishment of state Higher Education Council is need of the hour. India lives in a plural society; each state has its own individual demands and priorities. Instead of a monolithic structure, the non-singular structure of governance serves the purpose that imbibes two academic constituents – quality and freedom. Through decentralisation, we can achieve academic freedom and the Concept of SHEC offers much needed academic freedom.

The institutes should adopt continuous improvement strategies to realise improvements in three primary domains: services for students and stakeholders, processes to make it easier for faculties to do their jobs, and institutional outcomes. The inclusion of reputed alumni into the governance mechanism can provide the much-needed dynamism that our higher education institution lacks.

Quality teaching initiatives provide an occasion for teachers to think about their own role in the enhancement of quality. Complete revamping of teaching /learning methods from instruction and rote learning to interactive process that encourages creativity and innovation that is based on compulsory seminar tutorials should be advocated in the universities and colleges. New pedagogical techniques should be adopted like blended learning, flipped classroom, and experiential learning.

Knowledge Economies and knowledge-based production should be Research driven. We need to encourage "Foundation Institutions" to conduct research that is relevant to the economic and social requirements.

Today, India's prime concern is the creation of an employable workforce to harness its demographic dividend to the maximum extent. To attain this objective the country needs an education system which can deliver quality in terms of skilled and employment ready workforce while focusing on world-class Research & Innovation.

We need to devise a model wherein industry and higher education institutions can work in harmony covering the areas of research that are relevant for industry, engaging industry to provide funding, mentor research projects and to set up sector-specific/horizontal focused centres of excellence. There is a need to introduce multi-disciplinary, industry-oriented and skilled-based courses by adopting a learner-cantered approach.

Openness to international academic ideas, international collaborations, standards and talent as well as attentiveness to world university rankings and attractiveness to foreign students, faculty and curricula should be explicitly endorsed.

One of the strategies is to create a knowledge-based society-in doing so; we need to create an education hub for attracting students from nearby countries like Nepal, Sri Lanka, Bhutan, etc. On the lines of a few foreign nations, we should emerge as one of the largest players in the trans-national education market.

REFERENCES

Alvesson, M., & Deetz, S. (2000). *Doing critical management research.* London: Sage

Alvesson, M., & Skoldberg, K. (2000). *Reflexive methodology: New vistas for qualitative research.* London: Sage.

Coghlan, D., & Brannick, T. (2005). *Doing Action research in your organisation.* London: Sage.

Dewey, J. (1934). *Art as experience.* NY: Pedigree.

Gabel, S.L. (2001). "I Wash My Face With Dirty Water". *Journal of Teacher Education.* 52, (1), 31-38.

Holmes, P., Cockburn-Wootten, C., Motion, J., Zorn, E.T., & Roper, J. (2005) "Critical reflexive practice in teaching management communication." *Business Communication Quarterly*, 68 (2), 247-257.

Ironside, P.M. (2001). *Creating a research base for nursing education: an interpretive review of conventional, critical, feminist, postmodern, and phenomenological pedagogies.*

Japee (2018), *Improving Quality in higher education through self-reflexivity*, India: Education, 139-151

Miles. M.B., & Huberman, A.M. (1994). *Qualitative data analysis.* (2nd Ed.). London: Sage.

Nielsen, F.S. (2003) *Dictionary of anthropology.* Retrieved November 20, 2003, from

www.anthrobase.com/Dic/eng/def/reflexivity.htm

Nightingale, D. & Cromby, J. (Eds) (1999). *Social constructionist psychology.* Buckingham: Open University Press. Retrieved November 18, 2003, from http://www.psy.dmu.ac.uk /michael/qual_reflexivity.htm

Ryan, T. G. (2005). *The reflexive classroom manager.* Temeron Books/Detselig, Publications. Calgary, AB. Canada.

Sandelowski. M., & Barroso, J. (2002). "Finding the findings in qualitative studies." *Journal of Nursing Scholarship*, 34, (3), 213-220.

Schön, D.A. (1987). *Educating the Reflective Practitioner. Presentation to the 1987 meeting of the American Educational Research Association* [online] Russell: Queens University, Ontario pp1-15. January 1998. Retrieved September 12, 2004, from http://edu.queensu.ca/~russellt /howteach /schon87.htm

Foucault (1972) *Archaeology of knowledge*, Routledge, UK

9

Enlightenment in Higher Education

Dr. Gurudutta P. Japee

Abstract

When the enlightenment occurred two hundred years ago, rational thinking and the scientific method slowly emerged as a way to understand the universe. Thousands of scientists and their scientific inquiries arose. A vigorous debate about these scientific findings began, based on the rules of reason and rational inquiry that were hundreds of years old. Instead of a reliance on previous knowledge, practice and tradition, careful observation and analysis coupled with rigorously agreed methods became the way the world around us was explored. Laziness and cowardice are the reasons why such a large part of mankind gladly remain minors all their lives, long after nature has freed them from external guidance. They are the reasons why it is so easy for others to set themselves up as guardians. Leading education out of panic and into play should be every teacher's life mission. But to do this, one must be simultaneously working on healing own panic-driven soul, and this will allow the transformation of panic into play. Rumi's lines are very relevant to this.

Dance when you're broken open.
Dance when you've torn the bandage off.
Dance in the middle of the fighting.
Dance in your blood.
Dance when you're perfectly free.
Struck, the dancer hears a tambourine inside her,
like a wave that crests into foam at the very top,
Begins.

> Maybe you don't hear that tambourine,
> or the tree leaves clapping time.
> Close the ears on your head,
> that listen mostly to lies and cynical jokes.
> There are other things to see and hear.
> Music. Dance.
> A brilliant city inside your soul!
>
> (Rumi, as cited in Barks, 2004, p. 281)

How to institutionalise enlightenment ideas which will make the people enlighten. In this paper need of enlightenment in higher education is discussed.

Keywords: Governance, Freedom, Listening, Echoing, Self-reflexivity

PHILOSOPHY OF ENLIGHTENMENT

The primary logic of enlightenment is to have the courage to think. The problem of existing higher education is that the students and teachers do not have the courage to think. It is possible when you follow structure ideology, the pursuit of reason flows to a particular ideology or ideas or system.

AUTHORITARIAN GOVERNANCE

In the case of authoritarian governance, self and society linkages cannot be established, if the main pursuit is individual oriented. You do not require a position to establishes linkages. I am because we are I.e. concern for others can be established only when one can have freedom. In higher education also, academic freedom is the main pillar for enlightenment. But the major question in academic freedom is:

- How to get academic freedom
- Why not getting academic freedom

When we follow the Dogmatic Academic structure in higher education, we rarely find academic freedom. In academic structure, blindness exists within the discipline and along with other discipline and are not eradicated through rational understanding. With this type of academic structure, neither society nor the individual will develop.

Socialism and democracy both should be reconstructed. At present both are in orthodox mode. In socialism where "I" is suspended similarly in Democracy "We" is suspended. Individual choice is being rubbed out in both the cases, therefore, it should be reconstructed. Both are equally important for development but to grow it, the academy should be wedded to freedom of expression and ideas. Academic structure level is a collaboration between the academy and dogmatisation. When dialogue or discourse is not possible such academic structure should be suspended immediately.

Such type of structure is academic myopia which creates and allow it to flow. Eg Seniority in Indian higher education time – frame is considered as seniority. Such type of seniority, generally shun down or rule over the ideas given by the person who is junior or below the position. Sometimes seniority also discourages the students and young faculties by their dogma and poor experience of repetitive time frame.

Such seniority has lost the capacity of listening and for discourse and dialoguing, listening is a primary condition.

The present structure of echoing has also ruined higher education on a large scale. The echoing process is shown in the following diagram.

Except echoing, we are not doing anything new, because of that, we have lost the capacity to listen. "Listening is a greater virtue than speaking" Echoing is the thing which started by few mediocre by showing their shallow competencies in the curriculum in the Board of studies meeting. In the majority of the public Universities, the members of the board of studies are selected on the basis of reciprocation and associations with political or other establishments. The same curriculum is echoing in the classroom by the teachers who are again non-competent and selected on the basis of loyalty which they have towards few associations and finally, it is reflected in examination answer sheets written by students.

Such echoing system kills

- Questioning spirit
- Courage to think
- Self-reflexivity
- No grand narrative

To create a tapestry where all the threads are woven following steps should be taken immediately:

- Faculty myopia should be irradiated
- Learning habit should be created
- Academic Freedom should be given
- Self-reflexive thinking should be encouraged

Electronic gadgets like laptop and computers will not help to think. They are useful to collect information. The information available on fingertips but how to use this information is suspended here. Data Collection and analysis are not research.

- Where is the research
- Where is the question

The so-called information society is only information society, which liquidates human potentialities to reason.

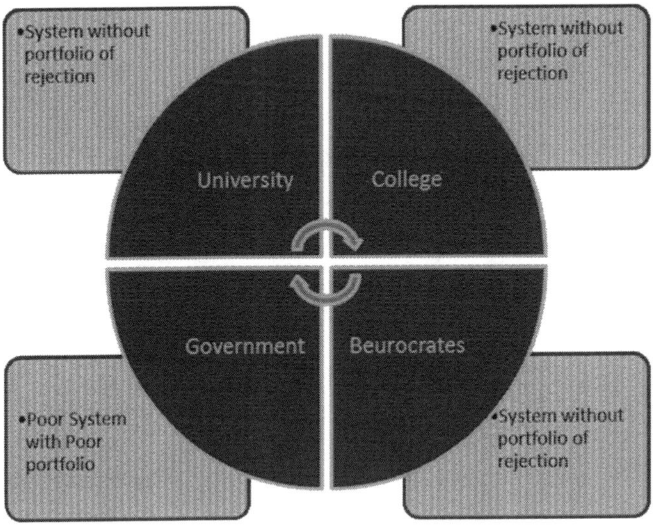

Do we have any system created by any of the above institutions? Who has given right to suspend, if they go wrong? Our entire system follows the vision of one person or party which has made a slave of the vision of the person and party.

They all are known as "Power Madness Dealers"

Power is for all it is for We. But unfortunately the above system of higher education where the university and college appoint the position of the leader who has only one portfolio which is developed by their political party. Their agenda is to please and convince about the portfolio which they have successfully completed with maximum participation of students and faculties to promote poor agenda of the party.

We have to delink the power and Vision of the party. Power should help to create two potentialities

- Creativity
- Social Creativity

There are very rare individuals who have potentialities to revolutionise. An adequate platform for such individuals should be provided by higher education.

Higher education should provide potentiality to understand the question and giving a solution not in a rudimental way but in a rational way.

One should welcome opinion and respect the opinion of all who are part of it.

There cannot be the second opinion, such attitude should not be developed by the educator.

The dissenting opinion is very much required in higher education. Voice of dissent is the other way of thinking. Such an environment in higher education should be created for enlightening values.

The environment should be created to develop the following ideas and this possibly can make higher education enlightened.

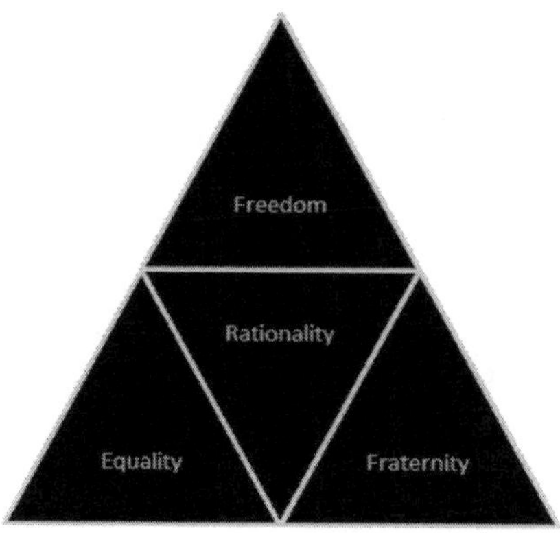

Potentiality to think and freedom to think both are important. The present system has a portfolio of infrastructure, Buildings, Heritage Hub, Research centre, MoU, etc., but how the quality is improved in higher education. How the students, teachers and other stakeholders will be enlightened by the higher education is not answered as yet.

We are good at parting ignorance rather than in knowledge. It is generated by so many bodies and empowered also. Knowledge and empowerment are different things. Such higher education is not useful where:

- You cannot have any dialogue
- You cannot have any say against authority
- You cannot challenge the credentials of anyone
- You cannot challenge guiding the institute

If it is decided on the basis of Loyalty, Reciprocation, Association, and if we do not have any criteria. (A person not known to operate sewing machine becomes Textile Minister}

How to Enlighten Leadership in Higher Education

Following steps should be followed by the leaders of the higher education,

1. Leading by listening
2. Demonstrating respect for the members of the campus community
3. Creating a healthy culture of evidence, inquiry and transparency
4. Rallying support for shared goals through explicit, consistent focus on student success
5. Incentivizing innovation and collaboration
6. Building on successes
7. Supporting risk-taking and allowing flops

There is an inherent conflict between blind faith and critical thinking. That is true whether it is religious fanaticism or the imposition of political ideologies or nationalistic or ethnic dogmas in colleges and Universities.

Placing education in such a straitjacket is having a major impact on development because it is affecting the way in which communities are conceived, justice is understood, and democracy is practiced.

If you examine the new apostles of education among many actors in so-called "reform", you will not find one trace of enlightenment DNA. There also seems to be no genetic link between market ideologues in education and the father of capitalism, Adam Smith. He said, "I have never known much good done by those who affected to trade for the public good."

But, there is another development in education that may be as dangerous as confusing the public interest with private gain. Even without the profit motive, it can denature the mission of education. And, its influence is spreading rapidly in the form of a market mentality alien to education and to public services in general.

As during the Enlightenment, education does not exist in a vacuum. It is a miniature of society. And, the Enlightenment rejected what the times meant for society. As Nietzsche said, "The essential element in the black art of obscurantism is not that it wants to darken individual understanding, but that it wants to blacken our picture of the world and darken our idea of existence."

The 21st-century battle against obscurantism requires us to deliberately provide that there is enough space for reason and for real debate to take place. It requires us to re-connect with our origins in the Enlightenment and in the centuries of thinking and practice since that time rather than accepting the blockages and limits of functioning within the rigid boundaries of simplistic market fashions.

In the world of good and evil, since the 1980s, good has increasingly been seen as private and public as evil. It is the perception of the weakening of the understanding of and support for the notion of the "public good" that has allowed much social and democratic progress to be reversed. The galloping inequalities and the loss of opportunities and hope that have afflicted many societies since this new definition of good and evil took hold, dramatically affects education in theory and in practice.

Without going into great detail, it is clear that, on a global basis, the language of management is defining education. As George Orwell argued, "…if thought corrupts language, language can also corrupt thought."

What is the relationship between the description of educators by Albert Einstein, "It is the supreme art of the teacher to awaken joy in creative expression and knowledge," and "Performance Management"?

In keeping with the management "party line", one could respond that there is no conflict; that, in fact, performance management is designed to ensure that teaching and education are of better quality and more efficient and effective. It is, in no way, intended to reduce education impact or quality. One could even argue that PM is the way to realise Einstein's vision.

But, there is "no management without measurement", so performance management means performance measurement. Only certain things can be measured, so what is the most easily measured, becomes most important. That becomes the basis for assessment of students and for the accountability of teachers.

These management systems define education. And yet, such systems leave little room for joy or creativity for the student or the teacher.

The connections between the elements of education are immediate; the links in the chain are tight. There is an interdependence that does not combine well with the separation of management from the profession and from the work at hand.

Teachers and their organisations are often excluded from education "reforms". New forms of organisation and management of education effectively shut out the public as well. It sometimes seems as if one has to be outside education and outside our communities to be inside the debate.

To the extent that reforms offer choices, they are rarely about policy; collective choices about how education should serve young people and society. Rather, they provide individual choices so that parents can "shop around" for schools.

The replacement of real democracy with the "democracy of the marketplace" will never bring about positive and sustainable improvements in education. Instead of increasing atomisation and feeding the forces that are breaking down the fabric of communities, we need to come together on values that will best serve education and society.

We need a real debate on education and we need serious reform to improve quality as well as access, one that does not exclude the very professionals that make education happen every day or parents or communities or elected officials. It makes sense to re-cast the debate so that it is about learners and teachers in the flesh unobscured by market dogma.

If we are going to discuss education based on the Enlightenment or create 21st-century enlightenment, it is not necessary to go back to the 18th century. The roots of "market babble" in the policy debate are shallow.

If, rather than beginning with performance management at the top of the hierarchy, we start with the purpose of education and, from there, make the logical and indispensable connection with the qualifications and status of teachers, the dots connect without elaborate gyrations or heroic efforts to put square pegs in round holes.

The Recommendation is informed by Enlightenment traditions and by the subsequent contributions of generations of education philosophers and educators. It is imbued with human values and with respect. It is based on experience, not theology and it is "tailor-made" for education rather than providing "off-the-rack" management tools.

One could argue that neither the Enlightenment nor the 20th century can provide useful guidance because so much has changed. However, that basic framework is better fitted to today's discussions that the framework under which we have failed to communicate in recent years.

Any fair examination of the future of education will show that it will depend on involving and serving the community, parents, and learners. But, in particular, it will recognise that good, quality education relies on professional teachers who are free to exercise their profession and maintain the highest standards without being micro-managed. It will show that the best role for school leadership is to supply teachers with the crucial support, trust, and respect that they need to educate. Recognition of the profession of teaching and for educators will not only lead to better quality education, but it will help overcome serious problems of recruitment and retention.

The Enlightenment and what we must strive to achieve in this century are about a lot more than opposing obscurantism.

They are about the free, critical thinking needed to support human rights, freedom, and democracy, and create and maintain tolerant and decent societies. In that context, there is an important contribution of the right kind of education to avoid what was described by Jean-Jacques Rousseau with these words,

> *"Once you teach people to say what they do not understand; it is easy enough to get them to say anything you like."*

REFERENCES

Bai, H. & Scutt, G. (2009). "Touching the earth with the heart of the enlightened mind: A Buddhist contribution to ecology as educational practice." *Canadian Journal of Environmental Education*, 14, 92-106.

Bai, H. (2001). "Challenge for education: Learning to value the world intrinsically." *Encounter*, 14(1), 4-16.

Barks, C., Rumi, J. & J. Moyne, J. (2004). *The essential Rumi* (A. Arberry, C. Barks, J. Moyne, & R. Nicholson, Transl.). New York: HarperCollins.

Cohen, A. (2009). *Gateway to the Dao-field: Essays for the awakening educator.* Amherst, NY: Cambria.

Fehmi, L. & Robbins, J. (2007), *The open-focus brain.* London: Trumpeter Books.

Noddings, N. (1992). *The challenge to care in schools.* New York: Teachers College Press, Columbia University.

Nhat Hahn, T. (1998). *Interbeing* (3rd ed.). Berkeley, CA: Parallax Press.

Palmer, P. (1998). *The courage to teach.* San Francisco: Jossey-Bass.

Tredennick, H. (1954). *Plato: The last days of Socrates.* Middlesex, England: Penguin Books.

Vokey, D. (2011). "Moral education for the 21st century: A Buddhist view." In J. DeVitis and T. Yu(Eds.), *Character and moral education: A reader.* New York: Peter Lang.

http://www.columbia.edu/acis/ets/CCREAD/etscc/kant.html

https://www.history.com/topics/british-history/enlightenment

https://www.publicagenda.org/pages/seven-practices-of-enlightened-leadership-in-higher-education

https://www.thersa.org/discover/publications-and-articles/rsa-blogs/2016/07/education-the-enlightenment-and-the-21st-century

10

Knowledge in Higher Education

Dr. Sai Madhavi D.

ABSTRACT

Knowledge in Higher education is seen with a different perspective altogether. Here teachers act as facilitators and play a key role in bringing out students hidden talents, identifying their strengths and weakness and focusing on how to empower those areas by applying various classroom strategies and activities by involving them in every day's class by communicating and collaborating constantly with them. At the same time igniting their critical thinking and creative skills. Institutions providing higher education should aim and work towards social, service-oriented, sustainable development, betterment, and improvement in living conditions of society. Their decisions, planning, and implementation should be focused on building solid education system which meets up with day to day technological changes coming up in the market thereby lending their hand in the technological growth of the community.

Keywords: Knowledge, facilitator, active learning activities, effective learning, collaboration.

AchAryAt pAdamAdatte, pAdam shiShyaH swamedhayA |

sa-brahmachAribhyaH pAdam, pAdam kAlakrameNa cha ||

आचार्यात् पादमादत्ते पादं शिष्यः स्वमेधया ।
सब्रह्मचारिभ्यः पादं पादं कालक्रमेण च ॥

Let me start the chapter with a subashitam. This sloka has four lines bringing out the essence of the art of learning. It clearly explains how the learning process should take place. Which is also the expectation of today's changed education system.

In Sanskrit, Padam means one fourth or 25%, and the first line from the above sloka means that 25% of learning happens because of our teacher, the teacher is the one who introduces us to this ocean of knowledge.

Here I would like to quote:

"Mediocakar Teacher Tells
Good Teacher Explains
Superior Teacher Demonstrates
Best Teacher Inspires"

What knowledge is known to the student can be compared to just a drop of water and what is unknown to an ocean. Therefore it is the duty of the teacher to inspire and create a fire inside the student so that student can fall in love with the subject.

The second line of the sloka says that next 25% of learning happens because of our own intelligence, which means the student has to contemplate and meditate what he has learned. He should put an effort to analyse what he is learning.

The third line of the sloka says that next 25% of learning happens on discussing the subject content with friends, and in the process of such discussion the student gets a better clarity.

The fourth line of the sloka says that last 25% of learning happens from our own experience. This experience is only possible with time and situation.

To summarise starting from what we learned from our teachers, then how we are able to contemplate it with our self as well as with friends and peers and when we put it in practice we get better and deeper understanding and also realisation about what we are learning.

Here I would like to quote one truth about a teacher and life:

> "Teacher teaches us a Lesson and the gives us a test". Which can be expected, but
>
> "Life keeps us a test which teaches us a lesson". Which is unexpected? Therefore we have to learn carefully and prepare our self so as to be able to face any unexpected tests in life and also we should grow so as to provide solutions for society and social cause. This is what is the expected an outcome and what the accreditation teams are looking or expecting from higher education systems to provide to their students.

Here I would like to take an example from nature and co-relate its essence to teacher and student fraternity:

> It's about sequoia redwood trees which are located in California, these are single stem strong, resilient trees that live on for thousands of years. These trees can grow up to 300 feet tall, 25 feet in diameter weighing up to 500 tons, live up to 2500 years. So now we can estimate how deep its root system must be, but the twist in the story is about its unique root system.

These trees have roots going down by 10 to 12 feet only, apart from having such huge heights, they stand very firm and withstand any sort of natural calamities like earthquakes, strong winds & storms. How is it possible that these trees are able to sustain and live on for so many years, it's because of its root system, these trees have a shallow root system, they do not have a tap root which goes deep into ground to hold them strong above the ground but their root system is intertwined underground with other redwood trees literally holding each other, supporting each other and also sharing nutrients with each other. So, these gigantic tall trees standing side by side under the surface have their entangled roots running around 100 to 150 feet interlocking with each other so as to face any sort of disasters that nature imposes on them.

Sequoia redwood trees instead of going deep down into the ground to hold itself alone firmly above the ground, they entangle their roots under the ground far and wide forming a sort of mesh in order to give good grip to hold themselves and parallelly hold all the trees as far as their roots are entangled, which is a unique phenomenon. This example from nature can be adopted by students in gaining knowledge in higher education.

When students come for higher education into college, each student steps into the campus with unique individual talents and each student also has a different pace of learning and understanding levels, keeping this in view the teacher has to plan his teaching strategies and activities in such a fashion which can give equal attention to each and every student.

In this new era of teaching-learning where priority is given to active learning within the classroom. The teacher has to conduct many activities in the classroom to make a real impact on the learning process. These activities make student participate in groups giving them a scope to participate in an intertwined manner. Interconnected with each other in group participation and supporting each other with one's own abilities and helping each other in the process of learning and doing.

In this whole process teacher teaches them to be intertwined, interconnected, supportive, dependent on each other and also interdependent on each other. If one team member has a "Failing Moment" entire team becomes supportive and helps him find a way to manage the "learn". As we all know "sometimes we win, sometimes we learn". This should teach the true essence of life in the whole process.

This chapter focuses on how knowledge transmission in the higher education system should take place, bringing into light the gradual changes from traditional teaching-learning practices to today's limelight, outcome-based practices their importance in today's education system and their overall impact on society at large. Higher Education in institutions play a key role and take responsibility in contributing to social change and the creation of a better possible world. Higher Education in institutions should act as active players in spreading today's current paradigms, perceptions of reality and beliefs. Higher Education educates the future generations who carry their professional activity at the same time able to deal with human problems.

KNOWLEDGE IN HIGHER EDUCATION

Traditional teaching practices Vs. Outcome-based practices:

- *Planning:* What content to teach Vs. What student will be able to do after learning.
- *Teaching:* To transmit knowledge to student Vs. Focus is on teaching-learning activities.
- *Assessment:* To assess students with a fixed set of tests Vs. Which requires the student to demonstrate what is learned in every class for a set of intended learning outcomes.
- *Approach:* Focus is on content-based input approach Vs. Competence-based output approach.

- *Achievement:* Achievement by all students was not sure Vs. Ensures all students achieve which is recorded with evidence.

This whole process requires a restructuring of the curriculum process, teaching process assessment process, and reporting practices to reflect the achievement of higher order learning and mastery rather than the accumulation of just courses by students. To accomplish this every institute should set a vision in the benefit of student fraternity and the institute works to reflect their goals by setting their plan and approach in a systematic representation to meet their Vision through Mission.

Mission in Higher Education

- *Preparation:* Students are prepared to successfully complete his/her higher education.
- *Core competency:* providing students with a solid foundation in fundamental subjects which will help in solving real-life problems.
- *Breadth:* He/she is trained so as to analyse, design and ability to create solutions for real-life problems.
- *Professionalism:* Building his/her ethical attitude, professional skills, communication skills, teamwork skills, leadership skills and exposure to multidisciplinary areas.
- *Learning environment:* Inspiring, filling motivation and inculcating the spirit of loving to learn.

KEY PRACTICES IN HIGHER EDUCATION

- *Key paradigm:* Way of viewing and doing things that are learned.
- *Key purpose:* Structuring learning environment so that outcome can be achieved and maximized for all categories of learners and to pay individual attention to each student.
- *Key premises:* Successful learning is promoted as an environment set makes student approach the teacher with different perspectives, all students learn not on same day and way.
- *Key Principles:* When a teacher teaches, he/she decides what the student learns.
- *Key Practices:* With the prior idea of what is expected an outcome from the student, the teacher teaches with clarity and focus straight on what the student should learn, this is possible with prior designing of course and activities.

In this change over the process from content-based input approach to competency-based output approach teacher's role changed from teacher to facilitator. The facilitator can be defined as one who intervenes when a student actually encounters problems during the learning process.

Knowledge and dissemination of knowledge are gradually undergoing a lot of changes, from traditional practices where the focus was laid on how best a teacher would teach to students to what students are able to do, how they are doing and to what extent they are doing.

With networking and internet facilities expanding rapidly, there is a huge volume of data that is made available to the student. The point here is how this information is processed or interpreted by the facilitator and how the student is able to use this knowledge in order to solve real-life problems. Teacher then designs his/her teaching-learning process with intended learning objectives, then to meet these learning objectives, every class is planned by facilitator with 2 or 3 breaks, in each break he should be able to complete his intended content and based on this content taught an activity should be planned by him/her which should not take more than 5 minutes time.

Active learning gives an opportunity for the student to think in the classroom for few minutes and develop an ability to collaborate, communicate with his group of students on the content taught and develop creative thinking skills on how content learned can be applied. Effective learning occurs with active classroom activities which involve 4c's among students.

DEFINING THE PRIME ROLE OF 4C'S

- *Collaboration:* Is an approach to bring the best understanding /outcome for a topic/task.
- *Creativity:* Is to bring out the best idea in order to deal/solve a problem.
- *Communication:* There is no point if you can't share /express that you are skilled enough to solve the problem or deal with the situation.
- *Critical thinking:* The ability to be able to analyse, conceptualise and apply innovatively based on context.

In order to accomplish 4 c outcomes in classrooms, tools are to be used for building interactive sessions in classrooms. Tools like Quiz, Games. Roleplay, Brainstorming, Think pair share, Focused learning etc. Based on the tool selected the activity is planned in the class for students by categorising them and grouping them accordingly.

- *Individual student activities:* Quiz, Brainstorming, focused learning.
- *Paired student activities:* Think-pair-share, Think-pair-solo.
- *Informal smaller groups activities:* Content matching, Games
- *Fixed group activities:* Role-play etc.

CONCLUSION

To actively participate in society and the global community at large students should be made to shift from 3R's to 4 C's by the facilitator. This change can be brought about in classroom learning, with a change in teaching. The technology could be the best choice to be used for facilitating in the classroom. Along with technology, tools, activities, and strategies help in overall engaging students with different bits of intelligence and interests, filling enthusiasm, encouragement, and energy to project their creativity and reflect their individuality and come up with their unique ideas. This process helps them in collaborating with students next to each other, other peers in the same domain, local experts available on campus, linking to global experts of the same domain of their interests using technology. The whole process helps them in learning the problem, their approach, discussions on suggestions, the technology available, how to deal with the situation and finally how to arrive at a solution.

REFERENCES

The John Maxwell team & Susan Williamson author (http://johnma xwellteam. com/2013/12/07/what-kind-of-root-system-do-you-have/)

Anantha Vallabh Das, *Art of Learning*. http://blog.practicalsanskrit. com/2009/12/how-we-learn-and-grow.html?m=1

Outcome-Based Education & Accreditation-by Dr. Urmila kar, workshop organised by (NITTTR-K)

11

Academic Freedom in Higher Education

Dr. Gurudutta P. Japee

ABSTRACT

Any frame of orthodoxy is an enemy of academic freedom. Any activity which suspends inquiry is against academic freedom. Academic Authoritarian is a prima facie hindrance to academic freedom. Though questions of academic freedom affect all of society and not just the society of scholars, though its fruits are reaped by everyone and by most of the institutions, a specific group that is most affected by its presence or absence is the faculty in the universities with their special duties of teaching and research. With this in mind, the paper is written to focus on the core areas of Academic Freedom.

Keywords: Academic freedom, History, Principles, challenges, Constitution.

INTRODUCTION

The limits of academic freedom should not be narrower than the limits of intellectual freedom, it is the right of the scholar to think, write and speak whatever he or she wants to think, speak and write. To defend academic freedom with the vigor, the task demands balance. The Defence of academic freedom is never easy. It is understandable that university leaders will react to outside attacks with caution. There is always a risk that taking a public position on a controversial matter may alienate potential donors or grants from government or offend one of the modern university's many and varied constituencies. In response to negative publicity, it is entirely natural for the vice chancellor and for trustees and regents to work feverishly to get this incident behind us and to reach or an accommodation that claims the critics and makes the problem go away. However, to act on such understandable impulses would be a grievous mistake. There are few matters on which universities must stand on absolute principle. Academic freedom is one of them. If we fail to defend this core value, then we jeopardise the global pre-eminence of our universities in the production and transmission of new knowledge in the sciences, Humanities, indeed in every field of inquiry. Whenever academic freedom is under fire, we must rise to its Défense with courage – and without compromise.

"For freedom of inquiry is our reason for being"

History of Academic Freedom

Although the struggle for academic freedom can be traced at least as far back as Socrates's eloquent Défense of himself against the change that he corrupted the youth of Athens, the modern history of this struggle, as it has played out in the university context, begins with the advent of universities, as we know from today, in the 12th century.

In the middle ages, Universities were the centre of power and prestige. They were largely autonomous institutions, conceived in the spirit of the guilds. There were, however, sharp limits on the scope of scholarly inquiry. When Galileo published his heretical telescopic observations, e.g. he was listed as a suspect in the secret books of the inquisition, threatened with torture, compelled publicly to disavow his views, and imprisoned for the remainder of his life.

Throughout the 17th-century university life remained largely bounded by the medieval curriculum. Real freedom of thought was neither practiced nor professed. In 1654, e.g. Harvard's president was forced to resign because he denied the scriptural validity of infant baptism.

The latter part of the 18th century saw a brief period of relative secularisation as part of the enlightenment.

We see today in the political realm on such issues as abortion, creationism, stem cell research, and same-sex marriages. The same pressure that now bears on the political process will likely be felt in Universities as well. This is perilous, for religion and academic freedom do not mix.

Universities must understand that at the very core of academic freedom is institutional neutrality. The role of Universities is not to take any positions on matters Political, moral, legal, economic, social, religious or international. For universities to promote academic freedom, they cannot themselves participate in the debate. Our responsibility is to create the conditions for free and open debate.

Too often, trustees, president, vice chancellor, deans, faculties, alumni and students want their universities to stand up and be counted. Unfortunately, in the last century, it is neither counted nor stand up. They should not endorse candidates, condemn policies, embrace causes or advocate positions not integrally related to higher education itself. If a university takes sides, it undermines its own neutrality, stifles free and open discourse and makes itself a target for others who will want it to take sides more often. In short, University that takes sides is not a university.

WHAT IS ACADEMIC FREEDOM FOR?

Academic freedom is a complex subject with many aspects and a rich history. Focusing on the question "what is academic freedom for?" is it near to a theological principle or peculiar entitlement for a privileged few.

The purpose of academic freedom is precisely to preserve the openness of inquiry and freedom of thought. In other words, academic freedom is designed to protect and preserve for the long run the unique capacity of universities to contribute to society. Fundamentally and historically Academic freedom to university is all about the capacity to fulfill mission effectively and efficiently. Universities by definition must seek to understand difficult ideas and answer complex questions. That requires rigorous inquiry, openness to all reasonable paths to illumination, and a willingness to challenge orthodoxy. Academic freedom protects the academy from efforts to impose restrictions on free inquiry, internally and externally. In turn, numbers of the academy are responsible for ensuring that such inquiry is pursued with integrity.

Academic freedom applies to both research and teaching. Freedom in research is fundamental to the advancement of the truth. Academic freedom in teaching aspect is fundamental for the protection of the rights of the teacher in teaching and of the student to freedom in learning. It carries with its duty's correlative with rights.

Academic freedom can serve the public good only if universities, as institutions are free from outside pressures in the realm of their academic mission and individual faculty, are free to pursue their research and teaching subject only to the academic judgment of their peers.

CHALLENGES TO ACADEMIC FREEDOM

The challenges to academic freedom can be directed at individuals or at the institution as a whole, and they can come from sources external or internal to the university. There are the following challenges to academic freedom

1. Internal forces on faculty or students intended to stifle the expression of individual views or perspectives that some deem objectionable
2. External forces on the university from the Government and other formal authorities, media, financial supporters, or alumni to take action against individual faculty members or students for their views; or external pressure directly against individual themselves.
3. External and Internal pressures on the university to take a political position that is widely perceived as just.
4. It often happens to Individual faculty doing good in teaching and research is also reprimanded by the undue influence of the authority because of jealousy.

THE FUNDAMENTAL ELEMENTS OF ACADEMIC FREEDOM

In affirming the value of academic freedom, we defend a notion that marks the convergence of three historical developments.

1. The evolution of the idea of faculty self-governance that emerged in medieval English universities.
2. The ascendancy of the 19th-century German concept of *Lehrfreiheit,* which emphasized the role of research in University life and

3. The modernizing impulses of early 20th century America that encouraged the professionalisation of academic activity.

Over the time, the founding principle gave rise to a basic norm of academic practice according to which person, groups and institutions constituting the academy may justly expect society to protect them in the exercise of a robust right of self-regulation. The robust right is actually a set of rights through which professional academics may dictate, within reasonable limits, the term of their work

1. The right to determine (which includes right to advocate, right to exclude and right to risk) fundamental content of research and publication
2. The right to make an important decision about the content of teaching
3. The right to make an important decision about the terms of teaching
4. The right to speak or write as citizens

In the last few years, critics have been increasingly likely to charge that academic freedom is too often a license for overtly coercive activity in the classroom. These critics claim that many faculty members are allowed to actively silence students who disagree with prevailing academic orthodoxies. They also charge that departments and institutions design curricula that ignore the diversity of moral and political conceptions.

ACADEMIC FREEDOM AND THE CONSTITUTION

The constitutional doctrine of academic freedom is incoherent because lacks an adequate theory of why the constitution should protect academic freedom. The supreme court believes that academic freedom should be protected because the constitution demands market place of ideas must be safeguarded, and the classroom is peculiarly market place of ideas. The nation's future depends upon leaders trained through wide exposure to that robust exchange of ideas which discovers truth out of a multitude of tongues, rather than through any kind of authoritative selection.

The question of whether an individual professor holds the constitutional right of academic freedom or whether these rights instead held by universities and institutions. The conflict between two respective comes in to view if a professor alleging a violation of academic freedom sues a university for denial of tenure. A university might well defend the suit on the ground of its own academic freedom to determine the quality of its faculty. A great deal of ink has been spoiled over the question of whether rights of constitutional academic freedom attach to individuals or to universities.

The tension between individual and institutional academic freedom can be reconciled if we appreciate that constitutional protection for academic freedom of research and publication serves the distinct value of democratic competence. This value encompasses both the on-going help of universities as institutions that promote the growth of knowledge and the capacity of individual's scholars to inquire and disseminate the results of their inquiry.

Therefore, from a constitutional point of view, academic freedom has nothing to do with the autonomy of institutions that happen to include the name university in their titles. It applies only to institutions that actually protect the application of professional scholarly standards to advance knowledge. Academic freedom does not entail deference to university administrators who have expertise in education. It instead entails deference to the professional scholarly standards by which knowledge is created. If a professor sues a university for a violation of academic freedom for its refusal to award him tenure, the right question for a court to decide is neither the individual rights of the professor nor the institutional prerogatives of the university. It is instead whether the tenure decision is made on the basis of the proper disciplinary standards.

In deciding this question, it is entirely appropriate for courts to conclude that when judges are asked to review the substance of genuinely academic decision... they should show great respect for the faculty's professional judgment.

Once appointed, the scholars have a professional function to perform in which the appointing authorities have neither competency nor moral right to intervene. The responsibility of the university teacher is primarily to the public itself, and to his judgment of his own profession; and while, with respect to certain external conditions of his vocation, he accepts a responsibility to the authority of the institution in which he serves, in the essentials of his professional activity his duty is to the wider public to which the institutional itself is morally amenable. So far as the university teacher's independence of thought and utterance is concerned – though not in other regards – the relationship of the professor to trustees may be compared to that between judges of the federal courts and the executives who appoint them. University teachers should be understood to be with respect to the conclusion reached and express by them, no more subject to the control of the trustees, they are the judges subject to the control of the Vice-chancellor with respect to their decision, while for the same reason, trustees are no more held responsible for, or to be presumed to agree with, the opinions or utterances of professors, than the vice chancellor can be assumed to approve of the legal reasoning of the courts.

Nevertheless, to link to academic freedom every policy and procedure that a professional association or any organisation might want for its members is to drain the concept of all meaning and to lend credence to the unfortunate view of some that academic freedom is no more than special pleading on behalf of a privileged elite. Because there are and will continue to be real and serious threats to academic freedom, it is important to all who care about universities to be as clear as possible about its meaning, to exercise restraint in its invocation, and to support true claims with vigor.

REFERENCES

Tisdel, Richard P. "Academic freedom-its constitutional context." *U. Colo. L. Rev.* 40 (1967)

Lotilla, Raphael Perpetuo M. "Student Academic Freedom in Institutions of Higher Learning." *Phil. LJ* 57 (1982)

Fernando, Enrique M. "Academic Freedom as a Constitutional Right." *Phil. LJ* 52 (1977)

Salmi, Jamil. "The road to academic excellence: Lessons of experience." *The road to academic excellence: The making of world-class research universities* (2011)

12

Imparting Skill-Education: Opportunity or Challenge

Dr. Mala Sharma

ABSTRACT

We take proud of being the world's youngest country in terms of demographic dividend, at the same time it should be realised that India has only 2.8% of the workforce currently enrolled for vocational training in India. (Labour Bureau-2013-14). Recent statistics and evidence direct that among all graduating today are not capable of developing the critical skills for vocational success and for squaring their role as a citizen in building the nation. Hence the very purpose of Higher education to develop High skill quotient for future employability and entrepreneurship is not satisfied.

Being one of the youngest countries of the world, skill development should be an integral part of our education policy which can prepare them for employability. Actually higher education authorities and policymakers should make the development of cognitive skills as one of the core objectives of higher education.

Currently, the country is facing the chronic problem of unadorned scarcity of exceedingly trained and quality labourers and on the other hand a big section of an educated workforce which has no employment because of fewer skills or no skills at all. Skill development and higher education go hand – in hand. Higher educational institutes have the responsibility of supplying skilled and talented workforce which industry can train categorically according to their requirement. But unfortunately, there exist a huge gap between industries requirement and level of skilled workers. The reasons can be many outdated curricula, low standard of education, lack of industry-institute linkages and less practical and applied training in higher education institutes. Hence the present paper tries to focus on below-mentioned areas related to skill generation.

- Role of Higher education in the development of skills
- The scenario of vocational training and skill development in India
- Connect between higher educational institute and skill development
- Problems generated due to Gap in skills and employability.
- The action was taken by stakeholders.

Keywords: skills, higher education, Employability, skilled workforce

INTRODUCTION

The council of National Academics awards (CNAA)Principle 3 has stated that the aims of Higher education program should include "*the development of Intellectual and imaginative powers, Students understanding and judgment, student's problem-solving skills, student's ability to communicate, their ability to see relationships within what they have learned*". (CNAA, 1989). The problem with Indian Higher education system is lack of development of the above skills and less focus on the same. UGC in its annual report certainly talks about "Growth of Higher education System" but it is only Quantitative growth i.e. Expansion in a number of universities, colleges, and student enrolment. This also can be considered as an achievement but simultaneously attention should be given to qualitative aspects of higher education.

The very basic purpose of Higher education is to increase the skills among students so that they can be well employed and can earn money and happiness in life.

It is important to note that in India both uneducated and educated youth is facing the problem of unemployment and the reasons are the same low skill quotient so less competency and hence less employment.

Hence the present paper tries to focus on below-mentioned areas related to skill generation.

- Role of Higher education in the development of skills
- The scenario of vocational training and skill development in India
- Connect between higher educational institute and skill development
- Problems generated due to Gap in skills and employability.
- The action was taken by stakeholders

LITERATURE REVIEW

Linda and Lian (2011) reviewed 42 Empirical studies of teaching critical thinking skills in higher secondary education which were published between 1994 and 2009. They reviewed the test measures used, instructional intervention, and research design used in studies. They suggested various methods which can be used in the future to improve teaching methods which can further enhance critical thinking. Multiple test measures (quantitative and qualitative) should be used to asses changes in student's critical thinking.

Dunber (2006) focused on oral communication skills in higher education. This study used "the competent speaker" a rubric developed by the National Communication Association to evaluate student performance in public speaking as a case study of student's skills and programmatic assessment.

Bacha (2002) tried to focus on problems of Arabic non-native speakers of English in the required English composition course. He delineated a few writing theories that can contribute to level 2 classroom methodologies.

Alemu (2003) find out that studies conducted in various developing countries have shown that even after the completion of primary education students do not acquire the basic skills of numerals and literacy.

Colclough (2009) explained the p-problem of developing nation emphasizing that increase in gross enrolment put a lot of pressure on limited resources results in the poor quality of education they attain.

Martin (2010) found that the Establishment of non-cognitive skills among young people improves academic achievement as well as have a positive impact on class retention by ten percent.

Krishnan and Kulikova (2010) examined the impact of a programme which aimed at increasing non-cognitive skills of children of a slum area in Mumbai. The focus was to enhance self-esteem and self-efficacy and it had a notable impact on academic achievement.

Adams(2007), Brewer (2004) have a similar view that in major developing countries young people leave school with very few skills and they face a lot of competition for the job, they often face the problem of unemployment, underemployment, and poverty.

Skill Development in True Sense

Skill is the ability to do your job well. There are general skills which are to be developed during school and higher education and in addition to that, there are skills which need to develop for employability. We can discuss skills in two ways

- *General Skills* (must be developed during school and college education)
- *Specific Skills For Employability* (Vocational Training)

It is sad to note that in our country we fail to develop both types of skill packages very poorly among youth. This is the reason for the large gap between demand and supply of employment.

General Skills

The very purpose of higher education is the same for years and that is to prepare the young generation for living life and work efficiently. These are a catalyst for success. These skills include

- The skill of listening, reading, writing, questioning
- Interactive skill
- To think critically (scientific)
- To solve complex problems

All of the above skills make us logical and rationale. Colleges should pay emphasis on critical thinking and analytical reasoning. Critical thinking benefits to taking day-to-day decision logically and teach us to govern ourselves during complex situations. Interactive skills are mandatory in the current situation. People should know what, when, and how to speak?

Higher education institution should have such a curriculum that all the above skills are developed. Curriculum, content, teaching pedagogy, quality of teachers, infrastructure facilities are core factors to develop these skills. Innovative methods and best practices, ICT also proves effective.

Skills Specific for Employability (Vocational Training /Internship/Apprentice)

The government in recent years focusing tremendously on vocational training. The biggest disadvantage of this is that we are preparing students for blue colour jobs. They are given job-specific training and then they work in that particular field, this is to improve their motor skills, but at the same time thought should be given to the loss of creativity, innovative thinking, out of box thinking, entrepreneurship skills, risk-taking ability, scientific thinking. As India overlays its path towards global economic powerhouse, it is very significant to sharpen the skills which can create marvels for its future.

Current Approach

As mentioned earlier that our education does not support much for the development of cognitive skills, they are paying attention to the development of vocational skills but the scenario is not that palpable there too. There is a wide gap between types of students adding to the labour force and the demand of the market. India has less percentage of vocationally trained (so-called skilled) people when compared to other nations. The current size of India's officially skilled workforce is very small. Labour Bureau 2013-14 survey says that only 6.8% of persons aged15 years and above have received vocational training Whereas in Korea 96%, Germany (75%) Japan (80%) and UK (68%) of the workforce is vocationally trained

Students Enrolment in Higher Education

It should be well understood that to equip the population with employability skills, improve their competence and productivity, the basic requirement is to focus on the development of cognitive skill at school level education. Skill development does not mean knowing one motor skill, but it enhances the ability to deal with each and every situation of life effectively. But our education system will take time to realise the actual meaning of skill development and implement the same.

Currently, the Government is trying to minimize the gap between demand for motor skills and supply for the same. In that case, also we are not moving in the correct direction. The data for the students enrolled in various courses at all levels in universities and colleges and other institutions of higher education gives us a clear picture of the type of workforce available to us in the near future. Below is the data on total students' enrolment which in an absolute sense is increasing, though the percentage varies.

All India Student Enrolment (2005-06 TO 2016-17)

Year	Total Enrolment	Percentage Increase
2005-06	12043050	9.1
2006-07	13163054	9.3
2007-08	14400381	9.4
2008-09	15768417	9.5
2009-10	17243352	9.4
2010-11	18670050	8.3
2011-12	20327478	8.9
2012-13	22302938	9.7
2013-14	23764960	6.6
2014-15	26585437	11.87
2015-16	28484746	7.14
2016-17	29427158	3.31

Note: data for the year 2016-17 is provisional data

Source: AISHE 2016-17

A look at students' enrolment by major discipline will give us a clear idea about the direction in which our youth is moving. Below is the data for the year 2016-17 by major discipline.

Out-Turn/Pass-Out at Undergraduate Level in Major Discipline/Subjects (2016-17)

Discipline	No. of students	% of students
Arts	2169351	33.60
Science	1021481	15.82
Commerce	948609	14.69
Engineering and tech	894437	13.85
Education	436472	6.76
Medical science	186832	289
Social science	179554	2.78
IT and computer	164239	2.54
Management	121114	1.88
Law	67973	1.05
Indian language	61623	0.95
Agriculture	42939	0.67
Oriental learning	38868	0.60
Foreign language	25052	0.39
Home science	17958	0.28
Library and information science	14155	0.22
Area studies	13305	0.21
Physical education	12915	0.20
Fine arts	9052	0.14
Linguistics	6648	0.10
Journalism & mass communication	5203	0.08
Social work	5140	0.08
Fashion technology	3256	0.05
Veterinary and animal sciences	2520	0.04
Design	2279	0.04
Cultural studies	1986	0.03

Religious studies	1903	0.03
Fisheries sciences	650	0.01
Defence studies	250	0.003872
Women studies	278	0.004305
Gender studies	134	0.002075
Criminology and forensic science	122	0.001889
Marine science	43	0.000666
Grand total	6456386	------
		Calculated

Source: AISHE 2016-17

The above data reveals that Arts, Science, and commerce are still the prominent fields for student enrolment. These are the streams were students generally lack professional training at the graduate level and lack employability skill too. It is strange that nearly 64% of total students are admitted in these three branches. Other streams have very few students. There can be two reasons for this. Firstly, Arts science and commerce are major categories from years and Rural and sub-urban people in India lack awareness about other branches. Secondly, there are a smaller number of seats available in the professional and technical course. Thirdly fees for such courses are very high. But specialisation is need of the hour. A bachelor's degree without specialisation is unable to earn a job in recent times. Moreover, in such courses in our country very less attention is paid to develop cognitive skills. Supply of students with Arts, commerce and Science degrees are much more than specialised degrees.

On the other hand, the government has identified 20 high-growth sectors and services that have the ability and requirement for employment in upcoming years.

Sectorwise Available Employment and its Annual Growth

Sector	Employment in 2008	Incremental HR requirement till 2022	CAGR (2008-2022)
Unorganised sector	35.9	41.1	5.6
Transportation, Logistics, warehousing and packaging sector	7.4	17.7	9.1
Tourism	3.5	3.6	5.2
Textile and clothing industry	35.4	26.2	4.0
Organised Retail	2.8	17.3	34.3
Media and entertainment	1.0	3.0	10.1
Leather industry	2.6	406	7.8
IT and ITES industry	2.2	5.3	9.2
Healthcare service industry	3.2	12.8	12.3
Furniture and furnishing industry	1.5	3.4	9.0
Food processing sector	8.5	9.3	5.4
Electronic and IT hardware industry	0.9	3.2	11.4
Education and vocational training	7.1	5.8	4.3
Construction Material and building hardware	1.1	1.4	5.8
Chemicals and pharmaceutical	1.7	1.9	5.5
Construction Industry	36.0	47.3	6.2
Banking, Financial Services, and Insurance Industry	4.3	4.2	5.0
Auto and auto component sector	13.0	35.0	9.8

Source: IMaCS Study

Looking at the demand side in the near future it is clear that the most prominent sectors are Manufacturing, textiles, construction, Automotive, and healthcare. It is necessary to develop proper skills in these areas. Even if our ITI's, Skill universities, and other agencies working on skill development manage to get data and encourage students to attain those skills which are required in the market, India can solve the problem of unemployment to great extent.

Problems Generated Due to Gap in Skills and Employability

- Massive unemployment and underemployment exist because industries are not eager to employ untrained people and that provided employment are also paid low.
- Improper development of skills results in lack of creativity, innovativeness, lack of communication skill, lack of interpersonal skill among youth.
- Unemployment and underemployment increase social unrest in nation.
- Improper skill development also affects negatively the production and productivity of the industrial sector.
- Distorted development of few sectors takes place. Other sectors which require trained, properly skilled labour force lag behind.

To solve the gap between demand and supply of skill and to generate more skilled workers, the government has taken a lot many policy initiatives and introduced a number of schemes which the training bodies are implementing.

The National policy on skill development was first framed in 2009 to produce skills ecosystem in India. It provides guidelines to formulate addressing challenges in skill development. Similarly, the National Skills Qualifications Framework established in 2013, is a competency-based framework. Most of the countries are in the process of developing a national qualification framework.

Planning commission declares that there are 1896 ITI's, 1244 polytechnics, 669 community polytechnics 9583 secondary schools with vocational education and training, 3218 industrial training centre in the private sector. Additionally, Ministries of Rural Development, MSME, Health, Tourism, and several others have their own training centre. The Director general of employment and training Co-ordinates all the program related to vocational training at the national level.

The key training schemes that have been undertaken at the national level are:

1. Craftsmen Training Scheme (CTS)
2. Apprenticeship Training Scheme (ATS)
3. Craft Instructors' Training Scheme (CITS)
4. Advanced Vocational Training Scheme (AVTS)
5. Supervisory/Foremen Training Scheme
6. Staff Training and Research Program
7. Instructional Media Development Program
8. Women's Training Scheme
9. Hi-Tech Training Scheme

The above schemes are working towards developing youth vocationally and to train them at-least one skill so that they can earn their living. But along with this, there are certain dodges in the functioning of higher education, the enterprises are not involved in curriculum design, teachers training, placement and system, which if taken care of, can solve a number of problems.

- Higher education has no back-up plan for drop-outs.
- There exists a lack of industry linkage at the school level. School education is majorly theoretical, where very less practical exposure is provided to students.
- The enterprise is not involved in curriculum design, teachers training, Placement and internship process in higher education institutes.
- Regional schools and colleges should design 1/3rd of its curriculum according to demand for local needs. For example, Gujarat has Chemical industries, pharmaceutical industries, fertilizer industries, handicraft then our curriculum must have incorporated in their study and tours, their understanding of skills required for those industries etc.

Conclusion

The term "Skill Development" has been used in a different manner in India. Skill development does not mean the development of motor skills or providing vocational training to students. It means to develop cognitive skills and social skills which can prepare the student for future challenges. The road towards success will not be easy, there will be all odds one can or cannot think of, but the students should be taught to deal with it effectively.

References

1. Adams, A. V. (2007) "The Role of Youth Skills Development in the Transition to Work." *A Global Review, Children and Youth The World Bank.* Washington D.C. Adams

2. *All India survey of Higher education* (2016-17).

3. Anita Ganesh, Sapna. H. Mogappagowda (2017) "Bridging the skill Vs. Employability – gap for a Smart India" *Project Management National Conference,* India.

4. FICCI-KAS (2015) "Skill Development in India"

5. George Brown "Effective Teaching" *Quality Assurance for University Teaching, Society for Research into Higher Education*, London, Open University Press.

6. The government of India (2014). *Demand responsive Vocational Training.* New Delhi: Directorate General of employment and training, Ministry of Labour and Employment, Ministry of Labour and Employment

7. *The government of India – Ministry of Skill Development & Entrepreneurship, National Skill Development Corporation and KPMG.* Human Resource and skill requirements in Food processing sector (2013-17, 2017-22).

8. IBEF (2013) "Skilling the workforce: Skill Development Initiative in India"-*A Study Report.*

9. Linda. S. Behar, Lian Niv (2011) "Teaching critical skills in Higher education: A review of Literature", *Journal of college teaching and learning,* volume 8, Number 2. University of Florida, USA

10. Nahla N. Bacha (2002) *Developing Learners' Academic Writing Skills in Higher Education.* A Study for Educational Reform, Language, and Education, 16:3, 161-177, DOI: 10.1080/09500780208666826

11. *National Skill Development Corporation* (2012-17,2017-22) Human Resource and skill requirements in the capital goods

12. Norah. E. Dunbar (2006) "Oral Communication Skills In Higher education" *Using a performance-based Evaluation Rubric to access communication skills*, Innovative Higher education.

Part III
Crown of Higher Education

13

Internationalisation of Higher Education: Hard Rock to Drill

Dr. Gurudutta P. Japee

Abstract

There is no denying the fact that Indian higher education is struggling to infuse quality at the systemic level and it has limited itself to a few institutions of excellence of IIMs and IITs. Instances like this, question the whole rhetoric that Indian higher education is reforming and expanding access. Indian institutions are facing a crisis of confidence where many students are aspiring for the same set of select few quality institutions.

A systematic approach to internationalisation May helps in bringing global good practices and more institutions with higher quality. It is a hallmark of adopting global practices ranging from admissions to teaching, research, and governance. In a country where absolute scores are still considered the only benchmark for admissions. According to one Survey by UNESCO The number of Indian students studying abroad rapidly increased by 163% between 1999 and 2006 to reach 145,539 as compared to slower growth of 25% between 2006 and 2013 to reach 181,872. This is not only brain drain but also the loss of economy and culture to the nation.

The purpose of this paper is to look at the concept and meaning of internationalisation and the strategies for integrating an international dimension into higher education institutions. This includes meaning and definition of the term, a description of the various approaches to internationalisation, an exploration of why it is important to internationalise the higher education sector and an analysis of which strategies are appropriate to integrate an international and intercultural dimension in a higher education institution. The paper may be useful to Indian higher education institutions opting for internationalisation and foreign collaboration...

Keywords: Strategies, Approaches, Internationalisation, HEI, Stakeholders

INTRODUCTION

Due to the increased interest in, and understanding of, the international dimension of higher education, the term "internationalisation" is being used customarily. Internationalisation means different things to different people. There are a number of terms which are often confused with or used in conjunction with internationalisation. The term which is most often used interchangeably with internationalisation is globalisation and thus it is important to explore further the relationship between globalisation and internationalisation. Globalisation can be described or defined in a vast number of ways. The description (Knight and de Wit, 1997) which is most relevant and appropriate to the discussion on the international dimension of the higher education sector is as follows:

- "Globalisation is the flow of technology, economy, knowledge, people, values, ideas... across borders. Globalisation affects each country in a different way due to a nation's individual history, traditions, culture, and priorities.
- Internationalisation of higher education is one of the ways a country responds to the impact of globalisation yet, at the same time respects the individuality of the nation." Thus, internationalisation and globalisation are seen as different but dynamically linked concepts.

APPROACHES TO INTERNATIONALISATION

Approaches to internationalisation there are a number of generic approaches that institutions are using as they plan and implement an institution-wide internationalisation strategy.

- *Activity:* Categories or types of activities used to describe internationalisation: such as curriculum, student/faculty exchanges, technical assistance, international students.
- *Competency:* Development of new skills, knowledge, attitudes, and values in students, faculty and staff. As the emphasis on outcomes of education grows there is increasing interest in identifying and defining global/international competencies
- *Ethos:* Emphasis is on creating a culture or climate on campus which promotes and supports international/intercultural initiatives
- *Process:* Integration or infusion of an international or intercultural dimension into teaching, research, and service through a combination of a wide range of activities, policies, and procedure

CONCEPT OF INTERNATIONALISATION

"Internationalisation of higher education is the process of integrating an international/intercultural dimension into the teaching, research and service functions of the institution" (Knight, 1994).

The idea of internationalisation is a dynamic process and not a set of isolated activities.

Integration or infusion is also key to this definition to ensure that the international dimension is a central part of programmes, policies, and procedures and not a marginal and easily expendable element.

It is short-sighted to think of internationalisation as only a geographically based concept.

By design, this definition is also rationale neutral. That is to say, the motivation for an institution to internationalise is not included in the definition.

A definition needs to be generic. Institutions have different rationales for internationalisation which need to be made clear and explicit. A definition, therefore, should not be linked to any particular set of rationales. Instead, the definition is better associated with the primary and universal functions of an institution of higher education, namely teaching, research and service to society.

It is challenging to find a definition of internationalisation which is appropriate and sensitive to the higher education systems in a wide variety of countries and cultures.

Perspective by Various Stakeholders on Internationalisation

Rationale	**Government Sector**	**Education sector**	**Private Sector**
Political Economical Academic Cultural/Social	The government sector includes the different levels of government ranging from supra-national bodies to national, regional and local. Within the government	The education sector is equally diverse because it is necessary to look at the sector from the system level, the institutional level, and the individual level. Among the many stakeholder groups in the	The private sector is another heterogeneous group due to the varied interests of the manufacturing, service or trade companies, the nature of their products and

	sector, there are, of course, many different stakeholder groups which have a vested interest in the international dimension of high education. The most obvious is the education departments. However, as the previous sections on rationale point out there are other governing units such as foreign affairs, culture, economic development and trade, science and technology which all have an interest in the international dimension of higher education	education sector are the different types of institutions (colleges, institutes, polytechnics, universities) which make up a system; the scholarly research and discipline groups; the professional and membership associations; the students, teachers, researchers, and administrators and of course other advocacy or issue groups	services as well as their geographical interests. Another influencing factor is the size of the company and whether it is local, national or transnational in ownership. It is important to recognise that the private sector is much broader than private education providers.

STRATEGIES FOR INTERNATIONALISATION OF HIGHER EDUCATION

In the process-oriented approach to internationalisation, the emphasis is placed on the concept of enhancing and sustaining the international dimensions of research, teaching, and service.

Integration is key to the process and strategies which focus on both academic activities as well as organisational factors are central to achieving a successful and sustainable integration of the international dimension. Therefore, two general types of strategies are discussed in this section, programme strategies and organisational strategies. Both types of strategies are needed to internationalise an education institution.

PROGRAMME STRATEGIES

Programme strategies are divided into the four groups Academic, Research and Collaboration, External participation and Extracurricular Activities. Following is the detail list of strategies can be adopted by any higher education institutions for each and every programme.

ACADEMIC PROGRAMMES

- Student exchange programmes
- Foreign language study
- Internationalised curricula
- Area of thematic studies
- Work/study abroad
- International students
- Teaching/learning process
- Joint and double degree programmes
- Cross-cultural training
- Faculty/staff mobility programmes
- Visiting lecturers and scholars
- The link between academic programmes and research,
- training and development assistance

Research and Collaboration

- Area and theme centres
- Joint research projects
- International conferences and seminars
- Published articles and papers
- International research agreements
- Researcher and graduate student exchange
- programmes
- International research partners in academic and
- other sectors
- The link between research, curriculum, and teaching

External Participation

- Community-based partnerships and projects with non-government groups or private sector companies
- International development assistance projects
- Customised/contract training programmes off-shore
- The link between development projects and training activities with teaching and research
- Community service and intercultural project work
- Off-shore teaching sites and distance education
- Participation in international networks
- Alumni development programmes abroad

Extra-Curricular Activities

- Student clubs and associations
- International and intercultural campus events

- Liaison with community-based cultural groups
- Peer groups and programmes
- Social, cultural and academic support systems

ORGANISATIONAL STRATEGIES

Organisational strategies are divided into four groups Governance, Operations, support services, and Human resource management. Following is the detail list of strategies can be adopted by any higher education institutions

GOVERNANCE

- Expressed commitment by senior leaders
- Active involvement of faculty and staff
- Articulated rationale and goals for internationalisation
- Recognition of an international dimension in mission
- statement and other policy documents

OPERATIONS

- Integrated into institution-wide and department planning, budgeting and quality review systems
- Appropriate organisational structures
- Communication systems (formal and informal) for liaison and co-ordinator
- The balance between centralised and decentralised promotion and management of internationalisation
- Adequate financial support and resource allocation Systems

SUPPORT SERVICES

- Support from institution-wide service units, i.e. student housing, registrar at, counselling, fund-raising, etc.
- Involvement of academic support units i.e. language training, curriculum development, library
- Student support services for international students studying on campus and domestic students going abroad, i.e. orientation programmes, counselling, cross-cultural training, student advisors, etc.

HUMAN RESOURCE DEVELOPMENT

- Recruitment and selection procedures which reorganise international and intercultural expertise
- Reward and promotion policies to reinforce faculty and staff contribution to internationalisation
- Faculty and staff professional development activities
- Support for international assignments and sabbaticals

The purpose of this paper is to introduce the key concepts behind what is meant by the term internationalisation of higher education; what are the different approaches to internationalisation; why is it important; what are the reasons why different stakeholder groups promote and support internationalisation; and what are the major strategies used to internationalise a higher education institution. This represents the international dimension of teaching/learning, research and service functions of higher education institutions.

REFERENCES

Aigner, J.S. et al. (1992), *Internationalising the University: Making it Work, CBIS Federal*, Inc., Springfield, Virginia.

Arum, S. and Van De Water, J. (1992), "The Need for a Definition of International Education in US Universities", in C. Klasek (ed.), *Bridges to the Future: Strategies for Internationalising Higher Education,* Association of International Education Administrators, Carbondale, Illinois, pp. 191-203.

Back, K., Davis, D. and Olsen, A. (1996), *Internationalisation of Higher Education: Goals and Strategies*, IDP Education Australia, Canberra.

Davies, J. (1992), "Developing a Strategy for Internationalisation in Universities: Towards a Conceptual Framework", in C. Klasek (ed.), *Bridges to the Future: Strategies for Internationalising Higher Education*, Association of International Education Administrators, Carbondale, Illinois, pp. 177-190.

De Wit, H. (1993), "On the Definition of International Education", *European Association for International Education* Newsletter, No. 11, pp. 7-10.

.... (1998), "Rationale for Internationalisation of Higher Education in Millennium", *Revista do Instituto Superior Politecnico de Viseu*, ano 3, No. 11, pp. 11-19.

Harari, M. (1989), *Internationalisation of Higher Education: Effecting Institutional Change in the Curriculum and Campus, Centre for International Education,* California State University, Long Beach, California

Harari, M. and Reiff, R. (1993), "Halfway There – A View from the Bridge", *International Educator*, Vol. 3, No. 1, pp. 16-19, 46.

Huntington, S. (1996), *The Clash of Civilisations and the Remaking of World Order*, Simon and Schuster, New York.

Kerr, C. (1991), "International Learning and National Purposes in Higher Education", *American Behavioural Scientist*, pp. 17-41.

Klasek, C. (1992), *Bridges to the Future: Strategies for Internationalising Higher Education,* Association of International Education Administrators, Carbondale, Illinois.

Knight, J. (1994), *Internationalisation: Elements and Checkpoints*, Canadian Bureau for International Education, Ottawa.

Knight, J. (1995), Internationalisation at Canadian Universities: The Changing Landscape, Association of Universities and Colleges of Canada, Ottawa.

Knight, J. and de Wit, H. (1995), "Strategies for Internationalisation of Higher Education: Historical and Conceptual Perspectives", in H. de Wit (ed.), *Strategies for Internationalisation of Higher Education* – A Comparative Study of Australia, Canada, Europe and the United States of America, European Association for International Education, Amsterdam.

.... (1997), *Internationalisation of Higher Education in Asia Pacific Countries*, European Association for International Education, Amsterdam.

Mestenhauser, J.A., and Ellingboe, B.J. (1998), *Reforming the Higher Education Curriculum: Internationalising the Campus*, The American Council on Education and Oryx Press, Arizona

OECD/IMHE, *Quality, and Internationalisation in Higher Education.* (1999)

https://www.oecd-ilibrary.org

http://digitallearning.eletsonline.com

https://en.wikipedia.org/wiki/Indian_students_abroad

14

Understanding Psychology in Higher Education – A Key Tool to Develop Professional Bonding

Dr. Krupa B. Bhatt

ABSTRACT

In general sense, it is rightly said that Psychology is the science of behaviour and mind, including conscious and unconscious phenomena, as well as feeling and thought. It is an academic discipline of immense scope and diverse interests that, when taken together, seek an understanding of the emergent properties of brains, and all the variety of epiphenomena they manifest. As a social science, it aims to understand individuals and groups by establishing general principles and researching specific cases. In this field, a professional practitioner or researcher is called a psychologist and can be classified as a social, behavioural, or cognitive scientist. Psychologists attempt to understand the role of mental functions in India.

Exploring the physiological and biological processes that underlie cognitive functions and behaviours, Psychology itself is a very vast subject and three are many para branches showing different aspects and angles of psychology. There are many types of research showing that psychology can be analysed at micro as well as macro level. Micro-level talks about individual psychological touch point showing the perception. It also includes attitude and thinking as well as changes in the thought process. Macro-level is about psychology with reference to group behaviour. It may be within a social group or reference group or may be within professional behavioural cases. In different situations, psychology affects human behaviour and the way an individual feels and approach is also upon the way of his thinking. Psychologists generally consider the organism the basis of the mind, and therefore a vitally related area of study. Psychiatrists and neuropsychologists work at the interface of mind and body Biological psychology, also known as physiological psychology, or neuropsychology is the study of the biological substrates of behaviour and mental processes. Key research topics in this field include comparative psychology, which studies humans in relation to other animals, and perception which involves the physical mechanics of sensation as well as neural and mental processing. This is with reference to technical terms.so far as higher education is concerned it's definitely connected with the education field.

Human development begins with the mobilisation of more primitive (innate) functions, with their natural use. Then goes through a training phase, in which, under the influence of external conditions, it changes its structure and starts to become from a natural process into a complex "cultural process" when it is a new form of behaviour with help of a number of external devices.

So far as syllabus viewpoint is concerned, at bachelor's level like in a B.Sc. or a B.A., the first year of an undergraduate degree covers the core elements: exploring mental health, childhood, and development, plus the required scientific fundamentals. Specialisation Psychology is the study of human behaviour, thoughts, actions, interactions and reactions, and a psychology student will demonstrate this through essays and experiments. The basis of most psychology degrees is in natural and life sciences, however, there is the opportunity to investigate social sciences and humanities too, for example in criminology and philosophy. Psychology degrees are either occur in the following years, covering topics like cognitive processes, neuroscience and the psychology of certain groups, such as trauma victims, the elderly and criminals. Sometimes it requires students to choose their own field of study, carry out original research, collect data and summarise their findings. Most psychology degrees last three to four years and some make a relevant work placement a requirement to pass the course. Placements could be in a range of establishments, for example in hospitals, prisons and rehabilitation centres. This is an important part of a course, so if a university doesn't offer placement as an option, it is worth pursuing work experience in the university breaks or part-time. The study of psychology is achieved through a variety of methods; practical sessions, lectures in the relevant theories and the learning of professional software programmes. Assessment is just as diverse in practice, from timed examinations to essays to lab reports to final project dissertations.

Career options are endless – those who become trained psychologists might pursue psychology-related fields, within healthcare, mental health support, an art therapist, social workers, speech and language therapists or counsellors. However, this degree does not limit you to the healthcare sector. Graduates thrive in every sector of society, including education, relationships, crime and punishment, advertising, human relations, and management. The above was the details of a career in psychology.

When it's a case of interactions between teacher and student, it's a must to understand psychological Growth mindset.

These are the Key points of learning enhancement through understanding psychology.

1. PRIOR KNOWLEDGE ABOUT TOPIC\FIELD

What Students Already Know Affects their Learning

Research shows that prior knowledge influences both conceptual growth and conceptual change in students. With conceptual growth, students add to their existing knowledge, and with conceptual change, students correct misconceptions or errors in existing knowledge. Facilitating conceptual growth or change requires first obtaining a baseline level of student knowledge prior to the start of each unit through formative assessment. Student's integrity and willingness also matter always.

2. IN-DEPTH ANALYTICAL SKILL

Another point to ponder upon is the hidden skill in a student. Most of the time they are not aware of their own skill. It comes with proper practice.in case of any problem solving it, matters to analyse all pros and cons with reference to depth analysis. After all, psychology plays a prime role here.

3. FACILITATING CONTEXT

Learning is based on context, so generalising learning to new contexts is not spontaneous, but rather needs to be facilitated.

Student growth and deeper learning are developed when instructors help students transfer learning from one context to another. Students will also be better able to generalise learning to new contexts if instructors invest time in focusing on deeper learning. It again depends upon developing a new angle of thinking.

5. PRACTICE

Acquiring long-term knowledge and skill is largely dependent on practice.

This principle details empirically based strategies that will help students more effectively encode learned materials into long-term memory. In addition to those in the memory unit, examples from this principle can help inform instruction throughout the course. It has been rightly said that practice makes a man perfect.

6. FEEDBACK

This principle highlights the importance of instructor responses and indicates the best manner in which to deliver feedback to students in order to maintain or increase motivation to learn. To make a proper connection it's a must to discuss feedback.

7. SELF-ASSESSMENT

Students' self-regulation assists in learning and self-regulatory skills can be taught.

Self-regulation skills, including attention, organisation, self-control, planning and memory strategies, improve learning and engagement and can be taught through direct instruction, modeling and classroom organisation. It is about the analysis of own self with reference to actions taken as well mistakes made.

8. CREATIVITY

Creativity is considered a critical skill for the technology-driven world of the 21st century and because it is not a stable trait, it can be taught, nurtured and increased. This principle describes specific methods of structuring assignments to increase creativity and ideas for how

9. Motivational Pushup

This principle is directed at how instructors can increase intrinsic motivation through classroom practices and activities that support the fundamental need of students to feel autonomous. It is important to note that not everything of importance is intrinsically motivating to all students and that there is a place for extrinsic motivation in education. Inspiration many times gives the best result. Due to motivation student takes action as per his best capacity due to inner confidence. It is helpful in his academic performance and also in career development.

10. Goal oriented

Students who form mastery goals are focused on attaining new skills or increasing existing ability, but students who develop performance goals typically are focused simply on showing adequate ability. Goal setting for long term creates a vision and for short term creates clarity to achieve long term.

All the above, are guidelines to enhance self-assessment skill and through that to understanding self-behaviour. It also helps to develop critical thinking ability and leads to overall development of a student subject to the condition that he should have basic knowledge about new techniques of behavioural science.

Conclusion

After all, it is universally accepted that psychology plays a great role to understand human behaviour. It may be evaluated from the individual angle or organisational angle. In all public relations at the workplace, psychology plays a prominent role. With special reference to higher education psychology is a connecting bridge of effective communication, conceiving ideas, generating knowledge-based thought process and a strong understanding followed by enhanced bonding between students and mentor.

15

Major Theoretical Aspects in Sociology of Higher Education

Dr. Rushiraj Upadhyay

Abstract

Sociology of higher education emerged at the end of the 20th century worldwide as a sub-branch of sociology. Socialisation through the educational system and Educationalisation through the social system are the important objectives of the sociology of higher education. As a matter of fact, there are very few studies conducting in the area of sociology of higher education by splitting from the sociology of education. Such studies accelerate with the clarification of theoretical perspectives in the same field. This paper includes the concept of sociology of higher education, an overview of higher education in India from past to present and functional and conflict theoretical aspects regarding sociology of higher education.

Introduction

Sociology is a subject connecting to the society which includes all the facts regarding human life. Groups – Community – its action, reaction, and interactions, Class – Creeds & Castes, institutes, and many more important points are the subject matter of sociology. Sociology begins with the French revolution and develops with the industrial revolution. Afterward, the process of its expansion and development does not stop worldwide. As per the needs of different countries of the world, the development of sociology continued to grow under the various branches i.e. medical sociology, urban sociology, rural sociology, regional sociology, sociology of sanitation etc. Sociology of education and higher education is one of the utmost important branches of sociology to scientifically analyse the relationship between education and society. When we specifically noting about the sociology of higher education, 'it is emerged as a sub-discipline in the 1960s coincided with a rapidly changing society and concomitant massification of higher education" (Andres, 2016). Sociology of higher education is a modern sub-branch of the sociology of education. It is in the roots of the sociology of higher education. "Sociology of education is developed in the western countries. Such educational problems rose during the twentieth century in America i.e. how to prepare the education programs in the schools? How to access the requirements of various ethnic and religious groups of foreign migrants whose learning and pattern behaviour was different? How to make equal educational opportunities to reach equal political goals in the field etc. were the questions rising with the complex industrial society for the education system. In this social condition, various approaches have been developed regarding the study of the sociology of education" (Shah, 2013). This paper includes the concept of sociology of higher education, higher education in the Indian context, and Major theoretical perspective of higher education.

THE CONCEPT OF SOCIOLOGY OF HIGHER EDUCATION

Patricia Gumport rendered Sociology of higher education as young and unformed till 1970. Moreover, after the publication of the foundational article by Barton Clark in the year 1973, various scholars began to define (Gumport, 2007). Anthony G.

defines education as a social institution which enables and promotes the acquisition of skills, knowledge, and broadening of personal horizons. Education can take place in many social settings". (2009; 834)

Sociology of education is not only focusing to study the relationship between the education system and social system but also focusing on the educational system as a social system. Socialisation through the education system and educationalisation through the social system is the main objective of the sociology of education. Socialisation is a process to educate the humans which makes them social from biological. Sociology of education includes the study of this entire process of socialisation. Study of educational institutions, its administration, and reformation, classroom relation and interactions, teacher-parent relationship, structure and functions of education system etc. are the subject matters of the sociology of education. Clark identifies two major areas of inquiry in sociology of higher education, "Study of educational inequality beyond secondary level" and the "Socio-Psychological effects of college on students," as well as "two smaller literatures" focused on "the study of academic man', or higher education as a profession", and "the organisations of higher education as the unit of study". Moreover, he extends earlier work to 'a more macrocosmic level' including the national system of higher education" (Gumport, 2007, p. 17:18)

Sociology of higher education is an evolving field in this contemporary era. In the Indian context, sociology of higher education, as a branch of sociology, is in the process of development. Very few studies are conducting regarding higher education in sociology since the 20th century. The need for the sociology of education has emerged with the establishment of colleges and universities in India during but as a matter of fact, till the independence sociology as a subject could not expand and grow. Mainly sociology was taught in two universities i.e. Bombay University and Lakhnow University. Moreover, needs of study regarding caste, creed and other socio-political structural-functional issues encompassed Indian sociologists, due to which sociology of education could not develop as an independent branch during that specific time of span. Though, some sociological concepts got space in the syllabus of the department of education in such universities of India. "Socio-educational researches i.e. 'environmental effects on the education of a child – 1926 by Sane and 'Interaction between education and social class – 1928 by Joglekar in historical context' etc. were conducted following the trend to analyse the social aspects of education. However, it was a period when mostly educational concepts of sociology were taught to train the teachers (Shah, 2013). Ultimately the development of educational sociology was in an initial stage during the British rule as well as colleges and university were not established in enough proportion. The proportion of people received primary education was also the law. Women education was also not promoted due to such traditional rigid perceptions, consequently, female education rate remained very low. During post-Independence, India's female literacy rate was only 8.86 present. However, the female literacy rate increased up to 64% till 2011. (Census, 1951-2011). It has been found that 'On the eve of the independence the women enrolment was less than 10 present of the total enrolment but in the academic year 2010-11 women enrolment increased up to 41.5 Percept. (Shanjendu, 2014) Need to increase rate of higher education, need to increase female participation in higher education, drop out ratio in higher education, educational inequalities, improve the needs of national and state universities and the study of its administration and structure etc. were the key factors for the emergence and development of sociology of higher education in India. Though, very few researches conducted in India considering the sociology of higher education compared to other branches of sociology.

HIGHER EDUCATION IN INDIA – AN OVERVIEW

Taxshila, Nalanda, Valabhi etc. were the oldest universities in India. It has also been found that many scientific types of research were conducted in the various field of education. British rule has commenced the western system of education, which has broken the Indian traditional education system. However, the proportions of higher education recipients were very few in the pre-independence era. Data shows that only 139 colleges and 16088 students were enrolled in the year 1883 which increased up to 591 colleges and 2,28881 enrolment in the year 1947. (Shanjendu, 2014) Today as on 2018 there are total 868 states, central, deemed and private universities and near about 50 thousand colleges and Stand Alone institutions remains in India. In the academic year 2015-16, there were 34,584,781 students were enrolled in various streams of higher education. (All India Survey on Higher Education, 2016) Data shows that India has made progress in higher education. Even after 7 decades of independence, female education ratio seems less compare to the male education ratio. Moreover, the drop out ratio in higher education is still noteworthy. "Since independence higher education in India has spread rapidly throughout India so much so that it is the third largest system in the world." (Shanjendu, 2014) Though, the higher education system needs changes and reformation in the contemporary era. As an independent branch, sociology of higher education has its own importance regarding these changes and reformation in the Indian education system.

THEORETICAL ASPECTS OF SOCIOLOGY OF HIGHER EDUCATION

Education is a formal system in the contemporary era which contributes to developing society as well as the nation. Sociological Theories can be seen in various aspects and sociology of higher education is one of them. Forefront theories i.e. Functional, Conflict, Structural, and Feminist etc. are described here with the various illustration in this educational branch of sociology.

Functional Theory

Society is a system comprising various parts and these parts are interconnected to each other. Various parts of the system and its interconnection is mean to sustain and integrate the social system. Functional approach depicts education as a part or as an institution for social integrity, sustainability, and development'. Classical sociological theorist Emile Durkheim sees education as a social fact. He emphasized to find the causes and effects of the various social facts. "The major functions of education are to provide require social glue in order to maintain solidarity; to supply necessary technical knowledge and skills in accordance with the needs of work-place and changing technological conditions; to socialise and humanise people "by providing the normative and cognitive frameworks they lack". (B, 1985) Strengthen the system of education in society makes it more functional as it derives the capacity to build social solidarity and integrity. Primary to secondary level education played an important role in socialisation process to control the pattern behaviour of students, make them enable for social adaptation, transfer the social values, norms, ends and through which prepare the responsible citizen. Higher education is generating skills and knowledge and being an important factor for economic institutions to provide skilled human resources.

Functionalism is one of the core perspectives of sociology. It assumed society as self-regulating and sustaining through the harmony and equilibrium of various integral and interrelated parts. Reciprocal relationship and Integration between the various parts of society enable the entire system to reduce the tensions created elements. The entire concept of functionalism in society could be described by the illustration of the human body. Various organs of the human body have particular functions through these organs are not independently working they are interrelated. A malfunction in a single organ of the boy can affect other body parts also. Similarly, society is like entirely a body and various organs or parts played an important role to sustain social system through their interrelated functions. Similarly, Education is a social institution which is a part of the social organism. Functionalism sociologist Emile Durkheim recommended to include the study of education in sociological boundaries. According to Durkheim, 'Society can survive only if there exists among its members a sufficient degree of homogeneity; education perpetuates and reinforce this homogeneity by fixing in the mind of the child, from the beginning the essential similarities that social life demands' (Giddens, Emile Durkheim; Selected Writings, 1972) Ultimately an important goal of education is to stimulate the social solidarity in the individual and from the childhood education plays an important role for that. It transmits the social values and ends, maintains and controlling the behaviour, attempt to maintain homogeneity and harmony and ultimately socialise people, increasing the knowledge and teaching the skills as per the requirements of advanced industrialised society and complex division of labour. Considering the higher education, it directly impacts on the economic system of society. Higher education plays an important role to fulfil the requirements of skills and knowledge in advanced industries as well as commerce and management sector. It builds the capacity of the individual to reach placement in various economic sectors. Examine the role of higher education to develop the skilled human resources as per contemporary demand of advanced economic society, role of higher education to instilling social solidarity and to functioning the socio-economic system, employability and unemployment, improve the living standard, socialise people to develop and maintain the commercial and industrial relations, personal development etc. are the important subject matter of sociology of higher education. Durkheim has focused on social solidarity in industrial society, and primary to higher education institutes play a role to preparing human resources for solidarity in a complex division of labour in industrial society as well as controlling the deviant behaviour to the functioning system through teaching self-discipline and explaining damage of system in front of students. To reinforce social solidarity, to train young people to maintain a social role, to maintain the division of labour through skill improvement and abilities in the socio-economic system are the important factors in the functionalist approach of the sociology of higher education.

Another functionalist approach has been introduced by Talcott Parson after Emile Durkheim in terms of education. Parson emphasized universalistic standards rather than a particularistic standard to mobilise the status of the child. As a matter of fact, the status of the child is ascribed within the family; which is decided by birth, not by ability, skills, and improvements. Standards of modern industrialised societies are universalistic and status in adult life can achieve. Educational institutes provide ground to students for their status achievement and occupational upliftment through creating require atmosphere. Maintain the universalistic standards in the educational institute are eradicating the differentiation and discrimination of sex, race, caste, class etc. and gave the importance to meritocratic principles. "Like Durkheim, Parsons argued that the school represents society in miniature. Modern industrial society is increasingly based on achievement rather than ascription, on universalistic rather than particularistic standards, on meritocratic principles which apply to all its members. By reflecting the operation of society as a whole, the school prepares young people for their adult roles" (Revise Sociology: 2017) According to the parsons, education is a most important agency of socialisation after the family. Educational institutes improve and internalise the knowledge and pattern behaviour of an individual. It internalises the values, norms, ends (and at some extent customs and assumption also) and other cultural elements of society which have to be applied in all the behaviour within the social system. Educational institutes are also teaching the goal attainment through adaptation and adjustment in society. Ultimately it prepares for the future social life as well. Higher educational institute role is as same as schools. For instance, examination system in all the educational institutes is same i.e. it held under equal condition and atmosphere in which all the pupils take the equal opportunity to rise up their rank, though on their ability they received the grade or rank. System examinations indirectly inculcate and prepare pupils to accept the fact that system is fair and equal and in that terms, they can be able to accept the status they achieved which played the role a role to maintain cohesion in society.

Conflict Theory

The roots of conflict theory in sociology remain in inequality and discrimination in society between two or more classes. Marxist thoughts are in the base to stimulate the conflict theory in all materialistic ideology. Karl Marx see the social system as a materialistic reality and evaluate it through indicating lack of amenities, goods, and services. Education is included in the essential service of any social system indicating the path of development from men to society. Though the critical approach of conflict theorists point out the other side of a coin, which is lack of equal opportunity to all in educational Institutes. "Conflict theorists do not believe that public schools reduce social inequality. Rather, they believe that the educational system reinforces and perpetuates social inequalities that arise from differences in class, gender, race, and ethnicity" (lumenlearning.com). However, by all mean in the Indian context, this can't be applicable. Contemporary Indian schooling condition seems different; in terms of caste discrimination public schools can reduce the gap between two castes. In fact, mostly so-called lower castes students and students belonging from poor families are studying in public schools, whereas, middle-upper middle and upper-class family's children are studying in private schools. However, higher education institutes scenario is different than schools. People prefer to take admission in public universities instead of private universities due to high fees. It has been found that those who didn't get admission in public universities due to the meritocratic system, they used to admit in private universities with high fees. The problem remains for those who are not able to pay high fees in private higher educational institutes and thus, from here, the seeds of dissatisfaction are planted against educational institutions.

The sociological view of conflict theorists clearly depicts that, unequal opportunities remain an entire education system for the students belonging from the different socio-economic background. Students of the lower socio-economic background are not getting the same opportunities as students from the higher socio-economic background. Moreover, the other educational facilities are affordable for the students of higher socioeconomic status compare to lower. Here the ability and quality of academia are less important. This discrimination creates the feelings of injustice for those who deprived from the educational facilities as well as education itself.

World's education system is working within a common circle. All institutes wanted to make silent effigy prepared under a particular syllabus frame as per the requirement of markets as well as the employer. History proved that students in a different way couldn't accept easily by our education system. The common circle of the education system is considering the quality of obedience not a quality of protest which produces the unimaginative and unquestioning workforce as employer's need. Syllabus framework prepares on the base of capitalists or employer requirements. As per Antonio Gramsci's theory of hegemony, economic dominant classes gain dominance over knowledge. In a very pragmatic language, the dominance over the thoughts by the leading group over the allied and subaltern groups is hegemony and in the Marxist term, economic competent classes are often leading. Interpreting this theory in terms of the education system, instead of building the independent mind-set, this system apparently builds a silent statue who work as per the mind-set of economic dominants and determinants.

In many cases, it has been found that students belonging from rich families are getting special private coaching – tuitions even in higher education whereas instead of getting special coaching, economically middle and lower classes students are finding jobs for income generation. Afterward, in such cases, jobs become more important than getting education seriously and making a degree base career. Even in private professional institutes are conducting special classes with getting extra fees which may not affordable for middle and lower class students. This class base segregation in education is a phenomenon to exist the class-based discrimination and inequality.

"Though education is free and open to all, Bowles and Ginh's claim that some have much greater opportunities than others. Bowles and Ginh's reject the view that capitalist societies are meritocratic and deny that they can do so within a capitalist framework they believe that class background is the most imp factor influencing levels of attainment" (archive.mu.ac.in). Bowles and Ginh's questioning the meritocratic system in capitalist societies. Rich students are getting higher educations in the frame of the requirement of higher level job opportunities, where cost is not affecting them. Middle-class people have high struggle from the initial level whereas lower class people mostly deprived to get higher level jobs. As per the conflict approach, Meritocratic system is one of the mechanisms in which the initial benefits are derived only by economically sound people.

References

(2016). *All India Survey on Higher Education.* New Delhi: Department of Higher Education, MHRD.

Talcott Parson's Perspective on Education. (2017). *Revise Sociology.*

Andres, L. (2016). "Theories of the sociology of higher education access and participation." In A. F. James E. Côté, *Routledge Handbook of Sociology of Higher Education* (pp. 29-39). London, UK: Routledge.

B, B. D. (1985). *Sociological Interpretations of Education.* London. Sydney. Dover, New Hampshire: Croom Helm.

Buddhischandra Shah and Kaushalya Shah. (2013). *Shixan nu Samajshastra.* Ahmedabad (Gujarat): University Granth Nirman Board.

Census. (1951-2011). *State of Literacy – Provisional Population Total.* New Delhi: Government of India.

Giddens, A. (1972). *Emile Durkheim; Selected Writings.* UK: Cambridge University Press.

Giddens, A. (2009). *Sociology.* UK: Cambridge: Polity Press.

Gumport, P. (2007). *Sociology of Higher Education – Contribution and their Context.* Baltimore: The John Hopkins University Press.

https://revisesociology.com/2017/09/05/taclott-parsons-perspective-on-education/. (2017). "Talcott Parsons' Perspective on Education." *Revised Sociology.*

Shanjendu, N. (2014). "Higher Education and Women Participation in India." *Journal of Business Management & Social Sciences Research*, 43-47.

16

Politics of Higher Education

Dr. Kamal. H. Kharecha

Abstract

With the second highest population in the world, it is obvious that it also has the highest number of student enrolled in education at a different level. In the year 2011, the overall literacy rate of population was 74% of which male literacy was 82.2% and female literacy was 65.5% in the country. In today's world where knowledge is a power which requires a significant increase in the number of institutions and an adequate number of qualified teachers for imparting education. Failure to redress the faculty shortage would hamper the achievement of the targets for increase in GER in higher education to 30 present by the year 2020. The universities (except private) mostly runs on government grants as higher education is highly subsidised in our country. All these universities receive large grants from various central and state funding agencies. This is one of the main reason of interest of people want to involve in the decision-making body and also for gaining a foothold in politics. The governing council or executive council is the highest decision making the body in universities which comprise of various ex-officio, elected and nominated representatives (preferably educationists). Nowadays, one can find a number of political representatives in various committees. The students have to give more preference to their own education than any other activities. Their active involvement in politics leads to damage of their own studies which is more necessary for them. Students should keep themselves out of this dirty game. They should think of entering into politics only after completing his / her desired qualifications. There is a famous quote "There is a greater politics in education and less education in politics", this symbolises our education system.

With the second highest population in the world, it is obvious that it also has the highest number of student enrolled in education at a different level. In the year 2011, the overall literacy rate of population was 74% of which male literacy was 82.2% and female literacy was 65.5% in the country.

There are four levels of schooling in India – Pre Primary, Primary, Secondary, and Higher Secondary. Primary education is made compulsory and covered under the right to education. The government schools, Grant-in-aid schools, and private schools provide schooling education. It is governed by various central and state education boards.

Higher education consists of three types – Vocational, University, and Technical education. The Vocational and University Education is looked after by the University Grants Commission (UGC) and Technical and Management Education is taken care of by the All India Council for Technical Education (AICTE). There are more than 15 regulating authorities to govern higher education in the country.

There are various types of universities and colleges like Central, State, Deemed to be, Private and Institute of National Importance. All these are governed and regulated by more than 15 professional bodies. The universities in India have affiliating colleges where undergraduate courses are being taught. The central and state government subsidises higher education through various schemes i.e. Grants, scholarships etc. The private institutions have to survive their own, however, there are some financial and other incentives available to these institutions and their students.

As per the latest UGC report – a total of 882 Recognised Universities in the country, of which 48 are Central Universities, 392 State Universities, 125 Deemed to be Universities and 317 private Universities.

The Gross Enrolment Ratio in higher education (GER) in the year 1950-51 was 0.7%. In 1960-61 it reached to 1.4%, in 2006-07 it was 11% which rose to 20% in 2012 and currently it's about 25% and up to the year 2020 the target is to reach 30%.

The Tamilnadu has the highest GER of 46.9% and Bihar holds the lowest 14.9%. There are 15 exclusive universities for women in 10 states and of total 40,000 plus colleges in the country, more than 1800 are exclusively for women.

There is a rise in the research programs also. In the year 2013-14 22,849 students registered for Ph.D. and 20,425 for M.Phil. Out of this half of them from Science, Technology, and agriculture. Overall 1,78,000 students enrolled for different research program across the country.

Distance learning is also a feature of the Indian higher education system. Indira Gandhi National Open University (IGNOU) is the central Open University and there were many state open universities catering the need for higher education to the unprivileged and working population.

There are many top rated universities in India which provide highly competitive world-class education in various discipline, at the same time it also has many universities which have been founded with the sole objective of making easy money. UGC and other Regulatory authorities have been trying very hard to extirpate the menace of private universities which are running courses without any recognition. Students from rural and semi-urban background often fall prey to these fake and unauthorised universities and colleges.

In today's world where knowledge is a power which requires a significant increase in the number of institutions and an adequate number of qualified teachers for imparting education. Failure to redress the faculty shortage would hamper the achievement of the targets for increase in GER in higher education to 30 present by the year 2020.

The higher education in India does not match with the global Quality standards. So there is a need for an assessment of the Quality of the country's educational institutions. Generally, the institutions assumed that Quality could be determined by faculty with impressive degrees, experience, a number of books and journals in the library, ultra-modern campus, and size of the endowment, efficient use of resources, producing uniquely educated, highly satisfied and employable graduates etc.

At present, the world-class institutions in India are mainly limited. Most of the Indian colleges and universities lack in high-end research facilities. Under-investment in libraries, information technology, laboratories, and classrooms makes it very difficult to provide top quality instruction or engage in cutting-edge research. It is time for all those who are concerned with policymaking, planning, administration and implementation of Higher Education to revitalise the very thinking on the subject and put it on the right track.

A report by the National Assessment and Accreditation Council (NAAC), which is affiliated to the University Grants Commission (UGC), reveal that two thirds (68%) of the country's universities and 90 present of its colleges are "of middling or poor quality" and that well over half of the faculty in India's colleges do not have the required qualifications. According to a study, only 25% of engineering graduates are directly employable. There is a lack of qualified persons perusing teaching as an attractive profession. It's the last choice in terms of career. In many institutions fresh graduates are employed to teach, leading to poor quality of classroom instruction.

The constituents of the university play a major role in politics. The Governors of the state are the Chancellors of the Universities in the states. The state government, with the approval of the chancellor, appoints Vice-Chancellors and Pro-Vice-Chancellors, which now has become a political post instead of educationist post. The governments appoint persons of their choice who can run and spread their ideologies and agenda. Many governments do not comply with the UGC regulations of various appointments which leads to litigations too.

The universities (except private) mostly runs on government grants as higher education is highly subsidised in our country. All these universities receive large grants from various central and state funding agencies. This is one of the main reason of interest of people want to involve in the decision-making body and also for gaining a foothold in politics. The governing council or executive council is the highest decision making the body in universities which comprise of various ex-officio, elected and nominated representatives (preferably educationists). Nowadays, one can find a number of political representatives in various committees.

The traditional universities and colleges offering regular courses of Arts, Commerce and Science are mostly subsidised and heavily depends on government funding. Naturally, they have to follow the agenda of the respective government. The faculty recruitments and student enrolment also govern by the governments. University's Act and statutes are made and amended in such a way that the government holds the indirect control of the institution. In many states, these type of universities and colleges suffered the most and gradually degraded.

The technological and another discipline like Medicine etc., the government has very few institutions and limited seats as it requires massive infrastructures and investments. The other interesting fact is that UGC, which regulates and monitors the universities across the country, plays an advisory role. It guides and recommends various regulations which are non-mandatory nature, so there are huge differences in the universities and colleges across the country as they adopt or ignore favourable guidelines.

On the other hand other regulators' like AICTE, MCI etc. make mandatory regulations which have to follow in total by the universities and colleges. The trend towards technical education rose in the recent past lead to mushrooming of private colleges and universities across the country. The affiliation of these is subjective many times as they cannot have the required capabilities. These leads to the degradation of higher education and students are the ultimate sufferer.

Higher fees structure of private universities is another phenomenon of politics in higher education. The fees of a private engineering college ranges from 50,000 to 5,00,000 rupees per annum, medical education fees ranges from 5 lakh to 20 lakh rupees per annum. So there is a large financial gap between technical education and traditional education in India. The private technical education is a highly profitable practice, although it believed to be a non-profit making and social obligation.

As a result, most of the educational institutions in India are owned by politicians and business tycoons. This Education system which is highly regulated by the government has been set up to benefit politicians. Most observers of higher education in India feel that the performance of higher education institutions has been less than satisfactory in terms of access, equity, and quality.

As a result, almost 45-50% of the total available seats in technical education remain vacant in the academic year 2018-19 in the country. On the other end, the meritorious students who are qualified to get admission do not afford the cost and subsequently less qualified and rich students get access to their desired course. In traditional courses, classrooms are filled with overcrowded students because of less costly and easily available education for mandatory requirements for jobs and social recognition. The trend of students perusing higher and advanced studies prefer to go abroad has increased over the year due to higher fees and lower quality education in the country.

The inadequate infrastructure, large vacancies of faculty, poor faculty, low student enrolment rate, outdated teaching methods, declining research standards, unmotivated students, overcrowded classrooms and widespread geographic, income, gender, and ethnic imbalances are main hurdles in the higher education system.

There is reported exploitation of students by many private providers. Access to quality higher education for students coming from poor families is a major challenge. Poor students are put to disadvantage since they are not academically prepared to crack highly competitive entrance examinations without access to private tuitions and coaching. Education in basic sciences and subjects that are not market friendly has suffered most. Many colleges established in rural areas are non-viable, are under-enrolled and have extremely poor infrastructure and facilities with just a few and non-qualified teachers.

Money also plays a vital role in the education system which needs to unique for all globally recognised syllabus and curricula. The standard education facilities are higher in the states which are much rich. There is a need to change such defects from the country education system which only can be influenced by increasing funding and providing better facilities to students.

Politics is an integral part of the operation of public education. Politics in education is not just about the ways of the election of college or university board members but it is an integral part of day-to-day life. Political activity is about negotiations over the allocation of scarce resources and about deciding who gets what. But all political activities are not the same. Political struggles in schools and colleges have different views and objectives.

The students have to give more preference to their own education than any other activities. Their active involvement in politics leads to damage of their own studies which is more necessary for them. Students should keep themselves out of this dirty game. They should think of entering into politics only after completing his / her desired qualifications. There is a famous quote "There is a greater politics in education and less education in politics", this symbolises our education system.

India has a lot of students who eventually became famous politicians. Almost every political parties promoting students caste politics, religious divisiveness and the commercialisation of education to gain their selfish purposes. Beset with violence, intimidation, and corruption, campus politics became increasingly dangerous. Every now and then we see disruption and violence in different educational institutions promoted by the so-called protector of education.

Student politicians earning multiple degrees so that they can continue to be in the institution and run their office. Clashes between student groups, harassments to teachers, molestation of girls and even murders are now a part of the political scenario every day. Rich national political parties are gaining a foothold in the colleges and universities. To restore peace many institutions have banned student elections.

The more students involved in Politics is primarily because student elections are views as steppingstones to national politics and ultimately a route to wealth and power. Another reason is the reduction of the minimum voting age from 21 to 18 during. This age generally coincides with students' entry into college. This aroused the interests of political parties as they are a vital source of votes. Politics has become a full-time profession in colleges and universities across the country and majority of the political parties created their own student wings i.e. ABVP of BJP, NSUI of Congress etc. It is a sad situation as these are the students who can really eradicate the politics based on the castes.

Politics is a social science and its study through organised movements can create a sound administration. The ignorance of politics among the masses of a country paves the way for the rise of tyranny and the fall of democracy. The ignorance of politics among the masses of a country paves the way for the rise of tyranny and the fall of democracy.

Today's education is about Influencing than being simply informative. Teachers have become the means of imparting government propaganda to students. Political discussions. Political magazines, political association and political seminars inside the premises translates into lawlessness and disorder. Student campaigns at the university are financed by their national affiliates and they spend thousands which a complete waste of money and time and other resources.

Students' groups are blank in ideology and never address issues of national concern. These students have to ultimately deal with problems at the national level – but they are woefully unequipped to do so.

Outside political parties also give tacit approval to their student affiliates to indulge in extortion. In return. The parties use their student wings during national and state elections both for conventional canvassing and for more dubious purposes like taking over polling booths to intimidate voters into choosing specific candidates.

For various political parties, the college campus is a training ground for their actual political life. The platforms are virtually identical to those of their national counterparts. They rarely raise issues of direct concern to students like housing shortages and the quality of cafeteria food. Instead, just like national candidates they often urge students to vote for them because of their caste or religion.

Students should be vigil about all types of development in the country, including politics. If students are prepared to be engineers or doctors, they can be a good politician too and serve the country. Universities are nurseries for future politicians and there is nothing wrong with them starting off at that level with the aim of joining mainstream politics.

The overall assessment of higher education over the recent past is not up to the mark. On one hand, the hunger for knowledge and higher education has increased but at the same time the pace of reforms and infrastructure facilities, cost of education, quality of education has suffered. Many institutions were closed due to the lake of students and there are many students who do not get admission in their preferred faculty or institution. There is also an imbalance of education in rural areas and urban areas.

With the holistic and long term thought to provoke planning, irrespective of any government at Centre or State, we need to reform our education system. In order to be in the race of developed countries, merely increasing Gross Enrolment Ratio (GER) and overlooking quality aspect will not be a good approach in the interest of the country the which has the highest number of young citizens in the world.

References

Anandakrishnan, M. (2006) *Privatisation of higher education: Opportunities and anomalies.* Privatisation and commercialisation of higher education organised by NIEPA, May 2, 2006., New Delhi

Kapur, D. (2010). "Indian Higher Education," in Clotfelter, C. (ed.), *American Universities in a Global Market.* Chicago, IL: University of Chicago Press.

Kohli, A. (2010). *State and Redistributive Development in India.* UNRISD Flagship Report on Poverty: Project of Poverty Reduction and Policy Regimes, India. New York: United Nations. 182-206.

World Bank (2004) *Measuring Trade in Services Liberalisation and its Impact on Economic Growth: an illustration,* World Bank Group Working Paper, downloadable from http://econ.worldbank.org/files/2373_wps 2655.pdf

Kumar. V. (1975). *Committees and Commissions in India,* 1947-1973. New Delhi: D.K. Publishing House.

MHRD (2006) *Annual Report. Ministry of Human Resource Development, Department of Secondary, and Higher education.* The government of India. New Delhi. Planning Commission (1999) Approach paper to the Tenth Five-year Plan (2002-2007). Planning Commission. New Delhi.

Stella, Antony (2002) *External quality assurance in Indian higher education: a Case study of the National Assessment and Accreditation Council* (NAAC).

International Institute for Educational Planning. Paris. UGC (2005) Research Handbook: Towards nurturing research culture in higher education institutions in India. University Grants Commission. New Delhi.

Agarwal, Pawan (2006) *Higher Education in India: The Need for Change* (ICIER Working Paper No. 180). New Delhi: Indian Council for Research on International Economic Relations, (http://www.icrier.org/publication/working_papers_180.html) Chronicle of Higher Education, various issues (cited as CHE) (http://chronicle.com/)

www.ugc.ac.in

www.mhrd.gov.in

17

Management of Higher Education

Dr. Gurudutta P. Japee

Abstract

Higher education created by any nation is created and built for a purpose. The purpose is to prepare the youth for today and tomorrow so that they can engage with life and living processes and their own identity. The identity is lost as the spaces for creators and generators of knowledge, new ideas and concepts are not available. Societies believe that higher education institutions should educate their students to be great citizens for tomorrow's world, a world which will be characterised by the necessity for more sophisticated skills, by the interaction between research and socio-economic development, and by a continuous cycle of innovation and knowledge transfer from academia to external stakeholders. From such a perspective, 'doing more with less' is now an imperative that characterises all of the public sector's activities, including the funding of higher education's operations and institutions. This paper is an attempt to focus on why, how and what type of management is required in higher education institutions in order to ensure quality.

Keywords: Management, Quality, Risk, Human Assets, Technology

Introduction

Management is a universal phenomenon. It is a very popular and widely used term. All organisations – business, political, cultural or social are involved in management because it is the management which helps and directs the various efforts towards a definite purpose.

According to Harold Koontz, "Management is an art of getting things done through and with the people in formally organised groups. It is an art of creating an environment in which people can perform and individuals and can co-operate towards the attainment of group goals".

According to F.W. Taylor, "Management is an art of knowing what to do when to do and see that it is done in the best and cheapest way".

Management is a purposive activity. It is something that directs group efforts towards the attainment of certain predetermined goals. It is the process of working with and through others to effectively achieve the goals of the organisation, by efficiently using limited resources in the changing world. Of course, these goals may vary from one enterprise to another. E.g.: For one enterprise it may be launching of new products by conducting market surveys and for others, it may be profit maximisation by minimising cost.

Management involves creating an internal environment: – It is the management which puts into use the various factors of production. Therefore, it is the responsibility of management to create such conditions which are conducive to maximum efforts so that people are able to perform their task efficiently and effectively. It includes ensuring availability of raw materials, determination of wages and salaries, formulation of rules & regulations etc.

Therefore, we can say that good management includes both being effective and efficient. Being effective means doing the appropriate task i.e., fitting the square pegs in square holes and round pegs in round holes. Being efficient means doing the task correctly, at least possible cost with minimum wastage of resources.

Higher education is becoming costly day by day and it is currently in a state of dismal conditions. Parents are not happy with the service delivered by educational institutions. There is unhealthy competition among the educational institutions and service both in terms of academic and administrative are of degraded in quality. We, therefore, required management which ensures better functioning of academic and administrative activities.

Management can be defined in detail in the following categories:

- Management as a Process
- Management as an Activity
- Management as a Discipline
- Management as a Group
- Management as a Science
- Management as an Art
- Management as a Profession

The concept of Management in HEI

Management of HEI is for measuring the strengths and areas for improvement of an organisation across all of its activities. It is non-prescriptive and does not involve strictly following a set of rules or standards but provides a broad and coherent set of assumptions about what is required for a good organisation and its management. Each organisation can use it in its own way to manage and develop improvement, under the control of those who use the methods rather than an external evaluator.

- *Leadership:* excellent leaders develop and facilitate the achievement of the mission and vision. They develop organisational values and systems required for sustainable success and implement these via their actions and behaviours
- *Policy and strategy:* excellent organisations implement their mission and vision by developing a stakeholder-focused strategy that takes account of the market and sector in which it operates. Policies, plans, objectives, and processes are developed and deployed to deliver the strategy
- *People management:* excellent organisations manage, develop and release the full potential of their people at an individual, team-based and organisational level. They promote fairness and equality and involve and empower their people. They care for, communicate, reward and recognise in a way that motivates staff and builds commitment to using their skills and knowledge for the benefit of the organisation
- *Partnerships and resources:* excellent organisations plan and manage external partnerships, suppliers and internal resources in order to support policy and strategy and the effective operation of processes. During the planning and whilst managing partnerships and resources they balance the current and future needs of the organisation, the community, and the environment
- *Process management:* excellent organisations design, manage and improve processes in order to fully satisfy and generate increasing value for customers and other stakeholders.

The concept of Quality Management in HEI

Concerns about the quality management of higher education are currently monopolising the policy agenda for any nation. The notion of quality is being viewed in a variety of ways, but two main approaches may be discerned. One approach uses "quality" to focus rather narrowly on performance, control and simple outcome measures. The other involves a broader, more comprehensive approach that accommodates more adequately the rich complexity and intangibility of higher education's processes and outcomes. Following points must be incorporated for the concept of quality management in higher education.

Purposeful

Institutional products and services conform to a stated mission/vision or a set of specifications, requirements, or standards, including those defined by accrediting and/or regulatory bodies

Exceptional

Institutional products and services achieve distinction and exclusivity through the fulfilment of high standards

Transformative

Institutional products and services affect positive change in student learning (affective, cognitive, and psychomotor domains) and personal and professional potential

Accountable

Institutions are accountable to stakeholders for the optimal use of resources and the delivery of accurate educational products and services with zero defects

Which Department should be Managed

The following departments in higher education institutions are required to be managed in order to ensure quality in higher education.

- strategy, organisation and quality management,
- teaching and learning process,
- research,
- human resources,
- students and Alumni
- infrastructure,
- financing,
- cooperation and openness of higher education institutions to the surrounding environment and the world at large.
- other stakeholders
- Activities of HEI
- Assessment and Accreditation

What is to be Kept in Mind while Managing HEI

While doing management of the above departments following points should be kept in mind in order to ensure that the institution is knowledge institutions.

- Empowering, people-centric practices
- A clear policy on talent attraction and retention
- Least rules so that they do not come in the way of innovation, autonomy, excellence
- Trusting practices, and not suspecting.

- At the same time, employees have to be responsible for the due discharge of their duties and realisation of goals of the organisation
- Management by exception is the best rule to manage them--the leader intervenes only when change is warranted or conflict occurs.
- Participatory and involved in decision making.
- Rules should be conducive towards building a learning organisation.
- careful selection of the leader/dean
- Competitive pay, and merit-based performance management

Types of Management used in HEI

Classroom Management

Effective Classroom Management Techniques Every Faculty Member Should Know

- Get the semester off on the right foot
- Prevent Cheating
- Incorporate classroom management principles into the syllabus
- Handle students who participate too much
- Establish relationships with students
- Use a contract to help get students to accept responsibility
- Employ humour to create conditions conducive to learning

Good classroom management doesn't just happen; you have to work at it. This collection of insightful classroom management articles is just the thing to help.

Faculty Focus contains a wealth of valuable material – not just about classroom management, but all of today's hot issues that are important to faculty and administrators.

- Educational Assessment
- Effective Classroom Management
- Effective Teaching Strategies
- Curriculum Development
- Instructional Design
- Faculty Development
- Faculty Evaluation
- Online Education
- Philosophy of Teaching
- Teaching and Learning

Human Assets Management

- To change a university, you need to change people's incentives
- To attract the best faculty, you need the best leaders without political association
- Control quality through hiring panels of industry-academia experts
- Hire the best international staff
- Know the talent list and congratulate people
- No pain, no gain increase the quality working hours
- Too much change, no gain

- Pay a top salary if you want the right department head
- Incentivise raising research money
- Cut the red tape and reduce the number of committees
- As a leader, be accessible
- Clarify the relationship between administrative and academic staff
- Start to train scholars in management when they are young
- Pick your board or council members because – and only because – they are good for the university, and then educate them
- Tell Government 'No!' on interference
- Give staff food for their tummies as well as thought
- Hire a scholar as leader
- Make sure the leader stays at least five years – and preferably more
- Give the leader plenty of power (or don't bother hiring one)
- Let the leader pick his or her own top team

Technology and Marketing Management

- Search engine optimisation
- Use of web analytics
- Strategic social media
- Mobile development
- CMS and CRM systems
- Flipped classroom
- Online certificate programmes

Risk Management

- Commitment and engagement of senior administration;
- Resource availability and capability;
- Failure to execute beyond initial assessment;
- Generating useful conclusions from assessment;
- Developing effective action plans to manage risks; and
- Sustainability of the risk management process.

Management Techniques must include

- strict financial management and devolved budgetary controls;
- efficient use of resources with an emphasis on productivity;
- extensive use of quantitative performance indicators;
- the development of consumerism and the discipline of the market;
- the manifestation of consumer charters as mechanisms of accountability;
- the creation of a disciplined, flexible workforce, using flexible/individualised contracts, staff appraisal systems, and performance-related pay;
- the assertion of managerial control and managers' right to manage.

References

Calvo-Mora, A. Leal, A., and Roldán, J. L. (2006), *Using enablers of the EFQM model to manage institutions of higher education*, Quality Assurance in Education 14: 2, pp.99 – 122

European Foundation for Quality Management, (2003), Modelo EFQM de Excelencia, European Foundation for Quality Management, Brussels.

Pollitt, C. (1990), *Managerialism and the Public Services*: The Anglo-American Experience, Basil Blackwell, London

Tommaso Agasisti (2017) *Management of Higher Education Institutions and the Evaluation of their Efficiency and Performance,* Tertiary Education and Management, 23:3, 187-190

http://www.fm-kp.si

https://www.hanoverresearch.com

https://www.marsh.com

http://www.dailyexcelsior.com

https://www.managementstudyguide.com

https://enqa.eu/indirme/papers-and-reports

https://www.hlrcjournals.com

18

Economics of Higher Education

Dr. Satyajeet S. Deshpande

ABSTRACT

Understanding the intricacies of higher education especially in a country like India with enormous diversities is not an easy task. It indeed requires a multi-disciplinary approach to understand various issues in higher education. Many branches like sociology, psychology, economics, politics etc. need to be visited for gauging various issues inflicting modern higher-education. The current paper tries to highlight various concepts and principles of economic theory which can improve our understanding of higher education. The major economic concepts described in the paper are an opportunity cost, labour economics, cost-benefit analysis, demand-supply analysis, merit goods etc. The first section describes the objectives of the study; the second section provides a detailed explanation of various economic notions and models which can help us in understanding the problems of higher education and finding their solutions. The final section concludes the paper.

Keywords: Economics, Higher Education, Demand and Supply Analysis, Cost-Benefit Analysis, Opportunity Cost, Labour Economics

INTRODUCTION

The paper attempts to examine how various concepts, theories, and principles of economics help us in understanding problems and issues in higher education. It tries to study how the knowledge of economics helps us in understanding the underlying principles of higher education much better and eventually in improving its quality.

The paper describes some of the economic principles and concepts like Human Capital Theory, Cost-Benefit Analysis, Opportunity Cost, Demand and Supply Analysis, Merit Goods and Externalities etc. It then evaluates how these concepts help us in understanding and resolving some of the issues in higher education.

Economic Concepts and Theories Used for Understanding the Issues in Higher Education:

The Human Capital Theory

The concept of human capital was originally given by Adam Smith in the 18th century. It was further developed by economists like Gary Becker, Jacob Mincer, and Theodore Schlutz. The skills, knowledge and the ability to perform the tasks efficiently were considered the human capital. The theory proposes a strong direct relationship between the value of human capital in an individual and his ability to generate income. An individual with lesser skills and knowledge will be able to generate lesser income compared to the one with higher skills. The theory brings out the importance of higher education in the economic prosperity of individuals and societies. The fact that people invest their time, effort and money in acquiring higher education is due to its ability to develop human capital and eventually generate higher incomes and better standards of living.

The important lesson from this theory is that if the youth is to be encouraged to take up higher education, there must be a mechanism in the country which rewards higher skills and knowledge. If the extent of educated-unemployment is high, gradually the youth will be discouraged from taking up higher qualification. The country in which the post-graduates, engineers, and doctorates remain unemployed or get low salaried jobs, the importance of higher education diminishes. Another lesson to be learned from the theory is related to the quality of higher education and its ability to make the students employable. The higher education which emphasizes more on abstract theoretical knowledge without imparting proper practical skills is bound to fail in creating human capital. This creates a strong case for adopting a case-study approach to higher education, application-oriented questions for evaluating the progress of the students and a greater number of projects and field visits.

Cost-Benefit Analysis

The concept of cost-benefit analysis has existed in economic literature ever-since its evolution. The concept is used by economists to explain why self-maximizing individuals take up certain activities whereas rejecting others. The simple proposition of the cost-benefit approach is that individuals have an inherent tendency to choose activities in which the perceived benefits are greater than the perceived costs. Similarly, the alternatives with higher relative costs are rejected. This is often termed as rational behaviour.

The concept is especially important in explaining the low literacy and enrolment among the girls in higher education institutes especially in the rural areas. The rural society in countries like India is still very orthodox with many families discouraging their young women from taking up jobs in the formal sector. Women are expected to cook, take care of house and children. As a result, many families send their daughters for school education but this percentage drops considerably when it comes to higher education. The obvious reason is the seeming absence of any benefit of educating the girls. The fact that there is no intention to utilise the knowledge acquired from education for doing a job for economic benefits makes higher education less lucrative in relation to its costs. The government has highly subsidised the higher-education for girls to bring down this cost. However, it is not the monetary cost which is discouraging rural girls from taking up higher education. There is a substantial opportunity cost, real cost and social cost in educating the girls. The general perception is that women should not work. The enrolment of girls in higher-education institutes can be expected to increase when the society accepts that girls are no lesser than boys in any aspect of life and they can equally participate in the work-force. Only when the girls' education will seem beneficial to society, the cost-benefit analysis will lead to gender-equality in higher education.

Opportunity Costs

The Economists define opportunity cost as the next best alternative sacrificed or foregone in doing something. The concept was first introduced in 1914 by Austrian economist Friedrich von Wieser in his book *Theory of Social Economy*. However, many previous writers including Benjamin Franklin and Frederic Bastiat had also made passing reference to the term. Franklin coined the phrase "Time is Money" in which the concept of opportunity cost was very much implicit.

Economists often use the concept of opportunity cost for advocating higher education. Some may decide against taking up higher education due to the income lost due to attending the college. The main cost of going to college is not the cost of tuition fees but the foregone earnings during college days.

However, eventually, the opportunity cost of not attending the college turns out to be very high due to the potential of higher education in making enormous value-addition in the students who pursue it. Studies have shown that higher education enhances the earnings of the candidates over the life course. The earnings of the college-degree holders have been found considerably more over the entire work-life as compared to the loss of earnings to the college goers in their early 20s due to attending the college. Economists often advocate higher education by comparing the earnings of college goers with that of non-goers who show similar academic performance in high schools. Another economic argument emphasizing the importance of higher education is the probability that a college degree results in higher cumulative earnings. The growth rates in earnings over the life course will also be higher for highly educated compared to those who haven't taken higher education.

Demand and Supply Analysis

Economics uses demand and supplies analysis to tell how many units of the product will be consumed and what price will be charged for it. The simple proposition is that the market clears where the demand and supply match each other. If the demand for a good or service is higher than its supply, the price tends to rise and if the supply exceeds demand, price falls. Price keeps on changing till both sides become the same.

The demand and supply analysis can be extremely useful in understanding some of the important issues related to higher education. It is a well-known fact that certain courses and certain institutes are more in demand by the students as compared to the others. This is mainly due to the differences in the rates of returns from them. The returns in terms of the annual salary packages in India for students from IIMs and IITs are higher as compared to the degree-holders from other institutes of management and engineering. This is true for most other courses as well. Certain institutes and universities have a proven track record in imparting quality education and ensuring rewarding placements. As a result, there is an imbalance between demand and supply of these institutes. The number of premier institutes in the country is limited signifying lesser supply whereas there are lakhs of aspirants who want to get admission in them.

In this context, economists have a unique conception of demand. Demand is not perceived as mere desire and willingness. It comes into existence only when this urge is backed by the ability. The decisions about which aspiring students to be admitted are taken on the basis of their ability or competence to take up difficult courses from premier institutes. An economist's solution would be conduction of a rigorous entrance test which would help in downsizing the demand to match the supply for different courses in different institutes. Similarly, over a period of time, the government has set up many new IIMs and IITs in the country.

Labour Economics

Labour economics plays a vital role in explaining wage differentials in higher education. The reasons for the difference in the wages or salaries of teachers with similar skills and qualifications can be explained through some established principles. The major reason for the unfortunate wage-differentials among college teachers in India has been privatisation. With extremely few exceptions, private institutes are grossly underpaying their qualified and competent teachers. The gap between the salaries of private and government funded colleges has been staggering with teachers in private colleges getting half the salary which they would have earned had they been in the government sector. On the other hand, the government colleges have their own issues with everybody getting paid handsomely irrespective of the level of competence. Similarly, the salaries of professors in developed countries are higher compared to those in developing countries. This can be attributed to the importance given to education by different societies. As the western countries value higher education and research more than the under-developed countries of Asia and Africa, they pay their teachers much better.

Privatisation

Economists have for long advocated privatisation of production processes for enhancing efficiency. One of the fundamental assumptions in economics is that the private sector primarily strives to maximize profits. This profit-maximizing behaviour inspires private entrepreneurs to raise productivity and improve quality. However, many economists are opposed to the idea of privatising the education sector. They strongly believe that what might work in production, certainly may not work in education. The initial experience of private institutes in higher education in India has been disappointing. In most cases, the quality of higher education has suffered significantly due to the profiteering motives of the private higher educational institutes. Most of them have been absorbing far too many students for generating revenues. This has resulted in a poor teacher-student ratio. Besides trying to maximize the revenues, these private institutes have left no stone unturned to cut the costs, the most dangerous among them being the payment of a very paltry salary to the teachers. Economists around the world have suggested that education and health are social sectors and hence should be governed by the state. Even if privatisation is encouraged, it should be done with caution and government regulations.

Merit Good and Externalities

Economists classify goods into various categories. One of them is merit goods. Merit goods are defined as goods which are under-consumed and under-produced when left to the private market. Merit goods are not only under-valued by their users; they also have significant positive externalities. This means that besides the one who consumes the product, others in society also get the benefit. The consumption of these goods is highly beneficial to society. Education is considered to be one of the top merit goods by economists. It has been found that poor people and in some cases certain rural populations do not understand the value of education. Poor send their children for work so that they can contribute to the family income. Rural societies consider girl education unnecessary as they believe that girls would be better off learning household chores compared to taking formal education. Besides, education has external benefits in terms of a more civilized society and neighbourhood. Due to all these reasons, economists feel that if the decision about higher education is left to markets, it will be grossly under-consumed. In economics parlance, the markets will fail to generate socially optimum outcomes as far as higher education is concerned. Hence the economists suggest that government-intervention of some sort is necessary to increase the spread of higher education. A lot of modern governments have subsidized higher education, especially for girls to encourage their consumption among them. Many grants, scholarships, and concessional loans are also provided to motivate the youth to take up higher and professional studies.

Conclusion

As observed from the discussion in the previous section, there are numerous concepts and principles of economics which guide us in understanding the intricacies of higher education.

These concepts not only improve our understanding but also guide us in improving the quality of higher education. The theory of human capital suggests that unless higher education enhances the value of human capital, its demand will be less. This would require higher education to be more practical & job-oriented and less theoretical. The cost-benefit analysis suggests that for improving the enrolment of girls in higher education, the perceptions about the benefits of education for girls must change, especially in the rural regions. The concept of opportunity cost tells us that although there is a short-term opportunity cost of pursuing higher education, the long-term opportunity cost of not taking higher education is much higher. This is because the higher-education results in phenomenal income generating capacity in the years to come. The demand-supply analysis tells us the way to bridge the mismatch between demand and supply of higher education. Rigorous entrance exams will rationalise the demand whereas setting up more and more institutes of eminence will enhance the supply. Labour economics explains the reasons for wage-differentials among the teachers in higher education. The paper also discusses how the privatisation of education without adequate government regulations can destroy its quality. Finally, the paper highlights the fact that education, though not pure public good, is certainly merit good. Therefore economists have always demanded some kind of government intervention in the education sector to ensure socially optimum outcomes. All in all, the paper has tried to highlight various concepts and principles of economics which enhance our understanding of higher education. At the same time, the paper is not all exhaustive as there are many other concepts and theories in economics from which a lot can be borrowed for understanding higher education.

19

Role of Finance in Higher Education

Dr. S.S.Sodha & Dr. Nimesh P. Bhojak

ABSTRACT

The education sector of India faces the challenges of the financing funding to provide the quality learning output, improve the skill of students to provide placement and uplift the standards of all stakeholders of the education institute. The higher education enrolment ratio decrease and the vacant seats in the higher education increase due to the high fee structure, poor quality output and lack of placement etc. This study focuses on the role of finance and different funding of finance in higher education. It also describes the current financing system in higher education. Education sector mainly in the India priority of the state list for the funding and implementing. There is the need to higher qualified person to meet the need of the Indian society in the next future. But the majority chunks of the social middle class and in the name of the better quality output and the uplift the standards of education and the fee structure of education institute increase. It is a challenging task to get higher education in India for the middle-income level group. There are many substitutes available like NGO funding, Student Loan, Private sector corporate social responsibility funding, Government education cess and subsidy for minorities and backward classes, weaker economics section of the society to fulfil the need and solve the problem of inequality in the nation. There is a need the different sources of funding to provide the efficiency and equity higher education to society of India.

Keyword: Finance, Higher Education, Subsidy etc.

INTRODUCTION

There is increasing financial management of higher educational institutions expressed by major stakeholders of higher education institute with reference to financing and pricing higher education and present accounting standards and gaps in accounting and auditing practices in universities and colleges. There are many researcher analyses the funding sources, current scenario, different methods and outlines of financing higher education in India. The education sector is mainly in the India priority of the state list for the funding and implementing. Stakeholders of higher education have the right to get accurate and smooth financial management in the Indian higher education system due to provide the education cess by the society of the nation. Higher education provides paybacks individual and society to uplift the standard of the living. There is a need for equity to share the financial burden on the individual, society, and government. There are many funding sources available like NGO funding, Student Loan, Private sector corporate social responsibility funding, Government education cess and subsidy for minorities and backward classes, weaker economics section of the society to manage financing higher education. The large numbers of the students are in the private higher education institute due to a shortage of public higher education. Though given the social, economic and political realities, the government has to continue to bear a large responsibility for funding higher education, instead of relying on a single form of funding in the rural and remote area with reference to the demographic, socioeconomic and political difference. There are need subsidy and other funding sources by the government to fulfil the gap.

Role and Development of Higher Educational Institutions

The National Policy on Education (1986) defines Higher Education as a vital aspect for survival providing the significant task of making moral populations and leaders for different walks of life. There were only 20 universities and about 500 colleges at the time India attained independence. In 2010 this increased to 611 universities and university-level institutions and 31,324 colleges, (UGC, 2011). Presently, in February 2014, there are 706 Universities and university-level institutions and 35539 colleges in India, (University News, 2014).

The annual growth rate of enrolment in private institutions was 11.2% and the same was 7.2% in government institutions, (FICCI, 2012). India's GER not only significantly lags behind that of developed countries such as the US, Switzerland, Japan, and the UK, but also that of developing countries including China, Brazil, Malaysia, and the Philippines, (FICCI, 2012). While enrolment in higher education has grown six times in the last 30 years, faculty strength has grown only four times, resulting in a shortage of faculty and high student-teacher ratios. Academics in China authored five times more research papers than India's in 2011. The relative impact of citations for India is half of that of the world average, (FICCI, 2012). As of March 2012, NAAC had rated 62% of the universities and 90% of the colleges as average (B) or below average (C) on specified quality parameters. Only two Indian higher education brands featured in the QS World University Rankings 2011-12 of the top 500 global Universities. Out of the 48 countries studied, India ranks last in the U21 rankings of national higher education systems, (FICCI, 2012).

FINANCIAL MANAGEMENT OF UNIVERSITIES AND COLLEGE

After Independence higher education in India has been largely financed by Government with social institutions progressively withdrawing. The Government is unable to make large allocations for higher education and so private initiatives become necessary. While mobilising resources from private sources it should not be forgotten that higher education is integrally related to socio-economic development and no government can afford to allow it to languish for want of funds. Higher education is being financed by the State Government, UGC, and other funding agencies.

We all know that our resources are limited. It is, therefore, necessary to ensure effective financial management in Universities, Colleges, and other higher education Institutions.

HIGHER EDUCATION AS A PUBLIC SERVICE

In 1776, Adam Smith, the father of modern political economy, published "An Enquiry into the Nature and Causes of the Wealth of Nations". He argued for the role of the state in providing funds for the education of those who could not afford it. And, it was Nobel laureate T.W. Schultz, who clearly showed that investment in education is an investment in human capital. He linked this with physical capital, as it reproduces not only knowledge but enhances it further thereby developing both man and material.

The relationship between education and economic development has been examined time and again by the economists as well as the educationists. Jan Tinbergen-H.C. Bos model 'for the planning of education' considered education as a factor of growth. Tinbergen and Bos argued that educational development must show both qualitative and quantitative aspects; the former refers to changes in methods of teaching and the subject matter of teaching; the latter refers to changes in the dimensions and the composition of the educational system.

The limitation of this model was examined and evaluated by Amartya K. Sen, this year's winner of the Nobel Prize for Economics. Sen said that the residual factor' concept of Tinbergen-Bos model did not take into account the external benefits of education which are not measured or not measurable. Sen has also emphasized the need to expand access to the higher education system on equitable terms, since academic excellence, in the long run, promotes social equity.

Education is a public good, private investment would not be coming in, so the State has got to intervene finally. Psychropolous, among others, has argued for more attention to primary education than to higher education, because for a developing country like India, returns are always higher in the former than the latter. His views dominated the development of higher education during the last one and a half decades, of course through RVIF and World Bank Publications and policy-influencing fora. This was despite several limitations of the concept of 'rates of return' analysis. One of the conditionality's for loans to developing countries (particularly India) was to cut investment in higher education by 10%. This has seriously affected the quality and growth of higher education in India. In contrast, some studies, carried out in the UK and USA, show that one unit of expenditure in higher education leads to four units of output. The World Conference on higher education held in Paris in October 1998 firmly stated that higher education is 'a public service'. Thus, any nation-state treating it otherwise may seriously affect its ability to face the challenges of knowledge society of the 21st century.

FINANCING HIGHER EDUCATION IN INDIA

After Independence higher education in India has been largely financed by the government with the social institutions progressively withdrawing. The government's share has steadily increased from 49% in 1950-51 to about 90% today. The government spends about 3.7% of GNP on the education of which the share of higher education is about 0.8% Amongst the different sectors of education the share of higher education was the highest, at 25%, during the Fourth Five year Plan (1969-74). It remained stable at 22% during the Fifth and Sixth Five Year Plans but declined to only 8% in the Eighth Five Year Plan (1992-97). It was 6% of GNP by the end of the Ninth Five Year Plan (1997-2002). However, the share of higher education is not likely to increase.

In India, over the last sixty years, there have been major changes in the level of financing of higher education and in priorities attached to different sectors within it. Higher Education had been rather neglected by early planners. The empirical study reveals that the various recommendations as also Five Year Plans and Policy statements recommend and emphasize to increase the percentage of plan expenses on higher education. The government is unable to make large allocations for higher education Private initiatives become necessary and society in general, and industry, in particular, will have to play a larger role in higher education. The industry should come forward to finance and design institutions that meet its specific requirement. It is hoped that an early decision will be taken on the Private Universities Bill that is on the agenda before Parliament.

While mobilisation of resources from private sources is a necessity, it should not be forgotten that higher education is integrally related to socio-economic development and no government can afford to allow it to languish for want of funds in this context, the suggestion made by Punnayya Committee of UGC (1994) is worth emphasizing: State or Government funding must continue to be an essential and mandatory requirement for support of higher education. The Government /State must continue to accept the major responsibility for funding the essential maintenance and development requirements of the Universities.

Indian higher education constructed up enormous infrastructure which, with marginal additional inputs, can be utilised with greater effectiveness and purpose. There should admit the actuality that improvements in Indian higher education system are not necessarily the function of additional resources. It requires a bold and imaginative approach to innovating, to experiment and to initiate a process of restructuring the entire edifice of our higher education.

PRICING HIGHER EDUCATION IN INDIA

Pricing social sector goods and services is a complicated issue from the point of view of both the theory of pricing and public finance as well as empiricism. Notwithstanding this, the need for re-examination of the several intricate issues relevant to pricing in social sectors like education, particularly higher education, is being felt with increasing intensity.

One might define 'Social sector goods' as those goods whose costs are incurred, and benefits are received, not by the consumer alone, but by the whole society. Once this definition is accepted, it becomes necessary to adopt an approach to pricing quite different from the standard economic approach to pricing, according to which the user or the consumer pays the marginal cost in full. Education being a social sector good, it's pricing becomes a complex proposition, particularly, because the mechanism of financing education has a very significant bearing on the outcomes of education. If education has to produce the desired results, decisions regarding its pricing and financing should be based on sound principles.

ACCOUNTING STANDARDS IN HIGHER EDUCATIONAL INSTITUTIONS

Admittedly, accounting is a language of a college or university, It speaks about the state of the financial management whether an institution is appearing well or not as the institutions have been financed by Government, UGC, industries, business houses, donors, the general public, so on and so far. What is required is the complete transparency in accounting methods and standards.

Accounting standards setting exercise has been initiated and persuaded by accounting bodies all over the world, during the past three decades. In India, the Accounting Standard Board constituted by ICAR shoulder the responsibility on formulating the accounting standards for various organisations in general and for business and industries in particulars.

It is necessary to understand the major users and their requirements with reference to education institutions. A set of standards for accounting information and guidelines for its communication depends upon an examination of who are the major users of accounting information and for what purpose they require such information. Following are the stakeholders, who have every right to the access of accounting information.

1. *State Government*: The State Government provides a maintenance grant for salary and non-salary expenses to colleges and universities. The Government through its

Regional Joint Director Office carries out yearly assessment and periodical audit. Therefore, the state government requires information about the receipts of tuition fee, other fees etc. and salary and non-salary expenses with reference to grantable criteria as laid down in grant-in-aid code, and the utilisation of other fees such as library fees, gymkhana fees, magazine fees, extension activities fees etc.

2. *UGC and other Funding Agencies such as S & T Department*: UGC and other agencies provide financial assistance for the development of undergraduate education and post-graduation departments which satisfy the conditions laid down by UGC & such funding agencies. The UGC and such funding agencies require information as per their requirements about the grants sanctioned, released and utilisation thereof, compliance of terms & conditions, completion of work, target etc.

3. *Trustees, members of the Society, Donors, etc.*: They provide initial finance for the establishment of colleges and fulfilling deficit in running the colleges. They require information about receipt of funds, donations, utilisation thereof and reasons of the deficit.

4. *Industries, Business houses, Alumni associations, NRIs, etc.:* With a view to mobilising external resources for various development plans and projects through participation, contributions from individual Indians or non-residential Indians, Alumni Associations, public and family trusts, industries, business houses, co-operatives, professional associations, employees' unions /associations, Municipalities, municipal corporations, are often contacted and funds are raised. This category of funding persons/agencies require information about the beneficiary of project/plans, funds raised and received

utilisation thereof and achievement of goals, targets, … etc.

5. *Employees' and Teachers' Organisation*: Employees and Teachers are concerned with the financial stability and sound financial management of the educational institutions. It indicates the scope for possible wage and fringe benefit increases and security of employment and retirement benefits, etc.
6. *Parents, Students*: They are the backbone of every educational institution. Students pay tuition fees and other fees to college; and eligibility fee, examination fee etc. to universalities. They are concerned with the effective utilisation of their fees and returns thereof with reference to quality teaching, good extension activities, souvenir/magazines, seminars, cultural activities, conduct of examination, timely declaration of eligibility and examinations results, timely issue of mark lists and degree certificates and counselling guidance and placement services, if possible.
7. *Society at Large*: As higher education is the main instrument of social transformation and the government funds are given to educational institutions out of taxes paid by the society at large, it is concerned with the effective and proper utilisation of funds and scarce resources by the educational institutions, universities, and colleges.

ACCOUNTING PRACTICES IN EDUCATIONAL INSTITUTIONS

There are defiantly gaps in accounting practices in mainly educational institutions, universities, and colleges. It is unfortunate to state that there is no transparency in financial management and accounting practices in educational institutions. It is also unfortunate that there is no mechanism to detect such gaps, misappropriation of funds and changes in the utilisation of funds.

SETTING ACCOUNTING STANDARDS FOR EDUCATION INSTITUTIONS

The main aim of setting Accounting Standard is to bring about uniformity in financial reporting and to ensure consistency and comparability in the data submitted by educational institutions. Standards for accounting information ought to be attended by an accounting system in providing information needed by the aforesaid seven types of users. The standards determine the quality of information. Hence the usefulness of accounting data is to be ensured. While standards are closely related to accounting theory, there is the difference between two in that accounting theory is concerned with attributes of the accounting system itself, whereas accounting standards are concerned with the quality of the information generated by that system.

As there are gaps in accounting standards laid down by Institute of Chartered Accountants of India (ICAI), standards may be set either by the government, university and/or management of the colleges or educational institutions. The concepts and standard underlying accounting for financial reporting purpose are called generally accepted accounting principles. There may be a number of approaches. The determination of certification of current major practice: a common law approach i.e. case by case as a distillation of experience and the use of an implicit or explicit conceptual framework is needed.

RESPONSIBILITIES OF GOVERNMENT AUDITOR AND INTERNAL AUDITOR

It is often noticed that these two agencies carry out their responsibility without any pre-set accounting standards. The entire task of auditing the accounts and financial management of educational institutions is taken very lightly. The control over the effective utilisation of scarce resources is often diluted.

It is, therefore, high time to define the role and responsibilities of auditors of educational institutions and the accounting standards and practices. No doubt the interest of all the aforesaid users of educational institutions must be safeguarded. Internal audit system must be implemented with quality and seriousness; management control system must be perfect and effective. Misappropriation, frauds, misrepresentations must be detected and curbed at their initial stage. Auditions must see whether the accounting standard has been strictly followed by the educational institutions or not.

CONCLUSION

The Financial management of higher education institution does include the aforesaid issues and problems pertaining to financing pricing, accounting standards and gaps in practices in universities and colleges. In the fast changing socio-economic context, the higher education system will be exposed to greater pressure for expansion, which needs effective pricing of higher education so as to provide comprehensive finances to university & colleges. At the same time utilisation of finance & funds must be strictly in accordance with the set terms and conditions, rules and regulations. The accounting standards must be widely accepted in practice in which the statutory obligation should be increased and ensured in consultations with the professional and regulatory bodies including ICAI, UGC, and NAAC etc. The gaps in practices should be seriously detected and checked so as to safeguard the interests of the persons and bodies financing higher education. The effective information system should be ensured to satisfy the aforesaid users of accounting information.

References

AIU (1991) *Decentralisation of Higher Education System*, AIU Publn; New Delhi, p. 101-116;

AIU (1991) *Financial Deficits in Universities*, AIU Publn. New Delhi, pp. 17-20, 31-38;

Anuradha De and Tanuka Endow, (2008), *Collaborative Research and Dissemination is the lead research organisation in India working with the Research Consortium on Educational Outcomes and Poverty* (RECOUP), a DFID supported research, ©2008 Research Consortium on Educational Outcomes and Poverty WP08/18

FICCI, (2012), *Higher Education in India in Twelfth Plan* (2012-2017) and beyond, FICCI Higher Education Summit 2012, Planning Commission of India

Financial Management in Higher Education – HIED 6/76666, Kent State.. . Retrieved from: -www.kent.edu/ ehhs/hied/degrees/upload /finance.pdf

Govt. of India (1985) *Challenge of Education Policy Perspective* GOI, New Delhi pp. 119;

Govt. of India (1986) *National Policy on Education* 1986 GOI N. Delhi pp. 29;

Govt. of India (1989) "Towards an Enlightened and Human Society," *reports of the Committee for Review of the National Policy on Education* 1986, GOI New Delhi pp. 409;

Govt. of India (1992) *Programme of Action 1992 National Policy on Education*, 1986, revised 1992 [Reprinted by UGC] New Delhi pp. 250;

Govt. of India (1997) *Govt. subsidies India.* Discussion Paper Department of Economic Affairs, Ministry of Finance pp. 20;

Govt. of Maharashtra (1992) *Report of Committee constituted to recommend revised draft of the proposed Non-Agricultural Universities Bill* – 1992;

Jafar M. Agrawal SS (1997) *Accounting Standards & Gaps in Practices Indian Journal of Commerce*, Dec 97, Qly public of ICA Bhubaneshwar, pp. 161-164;

Tilak, Jandhyala B.G., Varghese, N.V. (1991), "Financing Higher Education in India, Higher Education," Vol. 21, No. 1, *Higher Education in Developing Countries*, (Jan. 1991), Springer Publn. pp. 83-101;

Natrajan S. (1990), *Economics of Education*, Sterling Public. New Delhi, pp. 51-56;

Powar K. B. (1996) *Unit Costs in Higher Education* AIU New Delhi pp. 14;

.... (1997) *Higher Education in India since Independence*: Retrospect and Future option AIU, New Delhi pp. 5;

Sahu S. C. (1996) "Accreditation of Universities and Colleges: to be linked with funding," College Post, *ICF journal,* New Delhi pp. 12;

Strategic Financial Analysis for Higher Education, Retrieved from =file:///C:/Documents%20and%20Settings/ Flatron/Desktop/raihe6. pdf ;

Tilak J.B.G., *Pricing Higher Education,* UGC. Occasional Paper No. 2 UGC New Delhi, pp. 6-8;

Turan M.S., Bodia B.S. (1997) "Accounting Standard – Some Issues," *Indian Journal of Commerce,* Dec 97, Qly public of ICA Bhubaneshwar, pp. 146-147;

UGC (1990) *Report of the UGC Committee* [Gnanam Committee] towards New Educational Management, New Delhi p. 82-84; UGC (1994) UGC Theme Paper on NAAC new Delhi pp. 8-11;

UGC (2002-10), Annual Report 2002-03, 2003-04, 2004-05, 2005-06, 2006-07, 2007-08, 2008-09, 2009-10, University Grants Commission, New Delhi;

UGC (2011), Booklet "Inclusive And Qualitative Expansion of Higher Education": *Compilation Based on the Deliberations of the Working Group for Higher Education in the 12th Five-Year Plan* (2012-17), UGC Publn. November 2011, Chapter 1, pp.1-10 and Chapter 4, pp.66-73;

University News, (2014), *Higher Education at a Glance,* Vol. 52, N0. 7, Special Issue, Feb. 14-23, 2014 AIU publn., New Delhi;

Verma H.I, Garg M.C., Singh K.P. (1997) "Disclosure of Accounting Standards," *Indian Journal of Commerce,* Dec 97, Qly publication of ICA Bhubaneshwar pp.

20

History of Higher Education – From Ancient to the Modern

Dr. Preeti Oza & Dr. Gurudutta P. Japee

ABSTRACT

It is often said that Knowledge Is Power. In an economy when knowledge is the most valuable commodity a person and a country must offer, the best jobs will go to the best educated – whether they live in the United States or India or China. – US President Barack Obama, Washington DC (July 25th, 2009).

Education helps us with many things, but most importantly, it empowers individuals to think, question, and see beyond the obvious. Human beings are born with a natural tendency to question. Education is the best way to satiate our curiosity, without extinguishing the burning desire to learn and explore more. To understand any system of ideology and belief, it is very important to know the roots and the systematic/ organic/inorganic developments in the sphere of education.

The Indian education system is the oldest in the world and had some peculiarities which are not found anywhere in the world and we are proud of turn even today. Maharishi Manu had declared the importance of education some thousands of years ago. Nalanda, Takshshila, Vikramshila, and Vallabhi were some of the well-known universities of ancient India. During British Period Three modern universities were established in 1857. After Independence Indian higher education expanded with the objective of equality, Quality and Access. This Paper extensively deals with all aspects of education that prevailed in India since the Vedic age.

This paper is an effort to get a comprehensive look at the history and the gradual development of higher education in the major civilisations of the world and in particular India over the period of last 2000 years with the help of the available documented history.

Keywords: Higher education, Vedic Period, Medieval India, British India, Independent India.

INTRODUCTION

Historically it has been a religious rationale that has celebrated much on the question of how to, to educate'. In Catholic social teaching, for example, we find that at its heart lays concern for human dignity. It starts from the position that human beings are created in the image and likeness of God. They have by the very existence an inherent value worth and distinction. The history of higher education is a history of Human Rights, human values, human exploration, and social inventions, Higher education is also a common thread which is fundamental to the formation of the groups, networks, and associations necessary for the common life which is also called the subsidiarity.

This principle which first found its institutional voice in the papal encyclical in 1881 holds that human affairs are best handled at the lowest possible level, the process to those affected. It's a principle that can both strengthen the civil society and the possibility of more mutual relationships for learning.

THE EMERGENCE OF 'IDEA' AND 'BEING' IN HUMAN LIFE AND HISTORY OF WRITING

The 'idea' got dynamic with the invention of writing/ printing. This has helped to spread a system of spreading 'education' which was more knowledge-based. Starting in about 3500 BC, various writing systems developed in ancient civilisations around the world. In Egypt, fully developed hieroglyphs were in use at

Adidas as early as 3400 BC. Though it is not at all close to the current understanding of the term 'higher education', it was the roots of today's all-encompassing concept of (formal) education. In the modern world, universities have two purposes: equip students with advanced skills useful in the workplace and to further human knowledge and understanding of the world.

History of Ancient Higher Education

A variety of ancient Higher Learning institutions developed in many cultures to provide the institutional framework for scholarly activities. Dissension centres were supported, sponsored and overseen by courts, by religious institutions which sponsored Cathedral schools, Monastic schools, and Madrasas. In the past, there were very few higher education institutions since only a small fraction of the population could read or write. During this early period, centres of education mostly had a religious focus and trained clergy. In Western Europe, these centres were monasteries, while in the Islamic world these were madrasas. Scientific Institutions such as museums, hospitals, and observatories were supported, individual scholars. They are to be distinguished from the western style University, an autonomous organisation of Scholars that originated in medieval Europe and has been adopted in other regions in modern times.

There has always been some difficulty in producing a seniority list for the earliest universities. It is impossible to do so with any degree of precision, largely because the first universities – those having their origins in the eleventh to thirteenth centuries – were the outcome of spontaneous social developments. As the earliest universities grew out of associations of students, many of them came into existence as a result of the migration of students from one centre to another.

Thus Padua was created by scholars from Bologna. Paris, the earliest of the northern type of university, was unusual in that it was created by its masters.

Most of the oldest confirmed centres of higher education in the world today still exist in the Middle East and Northern Africa. According to the Guinness Book of World records, the oldest degree-granting university in the world is the Al-Karaouine mosque and university in Fes, Morocco (talk about some real history of higher education!). Established in 859 AD by Fatima al-Fihri, the daughter of a wealthy merchant, the school was based in Islamic tradition, but also taught grammar, mathematics, astronomy, and medicine. In the 1950s, the mosque school also added chemistry and physics to its areas of study.

Another ancient centre of Islamic scholarship, Al-Azhar University, was founded by the Shi'ites around 970-972 AD. It is the second oldest university in the world. Like Al-Karaouine, the university is also a mosque school and centres around Arabic and Sunni literature.

Many of Europe's first schools to offer higher education were formed during the Middle Ages. The University of Bologna (Italy) is thought to be the first higher-learning centre known as a "university," and also the first in the Western World. Its establishment has been estimated at around 1088.

Founded in 1170, the University of Paris more or less arose from the cathedral schools of Notre-Dame. Soon after, it developed into a centre of orthodox Christian teachings. It boasted many famous professors and thinkers of the era, including Thomas Aquinas and Albertus Magnus.

The University of Oxford is considered to be the English-speaking world's oldest university. While the actual date of its establishment is unclear, it is thought that teaching in some form has existed there since around 1096. What is certain, however, is that the school began developing at an accelerated rate in 1167, when Henry II banished English students from the University of Paris. Master scholars who headed the school were recognised as an "Universitas" in 1231, and the school was already accepting international students at that time.

In colonial America, only nine higher-learning institutions had obtained official "college" status by that time. They included Yale (established 1701 in New Haven, CT) and the College of William and Mary (established 1697 in Williamsburg, VA.)

By the twelfth century, there had emerged two outstanding seats of learning in Europe, Bologna, and Paris. At the first, the jurist Irnerius between 1116 and 1140 introduced the Corpus juris civilians to Europe, and at the second a group of masters with the blessing of the Church occupied themselves with the liberal arts and theology. At Paris, by 1150, the theologians occupied the cathedral area and the masters and students of the liberal arts the left bank of the Seine. Oxford's right to confer advanced degrees was confirmed by Innocent IV only in 1254. There were 11 in Italy, 5 in France, 2 in England, and 5 on the Iberian Peninsula. Some were imperial; others (such as Oxford) have enjoyed continuous existence since their establishment.

Eastern World versus Europe

The university, which developed and matured at the height of Catholic Europe, was a new phenomenon in European history. Nothing like it had existed in ancient Greece or Rome. The institution that we recognise today, with its faculties, courses of study, examinations, and degrees, as well as the familiar distinction between undergraduate and graduate study, comes to us directly from the medieval world. And it is no surprise that the Church should have done so much to foster the nascent university system since, according to historian Lowrie Daly, it was "the only institution in Europe that showed consistent interest in the preservation and cultivation of knowledge."

Total 81 universities had been established by the time of the Reformation. Of these 33 possessed a papal charter, 15 a royal or imperial one, 20 possessed both, and 13 had none. In addition, it was the accepted view that a university could not award degrees without the approbation of pope, king, or emperor. Pope Innocent IV officially granted this privilege to Oxford University,

According to the historian of science Edward Grant, the creation of the university, the commitment to reason and rational argument, and the overall spirit of inquiry that characterised medieval intellectual life amounted to "a gift from the Latin Middle Ages to the modern world...though it is a gift that may never be acknowledged. Perhaps it will always retain the status it has had for the past four centuries as the best-kept secret of Western civilisation."

The university culture developed differently in northern Europe than it did in the south, although the northern (primarily Germany, France and Great Britain) and southern universities (primarily Italy) did have many elements in common. Latin was the language of the university, used for all texts, lectures, disputations, and examinations. Professors lectured on the books of Aristotle for logic, natural philosophy, and metaphysics.

Hippocrates, Galen, and Avicenna were used for medicine. Outside of these commonalities, great differences separated north and south, primarily in the subject matter. Italian universities focused on law and medicine, while the northern universities focused on the arts and theology.

The 17th century was rife with events that adversely affected university expansion. Many wars like the Thirty Years' War, disrupted the university landscape throughout Europe at different times. War, plague, famine, regicide, and changes in religious power and structure often adversely affected the societies that provided support for universities.

Internal strife within the universities themselves, such as student brawling and absentee professors, acted to destabilise these institutions as well. Universities were also reluctant to give up older curricula, and the continued reliance on the works of Aristotle defied contemporary advancements in science and the arts.

The reputation of these Greek Institutions was such that at least four central modern educational terms derived from them – The Academy, the Lyceum, gymnasium, and the Museum.

The word 'University' came into practice during the medieval ages. It is derived from the Latin Universities which roughly means the community of teachers and scholars. Universities were created in Italy and a word from Cathedral schools for the clergy mainly for the religious education.

In the early period Rome, Athens and Alexandria what the main centres of learning but was overtaken in the 5th century by the new capital Constantinople. After the academy in Athens closed in 529, and the conquests of Alexandria and Beirut by the Arabs in the mid-7th century, the focus of all Higher Learning moved to Constantinople.

Medieval Universities

University is generally regarded as a formal institution that has its origin in the medieval Christian setting. European higher education was a place for hundreds of years in Christian Cathedral schools or monastic schools where nuns and priests taught classes as a part of religious education.

The earliest universities were developed under the aegis of Latin Church by papal as Studia generalia. But the development of Cathedral schools into universities was quite rare with the only exception of the University of Paris.

The first universities in Europe with the form of Corporate structure for the University of Bologna (1088) the University of Paris (1150) and the University of Oxford (1167).

Subjects-curriculum-research

1. *Platonic influence:* The Platina Academy which is referred to as the University of Athens was founded CA 387 BC in Athens, Greece by the philosopher Plato, lasted 916 years, until AD 529. It was supported later during the Renaissance by the Florentin Electronyk Academy whose members were following plateaus tradition.
2. *Aristotle's influence:* Around 335 BC, Plato's successor Aristotle founded the Peripatetic school for t students of which met at the Lyceum gymnasium in Athens.
3. *Hellenistic period:* The Museum in Alexandria which included the library of Alexandria became the leading research institution for science and technology from which many Greek innovations prank between AD 216 and 272.

Early Modern universities initially continued the curriculum and research of the Middle Ages: natural philosophy, logic, medicine, theology, mathematics, astronomy (and astrology), law, grammar, and rhetoric.

Humanities

Started with the gradual stress on the humanities the initial focus of the humanist scholars in the university was the discovery, exposition, and insertion of ancient texts and languages into the university, and the ideas of those texts into society generally, their influence was ultimately quite progressive.

The influence of humanism on scholars in medicine, mathematics, astronomy, and physics may suggest that humanism and universities were a strong impetus for the scientific revolution.

Professors of medicine such as Niccolò Leoniceno, Thomas Linacre and William Cop were often trained in and taught from a humanist perspective as well as translated important ancient medical texts. The critical mind-set imparted by humanism was imperative for changes in universities and scholarship.

Aristotelian Epistemology

Aristotelian epistemology provided a coherent framework not simply for knowledge and knowledge construction, but also for the training of scholars within the higher education setting. The creation of new scientific constructs during the scientific revolution and the epistemological challenges that were inherent within this creation initiated the idea of both the autonomy of science and the hierarchy of the disciplines. Instead of entering higher education to become a "general scholar" immersed in becoming proficient in the entire curriculum, there emerged a type of scholar that put science first and viewed it as a vocation. The divergence between those focused on science and those still entrenched in the idea of a general scholar exacerbated the epistemological tensions that were already beginning to emerge.

Humboldt and Schleiermacher models

The German, or Humboldtian model, was conceived by Wilhelm von Humboldt and based on Friedrich Schleiermacher's liberal ideas pertaining to the importance of freedom, seminars, and laboratories in universities. The French university model involved strict discipline and control over every aspect of the university.

Renaissance or New Age

Renaissance humanists studied the literature of ancient Greece and Rome, believing that these classical works represented the height of human knowledge and were important models for a new age.

Humanist educators found their models of literary style in the classics. The Renaissance was a particularly powerful force in Italy, most notably in art, literature, and architecture. In literature, the works of such Italian writers as Dante Alighieri, Petrarch, and Giovanni Boccaccio became especially important.

Printing Press

The invention of the printing press in the mid-15th century made books more widely available and increased literacy rates. But school attendance did not increase greatly during the Renaissance. Elementary schools educated middle-class children while lower-class children received little if any, formal schooling.

Children of the nobility and upper classes attended humanist secondary schools.

John Calvin, Martin Luther, and Huldreich Zwingli and the Protestant Reformation

The religious Reformation of the 16th century marked a decline in the authority of the Catholic Church. They rejected the authority of the Catholic pope and created reformed Christian, or Protestant, churches. In their ardent determination to instruct followers to read the Bible in their native language, reformers extended literacy to the masses.

John Locke, Jacques Rousseau, and early 17th Century

A major shift in higher education –

> John Locke in English and Jean Jacques Rousseau in French authored influential works on education. Both emphasized the importance of shaping young minds early. By the late Enlightenment, there was a rising demand for a more universal approach to education, particularly after the American and French Revolutions. Educators of the 17th century developed new ways of thinking about education. The work of English philosopher John Locke influenced education in Britain and North America. Locke examined how people acquire ideas in An Essay Concerning Human Understanding (1690). He asserted that at birth the human mind is a blank slate, or tabula rasa, and empty of ideas.

Indian Subcontinent

In ancient India during the Vedic period between 1500 BC to 600 BC, most higher education was based on the Veda and later Hindu text and scriptures. Gradually the education which was freely available in the Vedic society became more institutionalised and restricted as the upper society started dictating the lineage and put the hierarchy of society to get the benefit of education.

The oldest of the scriptures like Upanishad dates back in 500 DC. These texts encourage the powerhouse of the learning process. It was a time when teachers and students were staying together and exploring the process of learning in a search for truth. The teaching methods were reasoning and questioning and nothing was labelled as the final answer.

The Gurukul system of education supported traditional Hindu residential schools of learning. Typically, the teacher's house was an open monastery. Education was free but students from well to do families paid Guru Dakshina a voluntary contribution when the study complete. The teachers imparted knowledge of religion, scriptures, philosophy, literature, medicine, astrology and history.

The only knowledge centres of learning in India dates to the 5th century BC where Takshila was a prestigious place to study the Vedas and other ancient scriptures. It was also an important Vedic Hindu and Buddhist centre of learning from the 6th century BC to the 5th century a.d. In the line of Takshila, ancient India also had Nalanda Ujjain and Vikramshila universities Takshila specialised in the study of medicine while Ujjain was known for astronomy and Nalanda being the biggest Centre had all branches of knowledge having more than 10000 students. Vikramshila Maha Vihara was another important Buddhist learning centre between 783 to 820.

China

During the Zhou dynasty, 1045 BC to 256 BC there were 5 National schools in the capital city Pi Yong. They had another 4 schools for the aristocrats and nobility. The schools mainly taught the 6 arts: rites music archery chartering calligraphy and mathematics. According to the book of rituals at age 12 boys and arts related to ritual like music and dance and when older archery and carrier driving. Girls learn rituals like correct department Silk production and weaving. It was during the dynasty that the Origins of native Chinese philosophy also developed. Confucius 551 BC to 479 BC founder of Confucianism was a Chinese philosopher who made a great impact on the later generation of Chinese and on the curriculum of the Chinese education system which lasted for almost 2000 years.

Greece and Rome

In ancient Greece, most education was private except in Sparta anyone could open a school and college and decide the curriculum. The major areas of studies were athletics sports wrestling music poetry drama and history.

During the early middle ages, the Mona stories of the Roman Catholic Church for the centres of education and literacy preserving the church is the selection from Latin learning and maintaining the art of writing.

The first vidamal Institutions generally considered to be universities for established in Italy France and England in the late XI and XII century where the subjects like arts law medicine and theology were taught.

Between the 11th and the 15 century, many universities were established in the kingdom of Italy the kingdom of England the kingdom of France the kingdom of Spain and the Kingdom of Portugal

Initially, the medical university does not have physical facilities such as the campus of modern university classes were taught where ever space was available such as churches and homes University was not a physical space but a collection of individuals which were put up together as a university.

University of the general structure along three types the first I was in Bologna, where students hired and paid for the Teachers the second time was in Paris by the teachers was paid by the church and the third type was in Oxford and Cambridge which was supported by the state and the Crown.

Islamic World

During the 6th and 7 centuries The Academy of Gundishapur, originally the intellectual centre of this Sassanid Empire, and subsequently a Muslim centre of learning of for training in medicine philosophy theology and Science the faculty were exports not only in the Zoroastrian and Persian traditions but also increase and Indian learning as well.

The University of al – Qarawiyyin located in Fes, Morocco is the oldest existing continually operating and the first-degree awarding educational institution in the world according to UNESCO and Guinness World Records.

The house of wisdom in Baghdad was the library translation and Educational Centre from the 9th to 13 centuries areas of studies was astrology mathematics agriculture medicine and philosophy. Books from many traditions like version Indian and Greek were taught. As a major Centre for the study of Humanities and Sciences there also teaching Pythagoras Plato, Aristotle hypocrite S Euclid proteinous Sushrut Charaka Aryabhatta and Brahma Gupta.

The Islamic Mosque School (madrasah) thought the Quran in Arabic and did not at all resemble the medieval European universities. 89th century Bimari Sthan medical schools perform in the medieval Islamic world. Al-Azhar University founded in Cairo Egypt in 975 was the university which offered a variety of post-graduate degrees had a Theological Seminary and thought Islam law jurisprudence Arabi grammar Islamic astronomy and Islamic philosophy.

Under the Ottoman Empire The towns Of Basra and Edirne BK major centres of learning. In the 15th and 16 centuries, the town of Timbuktu in the West African nation of Marley became an Islamic Centre of learning with students coming from even the Middle East the town was home to the prestigious Sankore University. Over time there was a great accumulation of manuscripts in the area and some of them dated from pre-Islamic X and 12 century.

Japan

The history of Higher Education in Japan dates back to the 6th century when Chinese learning was introduced at the Yamato court. Foreign civilisations have often provided new ideas for the development of Japan's own culture.

By the 9 century Heian-Kyo (today's Kyoto) Imperial capital had 5 Institutions Of Higher Learning. During the medieval period, 1185 to 1600 Zen Buddhist monasteries were especially important centres of learning and the Ashikaga Schools flourish in the 15 century as a centre of Higher Learning.

Central and South American Civilisations

The Aztec which refers to certain three groups of Central Mexico achieved political and military dominance over large parts of Mesoamerican in the 14th 15 and 16 centuries. Other important areas were Inca and Ametus. The constituted a special class of wise man like the bards of Great Britain. The included industrious philosophers poets and priests who kept the oral histories of Incas alive.

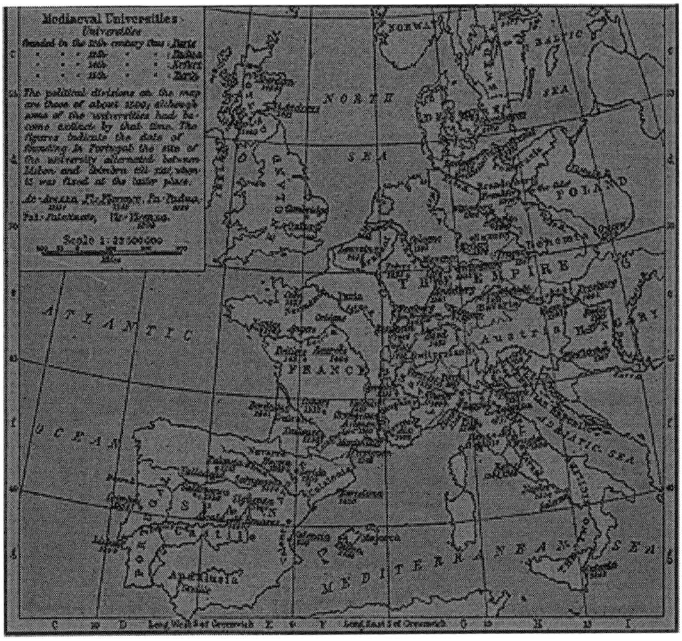

Modern systems of education in Europe derive their origins from the schools of the High Middle Ages. Most schools during this era were founded upon religious principles with the primary purpose of training the clergy.

Many of the earliest universities, such as the University of Paris founded in 1160, had a Christian basis. In addition to this, several secular universities existed, such as the University of Bologna, founded in 1088. The idea of Free education for the poor was officially mandated by the Church in 1179 when it decreed that every cathedral must assign a master to teach boys too poor to pay the regular fee; parishes and monasteries also established free schools teaching at least basic literacy skills.

France: The modern era of French education begins in the 1790s. The Revolution in the 1790s abolished the traditional universities. Napoleon sought to replace them with new institutions, the Polytechnique, focused on technology. The elementary schools received little attention until 1830 when France copied the Prussian system.

The Higher education System has now become very complex with a large variety of institutions. – Central Universities, State Universities Deemed Universities, Unitary and affiliating Universities, Sectorial Universities, Private Universities, and Undergraduate and Postgraduate colleges.

In recent years, with the growth of the Information technology related service sector, the nature and demand for higher education have changed dramatically. Earlier the system was managed by a guru (teacher/saint) Now it is managed by businessman and Industrialist on approval of political party. Before going to the history of higher education let us understand what higher education is all about.

EDUCATION IN ANCIENT INDIA

In Ancient India Knowledge was gained to attain salvation (Moksha) Education in ancient India can be understood by following.

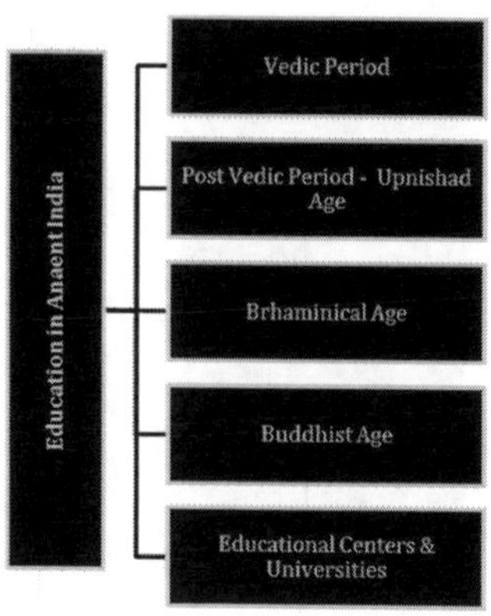

(1) Vedic Age

Vedic Education was based on an organised and thought out the scheme with a message to humanity. Vedic Literature is considered as the mean basic for Vedic education. The literal meaning of 'Vedas' is Knowledge. The word is derived from 'Vid' root meaning 'to know' thus 'Veda' means the knowledge of various types. The four Vedas are composed in verses but some portion of, it is written in prose the four Vedas are Rig Veda, Yajur Veda, Sama Veda, and Atharva Veda.

The hymns of Rig Veda show that Vedic education was carried on verbally, but here two methods of Vedic education:

1. First, the Rig Vedic hymns were composed.
2. Second, they were preserved.

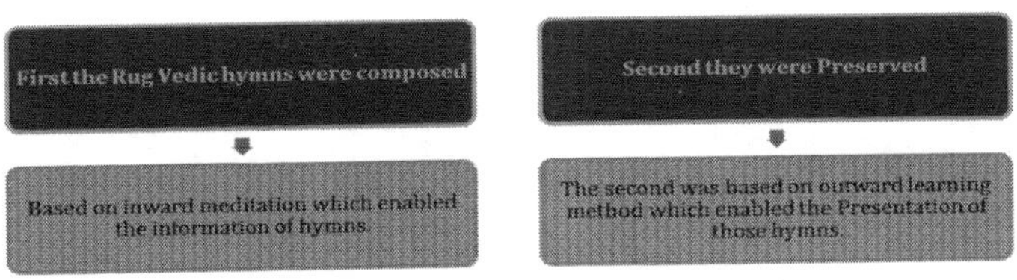

Vedic hymns were the traditional Properties of the various families of the Rushis. They Verbally Preserved in the families of Vamdeva, Attri, Bhardwaja, Vashistha etc.

The following are the characteristics of Vedic education

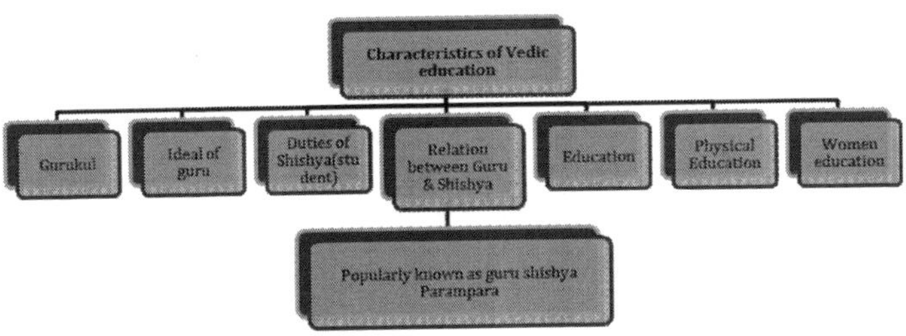

(2) Post-Vedic Period (UPNISHAD AGE)

Post-Vedic period is generally the period between 1400 B. C. to 600 B. C. i.e. from the end of the Rug Vedic period to the beginning of Buddhism and Jainism. During this period priests were divided into four categories.

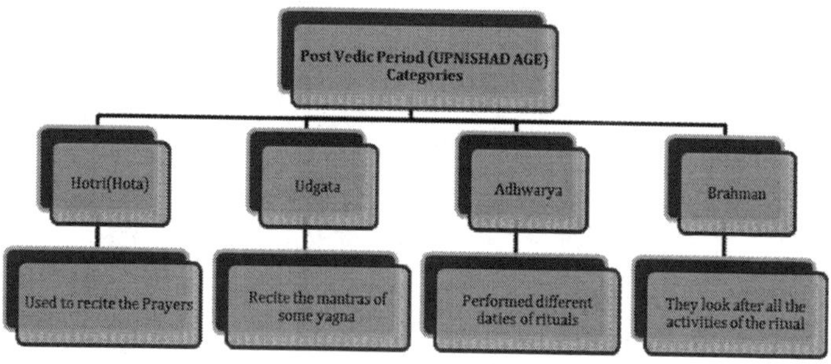

Among the available Brahmans following are worth mentioning

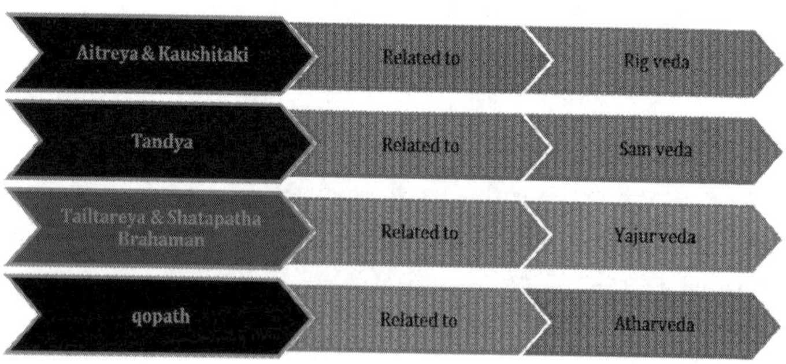

The aim of education enables the realisation of true Knowledge and achievement of absolute (Brahma). The education was considered to be a process of inwardly med. Taken and thinking.

Method of Teaching: The following three methods existed during this period.

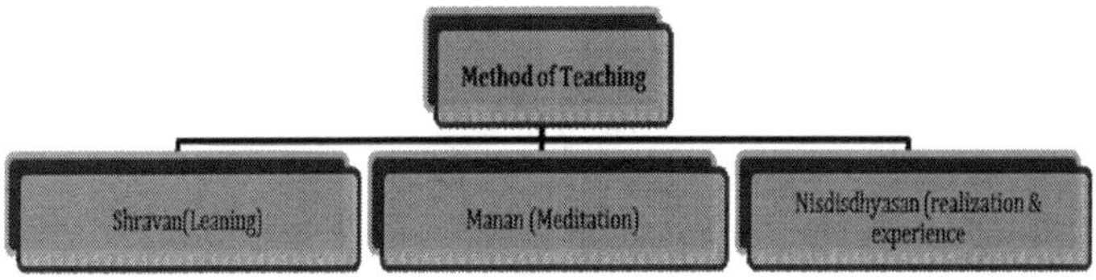

AGENCIES OF EDUCATION – EXPANSION

- Branch or shakhas ->Denotes all three branches of Vedas
- Charans -> According to Panini only a group of disciples who studies in one branch or Shakhas was Charan
- Parishad -> Parishad means all things expanded on all sides.
- Gotra or kala -> It was based on family traditions which might be real or imaginary various Gotra or kula were related to ancient 'Rishis'

BRAHMANICAL SYSTEM

Mr. F. E. Keay in his book named history of Indian education, Ancient and later Times observes, "Not only did Brahman educators develop a system of education which survived the crumbling empires and the changes of the society, but they also, through all these thousands of years, kept a glow of the torch of Higher learning and numbered amongst them. Many great thinkers who have left their mark not only on the learning of India but upon the intellectual life of the world" with this aim of Brahmanic education becomes clear.

The following were the chief characteristics of the Brhamical system of education Characteristics:

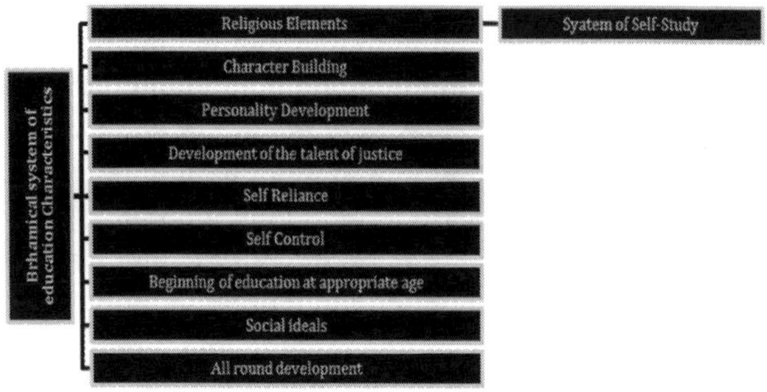

The students had to study in the gurukuls for about 12 years.

BUDDHIST PERIOD

The history of education in Buddha Period is interrelated with the history of monasteries and Vihars because there were no independent educational institutions or centres, of the than those religious centres. Those centres were highly responsible for the spread of Buddhism in India by 600 B. C. In the Buddhist period, there were no organised gurukuls like that of the Vedic period. But the education was imported through monasteries and Vihars these the monks (Bhikshu), the education like Vedic education was also monthly religious. The aim was to gain salvation (Nirvana).

There were two stages of education during this period

- Primary
- Higher

EDUCATION CENTRES AND UNIVERSITIES

(1) Takshshila

- Situated at the distance of 20 miles in the west of Rawalpindi, Takshshila was the capital of Gandhara Kingdom.

- This place was conquered by Ephesians in the 6th century in 2nd century B.C by Greeks in the 1st century BC by Sakas. In the 1st century AD by Kushans and in 5th century AD by Huns.
- Only higher studies were conducted.
- Minimum age 16 years to get admission.
- Literary or general and scientific or Industrial education was key areas.

(2) Kashi

- The modern name of the city is Varanasi formerly it was Banaras situated in the North part of India.
- Many Acharya of kasha were the scholars of Takshshila.
- In the 7th century, BC kasha became the most famous centre of learning in northern India.
- Kashi was the greatest centre of Brhamnical Learning.
- In the 11th century, Kashmir and Kashi were the two greatest centres of learning.
- In the 12th century when Kashi was annexed by Muslim rulers then the educational system the centre was badly damaged.

(3) Nalanda

- In the state of Bihar at a distance of 7 miles in the north of Rajgir and in the southeast of Patna at a distance of 43 miles, is situated Nalanda. In the beginning, it was a small village, which later on flourished as the centre of the Buddhist religion.
- In Nalanda, the Vihara was established by Emperor Asoka. He had built a Sangharama (residence of Buddhist nuns) but as a university, it did not flourish before 3rd century A.D. Nagarjuna came to study here about 300 A.D.

- Boarding and lodging were provided to the students free of cost by the university.
- Yog Shastra, Jyotish, Hetuvidya, Shabdavidya, Brahminic subject, Vyakaran, various philosophies etc.

(4) Valabhi

- Nalanda could be compared with the educational and cultural centre of valabhi, situated on the eastern side of Kathiawar.
- It is said that Princess Dudda, daughter of king Dhruva-1 had built the Vihar in Valbhi and in 580 A.D. Dharasena-1 ordered for the construction of one more monastery. In 640. A. D. there were about 100 Vihars in the city, where 6000 Bhikshus were studying.
- Vyakaran, Bookkeeping, literature etc. were the subjects imparted.

(5) Vikramshila

- The Vihar of Vikramshala was established by the famous emperor Dharampal of Pal dynasty in the 8th century in Northen Magadh at a bank of the Ganga river.
- In Vikramshila 108 scholars were appointed as the in-charge and acharyas of various temples. 6 additional pandits were also appointed as general manager.
- Logic, Philosophy, Vyakaran, Tantra Shastra and Karamkanda were the main subjects.

(6) Odantpuri

- University of odantpuri perhaps the university was established before the prominence of Pal dynasty in Magadh.

- University assisted the development of Buddhist to a great extent and many scholars from Tibet etc.
- It is said that the first monastery of Tibet was built on the lines of Odantpuri Vihar in 949 A.D.

(7) Jagaddala

- Pal kings, Raja Rampal of Bengal had set a city on the banks of Ganga. It was the beginning of the 11th century and named Runavati.
- This University became the centre of learning and renamed the centre of Buddhist culture for about 100 years it was destroyed by Muslim in 1203. A.D.
- Bibhuti Chandra, Dansheel Sudharkar and Moostakar Gupta are few eminent scholars.

(8) Mithila

- Rajshri Janak used to hold a religious conference, wherein learned Rishis and Pandits took part in the religious discussions.
- Later on devotees of Shri Krishna like famous poet Vidyapati, Jaideo were born here.
- 12th to 15th century Mithila was a very important place for learning and culture.

(9) Nadia

- Known as Navadweep
- Situated at the bank of Ganga and Jalangi rivers in Bengal.
- Centre for trade and commerce.
- Education in Nadia University was imparted in 3 centres – Shantipur, Gopalpura, and Navadweep.

(10) Kanchi

- Kanchi was the capital of Pallava dynasty of South India. It was famous for learning and culture and was called Kashi of the South.
- Famous Chinese pilgrim Yuan having has visited Kanchi in about 642 A.D.

EDUCATION IN MEDIEVAL INDIA (MUSLIM PERIOD)

8th century A.D. Mahmud Ghazni invaded India and established a large number of schools by looted wealth. Education during the Muslim period was much inferior to that of the Hindu period, only Akbar did commendable work in the field of Education. During the Muslim period education was organised in Maktabs and Madrasas. Primary education was given in Maktabs and higher education was given in Madrasas.

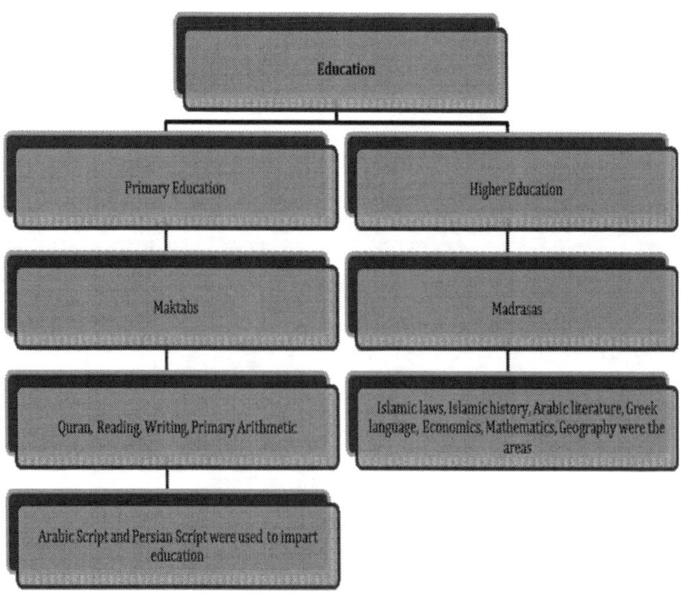

CHARACTERISTICS OF EDUCATION

- Patronage
- Teacher-Pupil relationship
- Lack of University
- Discipline and Punishment
- Examination
- Military Education

Delhi, Agra, Jaipur, and Bihar were an important place where education was given to all disciples.

EDUCATION IN BRITISH INDIA

In the last Quarter of the 15th century, the European from different countries had started visiting India in connection with their trade. The Portuguese were the first among the European who come to India. Vasco-De-Gama discovered the sea route to India and landed in 1498. Afterward, the Dutch, the French, The Spanish, the Danes, and the English people came here and started their businesses. During the period they began to spread their religion, Christianity in the land. East India Company also made education as a means of publicity of religion. Besides, Christian, Missionaries played a significant role in spreading education in India.

1. The Portuguese

- St. Francis Xavier the follower of Jesuits religious sect came to India in 1542 A.D.
- He started University named Kochin
- Their main centre of activities was Bombay, Goa, Diu, Daman, Ceylon, Hugli, and Chittagong.

- Started 1st graduate college in Goa in 1575 name of the college was St. Anne College.
- Christianity, logic, grammar, and music were the main subjects.

2. The Dutch

Dutch came to India in the 17th century. They have started college in Ceylon, but due to enmity with Britishers, they could not stay in India for long. To carry the trade, the factories were set-up in Chin surah and Hubli in Bengal and in Nagapattinam coast of Madras.

3. The French

French also established a trading company in 1664. They started primary schools in Pondicherry, Mahi, Yenam, and kanikal. They also started higher secondary schools where the French language was taught. They had to face the opposition of English and later their land schools were captured by an English company.

4. The Denes

On the 17th century some inhabitants of Denmark also came to India and started factories in Travancore and Srirampore. In 1845 they sold their colonies to Britishers and left India. They converted about 50,000 people to Christianity.

The Contribution of Lord Macaulay in Indian Education

Lord Macaulay was appointed by Governor General Lord William Bentinck as the chairman of the committee of public instruction on 07.03.1835, he passed a resolution in his council and emphasized on following:

1. All the funds of government to be spent in imparting to the Indians the knowledge of English literature and Science.
2. The government funds were not to be spent on printing oriental works.

The Years between 1836 to 1853

Many schools & colleges were established in various parts of the country. Lord William Bentincks founded a Medical College of Calcutta, the Engineering College at Roorkee by Lord Dalhousie. In 1857 the Calcutta, Bombay and Madras Universities were established. In 1878, Punjab University was founded. In 1860 St. Xavier's College Calcutta, In 1864 Foreman College Lahore, In 1869 St. Xavier's College Bombay. In 1877, Red college Lukhnow. In 1882 St. Stephen's College, Delhi was established. Thus the number of colleges rose from 23, in 1854 to 72 in 1882.

The recommendations & Lord Curzon for establishing Indian University commission was not welcomed by countrymen or people of India, but for the first time in the history of India. The education act was established on 11th Mar 1904. This, later on, became the law to govern Indian education. Gopal Krishna Gokhale rendered remarkable service for primary education in India. He contacted Maharaja Sayajirao of Baroda in 1906. He made primary education free and compulsory within the territory of this state. Hartog committee repair was presented in Sept 1929 where the recommendation was given for primary, secondary, higher, technological and vocational education, as well as committee, emphasized the education of Women and Muslims.

In 1937, Abbott and Wood submitted a report when was divided into two parts:

1. General Education
2. Vocational Education.

In 1937, All India National educational conference was held, also known as Wardha education and conference which was held under the presidentship of Mahatma Gandhi, where following resolution was passed after a long discussion.

1. Free and compulsory education be provided medium of instruction in the mother tongue and the basic education for all.
2. One of the landmarks in the history of education was the report of sergeant commission on the post was an educational department in India. Where the recommendation was given for pre-primary education, primary or basic education, secondary education, University education, Industrial and vocational education, education of the adults, training & the teacher's educations of the physically challenged etc.

EDUCATION IN FREE INDIA

Sergeant scheme of education has suggested a 3-year degree course as is very much in practice today. University Grant Commission under the Ministry of Human Resource Development was established in India in the year 1956 with three objectives i.e. Access, equally and quality and is charged with coordination, determination and maintenance of standards of Higher education in India time to time the various commission was appointed by the government of India the list of the commission are as under

Year	Name of the commission	Chairman of commission
1948-49	Radhakrishnan Commission	Dr. S. Radhakrishnan
1952-53	Mudaliar Commission	Dr. A. L. Swami Mudaliar
1953	Acharya Narendra dev Committee	Acharya Narendra dev
1965-66	Kothari Commission (Indian Education Commission)	Dr. S. Kothari

Apart from this commission, Other commissions and committee were constituted which were the National Commission on teachers (1983), Mobilisation of Resources in central Universities (1993), AICTE committee on technical education (1994). National Policy on education was also announced in the year 1968, 1986 and 2016.

The five-year plan was started in the year 1951. The first five-year plan for education was for the period of (1951-56). At present 13th five-year plan is in force from (2017 to 2022).

Modern Indian Higher Education

The modern education system in India is identified with Lord Macaulay and his initiatives for English education. He advocated for the teaching of English in schools and the formation of a class of anglicised Indian interpreters. Traditional structures were not recognised by the British government and have been on the decline since.

Public education expenditures in the late 19th and early 20th centuries varied dramatically across regions with the western and southern provinces spending three to four times as much as the eastern provinces. Much of the inter-regional differential was due to historical differences in land taxes, the major source of revenue.

Lord Macaulay and Lord Curzon are the pioneers of the modern English education system in India. Lord Curzon, the Viceroy 1899-1905, made mass education a high priority after finding that no more than 20% of India's children attended school. His reforms cantered on literacy training and on the restructuring of the university systems. They stressed upgraded curricula, modern textbooks, and new examination systems. Curzon's plans for technical education laid the foundations which were acted upon by later governments.

Indian Higher Education after Independence

India has grown tremendously post-independence and in the last two decades, post-globalisation and liberalisation of the Indian economy, India is now the third largest education system in the world. After China and the United States.

Under MHRD, higher education in India is governed by bodies such as UGC, AICTE, DEC (Distance Education Council) and CoA (Council of Architecture), MCI (Medical Council of India), VCI (Veterinary Council of India), BCI (Bar Council of India), DCI (Dental Council of India), INC (Indian Nursing Council, PCI (Pharmacy Council of India), Central Council of Homeopathy, Central Council of Indian Medicine and Rehabilitation Council of India., the Indian Council of Agriculture Research (ICAR). These bodies are supported by the State Council of Higher Education and University Grants Commission (UGC) is an Autonomous Body which governs the general education system in colleges and universities. UGC enforces its standards, advises the government, and coordinate between the centre and the state.

NUMBER OF HIGHER EDUCATION INSTITUTIONS IN INDIA (AS PER ANNUAL REPORT UGC 2014-15)

	Higher Education		Institutions in		Students'	
		Absolute figure			Enrolment in lakh	
	Colleges		University		Enrolment in Higher	
					Education	
	Nos.	Trend %	Nos	Trend %	Fig.in lakh	Trend %
1950-51	578	100	27	100	4	100
1960-61	1819	314.71	45	166.67	10	250
1970-71	3277	566.96	82	303.70	33	825
1980-81	6963	1204.67	110	407.41	48	1200
1990-91	5748	994.46	184	681.48	49	1225
2000-01	10152	1756.40	254	940.74	86	2150
2005-06	16982	2938.06	350	1296.30	143	3575
2006-07	19812	3427.68	371	1374.07	156	3900
2007-08	23099	3396.37	406	1503.70	172	4300
2008-09	27882	4823.88	440	1629.63	185	4625
2009-10	25938	4487.54	436	1614.81	207	5175
2010-11	32974	5704.84	621	2300.00	275	6875
2011-12	34852	6029.76	642	2377.78	292	7300
2012-13 (p)	35829	6198.79	665	2462.96	296	7400
2013-14 (p)	36671	6344.46	712	2637.03	NA	
2014-15	40760	7051.90	761	9766.67	NA	

THE STRUCTURE OF THE HIGHER EDUCATION SYSTEM IN INDIA TODAY

Institutions of Higher Education in India –

The institutions of higher learning in India fall into the following broad categories:

- *Universities:* These are established by an Act of Parliament or State Legislature and are of a unitary or affiliating type. They are called Central Universities and State Universities respectively.
- *Deemed to be Universities*: These institutions are given deemed to be university status by the Central Government on the recommendation of the UGC in terms of Section 3 of the UGC Act. Some of these institutions offer advanced level courses in a field or specialisation while others award general degrees.
- *Private Universities:* These are established by various State governments through their own legislation.
- *Institutes of National Importance:* These Institutes are declared as such by the Government of India by an Act of Parliament and are empowered to award degrees. In some cases, such Institutes are also set up by the Government through an Act of State Legislation.
- *Premier Institutes of Management:* These are the Institutes that have been set up by the Central Government and are outside the formal university system. They offer Post-Graduate Diploma Programmes which are equivalent to Master's Degree Programmes in the area of management.

CONCLUSION

As per the UNESCO's WORLD DECLARATION ON HIGHER EDUCATION FOR THE TWENTY-FIRST CENTURY: VISION AND ACTION, higher education in the future world is one of the most important aspects of the civilised world. It can be summed up in the following articles of the declaration:

- Article 1 – Mission to educate, to train and to undertake research
- Article 2 – Ethical role, autonomy, responsibility, and anticipatory function
- Article 3 – Equity of access
- Article 4 – Enhancing participation and promoting the role of women
- Article 5 – Advancing knowledge through research in science, the arts and humanities and the dissemination of its results
- Article 6 – Long-term orientation based on relevance
- Article 7 – Strengthening co-operation with the world of work and analysing and anticipating societal needs
- Article 8 – Diversification for enhanced equity of opportunity
- Article 9 – Innovative educational approaches: critical thinking and creativity
- Article 10 – Higher education personnel and students as major actors
- Article 11 – Qualitative evaluation
- Article 12 – The potential and the challenge of technology
- Article 13 – Strengthening higher education management and financing

- Article 14 – Financing of higher education as a public service

In 7 decades of Independence, the higher education system in India has grown remarkably in quantitative terms. It is also quite diverse and democratic. It is also quite diverse and democratic. It is largest in the world in terms of institutions. This massive expansion during the post-independence period was unavoidable because access to higher education but till date following challenges are faced/encountered by Indian higher education they are

1. Employability
2. Quality of Research
3. Financing in higher education
4. Infrastructure facilities
5. Foreign enrolment of students
6. Examination oriented education
7. Lack of Internationalisation
8. Reservation System
9. Social behaviour of family
10. Lack of reforms
11. Regulatory System
12. Academic freedom

Let us hope Indian higher education will be able to overcome aforesaid challenges in the very near future as the Government is more conscious and political will is also positive for higher education in India.

References

http://collegestats.org/articles/2009/12/top-10-oldest-universities-in-the-world-ancient-colleges/

http://www.islamiclandmarks.com/various/al_azhar_university.html

http://www.eng.unibo.it/PortaleEn/University/Our+History/default.htm

http://www.britannica.com/EBchecked/topic/443814/Universities-of-Paris-I-XII

https://ourworldindata.org/higher-education/

Alatas, S. F. (2006), "From Jami'ah to University: Multiculturalism and Christian–Muslim Dialogue", *Current Sociology*, 54 (1): 112–132 [123–4], doi:10.1177/0011392106058837

Arthur Lovejoy: *The Great Chain of Being: A Study of the History of an Idea* (1936), ISBN 0-674-36153-9

Boud, D., Keogh, R., and Walker, D. (eds.) (1985). *Reflection. Turning experience into learning.* London: Kogan Page.

Brookfield, S. (1984). *Adult learners, adult education and the community.* Milton Keynes, PA: Open University Press.

Buber, Martin (1947). *Between Man and Man.* Transl. R. G. Smith. London: Kegan Paul.

Carr, W. and Kemmis, S. (1986). *Becoming Critical. Education, knowledge and action research.* Lewes: Falmer.

Dewey, J. (1916), *Democracy and Education. An introduction to the philosophy of education* (1966 edn.). New York: Free Press.

Dewey, J. (1933). *How We Think. A restatement of the relation of reflective thinking to the educative* process. (Revised edn.), Boston: D. C. Heath.

Dewey, J. (1938). *Experience and Education.* New York: Collier Books. (Collier edition first published 1963).

Encyclopædia Britannica: *History of Education.* The development of the universities.

G. Leff and J. North, Chapter 10: "The Faculty of Arts," in *A History of the University in Europe*, Volume I: Universities in the Middle Ages, W. Ruegg (ed.), Cambridge University Press, 1992.

George Makdisi: "Madrasa and University in the Middle Ages", in *StudiaIslamica,* Vol. 32 (1970), S. 255-264 (264):

H. Rashdall, *The Universities of Europe in the Middle Ages*, 3 Volumes, F.M. Powicke, A.B. Emden (Eds. of 2nd Edition), Oxford University Press, 1936.

Pandey, D. (2016). "Growth Of Higher Education In India After Independence." *International Education And Research Journal*, 2(10). Retrieved fromhttp://ierj.in/journal/index.php/ierj/article/view/510/482

Rait, R.S. 1912. *Life in the Medieval University*, p.133

Rait, R.S. 1912. *Life in the Medieval University*, p.138

Rait, R.S. 1912. *Life in the Medieval University*, pp.138-139

Riché, Pierre (1978): *Education and Culture in the Barbarian West: From the Sixth through the Eighth Century*, Columbia: University of South Carolina Press, ISBN 0-87249-376-8, pp. 126-7, 282-98

Rüegg, Walter (ed.): *Geschichte der Universität in Europa*, 3 vols., C.H. Beck, München 1993, ISBN 3-406-36956-1

Rüegg, Walter: "Foreword. The University as a European Institution", in *A History of the University in Europe*. Vol. 1: Universities in the Middle Ages, Cambridge University Press, 1992, ISBN 0-521-36105-2, pp. XIX-XX Verger 1999

Agrawal, p. (2012). *A Half Century of Indian Higher Education essay* by Philip G. Altbach. New Delhi: Sage Publications.

Gurudutta, J. (2015). "Building Quality Education in India: Review and Conceptual Model." *Zenith International Journal of Multidisciplinary Research*, 17-23.

Jayapalan, N. (2005). *History of Education in India*. New Delhi: Atlantic Publishers.

Tilak, J. B. (2014). *Higher Education in India*. New Delhi: Orient Black Swan.

21

Language and Literature of Higher Education

Gargi Gohil

ABSTRACT

India is the first Asian country, and amongst the first in the world, where English Studies was established as an academic discipline in higher education (HE). Developments therein from the mid-nineteenth century onwards have often been significant for disciplinary pursuits elsewhere, especially as the study of English language and literature tried to accommodate diverse cultural contexts, and insofar as the postcolonial condition came to be regarded as a fulcrum for understanding past and current political dimensions of such study.

The language is the most important medium of communication and education, its development occupies an important place in the National Policy on Education and Programme of Action. Therefore, promotion and development of Hindi and other 21 languages listed in the Schedule VIII of the Constitution including Sanskrit and Urdu have received due attention. In fulfilling the constitutional responsibility, the Department of Higher Education is assisted by the autonomous organisation and subordinate offices.

Keywords: Language, Literature, Colonial India, Post-colonial India, Language Policy, Multiligualism.

India's higher education system is the third largest in the world, next to the United States and China. The main governing body at the tertiary level is the University Grants Commission, which enforces its standards, advises the government, and helps coordinate between the centre and the state. Accreditation for higher learning is overseen by 15 autonomous institutions established by the University Grants Commission (UGC).

The language is the most important medium of communication and education, its development occupies an important place in the National Policy on Education and Programme of Action. Therefore, promotion and development of Hindi and other 21 languages listed in the Schedule VIII of the Constitution including Sanskrit and Urdu have received due attention. In fulfilling the constitutional responsibility, the Department of Higher Education is assisted by the autonomous organisation and subordinate offices.

Language Policy

The Language Policy of India relates to the use of languages in various fields and is pluralistic in its scope, it's language-survival oriented. This policy intends to encourage the citizens to use their mother tongue at certain levels through some processes, but the main goal of the policy is to help all languages to develop into fit mediums of communication in their areas of use, irrespective of their nature or status like major, minor, or tribal languages. The policy is ever-evolving, through mutual adjustment, consensus, and judicial processes. Evolving language policy is a major endeavour of the Language Bureau of the Ministry of Human Resource Development, Government of India. This is done by the Bureau through language institutions set up for the purpose under its aegis: Central Hindi Directorate, Centre for Scientific and Technical Terminology, Central Hindi Institute, Central Institute of Indian Languages, National Council for Promotion of Sindhi Language, National Council for Promotion of Urdu Language, Rashtriya Sanskrit Sansthan

(RSKS), Maharishi Sandipani Rashtriya Vedavidya Pratishthan (MSRVVP), Central Institute of English and Foreign Languages.

India is the first Asian country, and amongst the first in the world, where English Studies was established as an academic discipline in higher education (HE). Mid-nineteenth century onwards developments have often been significant for disciplinary pursuits especially as the study of English language and literature tried to accommodate diverse cultural contexts, so far as the postcolonial condition came to be regarded to understand past and current political dimensions. Equally, debates about English Studies in HE provide a useful index of social developments in India after independence. Some of the developments and debates are presented with a view to assess the current condition of English Studies in India and consider its future prospects, the discipline consists in whatever is regarded as the professional concern of HE English teachers and English departments. That could include any variety of English language teaching as well as, linguistics.

HIGHER EDUCATION SYSTEM IN INDIA

Education in India dates back to its early civilisation time where the teaching and learning process revolved around the 'Gurukal system'. This system was a residential concept wherein the students were educated under the tutorship of a teacher in different areas of religion, philosophy, and science. The modern concept of University style education centres was established around 6 BC at Nalanda and Takshila. The concept of centralised learning centres with multiple streams continued till the arrival of Europeans to the Indian subcontinent. These higher learning centres were the nerve centre of different dynasties which ruled across India for thousands of years and generated the required human resources.

In the middle ages up to 1200 AD, the religion based on higher learning centres were established throughout the Indian peninsula. These learning centres attracted students from Central Asia, China, Middle East, South East Asia and Rome focusing on Literature, Philosophy, Astronomy Architecture influences of which can be seen across the world in terms of temples, construction and irrigation systems.

In the early modern age after 1200 AD, the Islamic influences enriched the traditional University learning centres and brought in the disciplines of Geography, Law, Administration and Arabic mathematics to Indian subcontinents.

HIGHER EDUCATION SYSTEM UNDER BRITISH RULE

The European Rulers brought a major change in the traditional style of higher education from 1600 AD. Informal European style learning centres existed across India till 1850, whose main focus was on the development of European language speaking administrators and clerks for helping the establishment of their rule. Through the East India Company, the British were successful by 1800 in controlling much of the Indian sub-continent. The British established a formal system of higher education which continues to date. Lord Macaulay had been responsible for making English the language of instruction across the education system in India. The British style University was established in Calcutta, Mumbai, and Chennai in the year 1857 based on the model of the University of London which has been the foundation of the modern higher education system in India. Universities focused on languages, literature, history, and philosophy. These learning centres were focused on generating English speaking working class for the British administrative services, army, and trade. Modern Science and engineering education which flourished in Europe and America during late 1800 weren't the main focus under the British rule. By 1903 the Indian Institute of Science was established by Tata with a focus on research in science and engineering which is the first higher technical learning system in modern India. The British model of University system continued to expand across India leading to a growing number of higher learning centres by 1947.

Higher Education and the University System in India

India is home to the third largest higher education system in the world by volume of students enrolled. The government of India through the Ministry of Human Resource Development (MHRD) under the Department of Higher Education shapes the policies related to higher education. The University Grants Commission (UGC) a statutory body established in 1956 through Parliament enacted law modelled on the UGC of United Kingdom is responsible for coordination, evaluation and maintaining standards of higher education in India. UGC funded through MHRD is responsible for establishing central universities across India and for recognising Deemed to be Universities run by privately funded trusts and Universities established by the 28 Federal State governments across India. UGC has established statutory Councils to promote, provide grants, set standards and establish professional education in different areas.

Language Studies in Higher Education

The key component of cultural identity is the language of that particular peninsula. However, multilingual proficiency is also essential to access various knowledge sources and a larger world with a broader outlook. In political unification and divisions of nations, language played a major role as multi or bilingualism often determines political discourse and political history.

India has its strength and weaknesses due to its cultural as well as linguistic diversity. Whether the colonial government or post-independent government, educational discourse cannot be complete without touching upon the linguistic concerns of the nation. Hence, the process of bringing about a unified governance structure in India by the colonial government revolved around the issue of education, specifically modern English education to the natives in the Indian subcontinent. Later the emergence of Swadeshi movement and the idea of Indian nationalism also deeply engaged in inculcating a national spirit by connecting diverse cultural, religious and ethnic communities in the subcontinent through a facilitating linguistic model. The evolution of discourse on multilingualism in Indian classrooms seemingly reflects the political agenda of the State which eventually resulted in the formation of the Indian state in the later period. The post independent India also constantly engaged in developing an appropriate strategy and methodology to deal with multilingualism in the classrooms. An inquiry into the strategy and the methodology delineated to handle the linguistic diversity of the nation as well as the socio-economic mobility of the people through classrooms by Indian state provides answers to:

(1) What is the objective of the Indian State (pre and post-independent) while dealing with the issue of multilingualism? (a) Is it just at to consolidate people and/ or provide a facilitative environment for the functioning of the State? and (b) Or has it an inclusive meaning that 'beyond Mother Tongue (MT)'?

(2) How did the State policy shape the idea of multilingualism in postindependence India? (a) Was it related to promoting the spirit of nationalism or aimed at the scientific-technical and knowledge development of India? and (b) Is the concept of multilingualism cater to the employability of the educated Indian?

The post-independent India geared up to address the increasing developments in the environment with regard to the national goals and changes in the rest of the world, at the same time including language and cultural diversity of India. Now the question is, whether this understanding emerged as a goal of the development or arose as a compulsion (just like the majority of Indians forced to speak more than one language of the nation due to either in or out migration in their localities). Briefly, multilingual education is an instance of bi-literacy, "in which communication occurs in two (or more) languages in or around writing". When we consider this, we realise that modern Indian education followed multilingualism incorporating modern Indian languages, the MT and the global language, English. Colonial classrooms in India were bilingual – MT and English and the language policy proposed multilingualism in the classrooms covering MT, English, and Hindi. The background paper of Education for All Monitoring Report 2004 (UNESCO) [8] argues that MT based bilingual education offers significant pedagogical advantages which have been reported consistently in the academic literature (Baker 2006; [9] and Cummins 2000) [10]. With this insight, the article tries to understand how India formed its policies to address the bilingual/ multilingual character of Indian classrooms.

During that time, Colonial Education Policy, its Experience, Linguistic diversity was an integral part of Indian social fabric. Ancient Indian education System of Gurukul aimed at a religious purpose, administrative and literacy activities. Keeping in mind its aim the Medium of instruction was mostly Sanskrit or Persian/ Urdu or Arabic as the proficiency in the classical language determined the scholarly status of a person, although each Republic had its own language, this education system had no place for vernacular language. When the Europeans came to India, they needed people with proficiency in the local language as well as English for expansion of their Empire. Education became a main engagement of the Company by the end of the 19th Century and missionaries were encouraged to open schools. Naturally, the controversy over the medium of instruction and language education in Indian schools begun. Many Indians developed an interest in learning English and reformers like Raja Ram Mohan Roy demanded to open an English college in Calcutta instead of Sanskrit or Persian. Language controversy in Indian education was whether the medium of education in higher level should be through classical languages (Sanskrit for Hindus and Arabic and Persian for Muslims) or modern Indian languages or through English (Orientalists and Anglicans). Even though, all these groups were agreed that Western science and knowledge should spread in India [16].

The Macaulay Minutes proposed a policy to undertake the formal Western type of education imparting knowledge of Western literature and science through English as a medium of instruction. English Education adopted, and encouraged by the Government, spread along with the vernacular language [18] schools. But due to the prevailing religious and cultural traditions, many looked at English and western science education with suspicion, resulting in a division of educated Indians as English knowing and non-English knowing. The English knowing educated class developed a superiority complex, and refused to mix with the rest which went against the "downward filtration theory". Therefore, in the Dispatch Commission Report, First Education Commission Report in 1854, brought a compromise formula to settle the controversy of the Orientalists and Anglicists groups on the issue of language and the medium of instruction such as vernacular languages were the medium of instruction for the masses and English language was taught wherever it was demanded. Further, it clarified that vernacular language as a medium of instruction in indigenous primary schools, but at high school level onwards, the medium of instruction should shift into English or modern Indian language in which modern science was taught only in English (Basu, 1989 [19] and Ghosh, 2013) [20].

In India during the post-independence time, the scenario of higher education, the debated issue was of linguistic minorities in one hand and need for a national language on the other hand. Even though, the Constitution does not provide any specific direction regarding the medium of instruction, Article 350-A of the Constitution of India points out that 'it shall be the endeavour of every state or of every local authority within the state to provide adequate facilities for instructions in the MT at the primary stage of education to children belonging to linguistic minority groups.' It means, the law laid down by the Supreme Court becomes binding to the educational institutions so English as a medium of instruction and examination also adopted at higher education level. However, the Central Advisory Board of Education (CABE) adapted the main content of the educational policy developed after the Wardha Conference (Kher and Zakir Hussain Committee recommendation) which has laid down the language policy start with MT at primary level and eventually incorporating English at middle and secondary level onwards. It was first briefed in the first Education Commission in independent India – National University Education Commission headed by Dr. S Radhakrishnan. It proposed a strategy to introduce multilingualism through a system of education at the university level by making provision for the study of several languages in the curriculum (Srivastava, 2007) [23]. The Three-Language Formula emerged out of this consideration.

The Kothari Commission in 1966 deliberated on it properly and the First National Policy on Education (NPE) in 1968 adapted it as the Three Tier Language Education Policy. The original principles that shaped the three language formula were that MT as the first language which children must learn from the primary levels both as a subject and as the medium of instruction in order to derive maximum advantage from education (Srivastava, 2007) [24]. This formula also includes the study of regional language – Hindi in non-Hindi speaking regions and the South Indian States or another non-Hindi language in Hindi speaking regions and English as the third language. Implementation of three language formula, the introduction of English and second language, is proposed to start from middle school level (class V onwards) and making it mandatory at high school. The objective of the three language policy was the development of regional/ modern Indian languages and the national language, and to connect India with the world through a global language, English. It is to be noted that three language formula has been adopted in all non-Hindi speaking regions except Tamilnadu, but Hindi speaking States ignored the proposal to learn [26]. The non-inclusive approach of the Hindi speaking States challenged the idea of national integration and developing mutual respect and understanding the diverse cultural spectrum of the country and the contemporary Indian history provides evidence to it. The

National Policy on Education (NPE), 1986 and modified in 1992 also addressed the issue of medium of instruction. The second education Commission – Ramamurti Committee in 1990 reviewed the NPE 1968 proposals and its status. Implementation of three language formula failed mainly due to the lack of teachers and pedagogy to handle modern Indian languages and English in the Hindi speaking regions. It has been proposed to set up institutions that provide support to the multilingual education system in India. Specified objectives of teaching different languages, levels of language proficiency to be achieved in respect of each language and specification of the class from and the duration for which the three languages will be taught are discussed in detail in the report. The Committee also reviewed the role of language in inclusive education especially the education of marginalised communities and groups in India.

The input document on NPE, 2016 also deliberated on language policy in a similar manner, without considering the larger challenges that the classrooms experience due to the inclusive education policies and the migration of people across the country. While emphasizing on MT education and Three Language Formula, NPE Report 2016 suggest flexibility in the concept of Three Language Formula, assuming that with the passage of time the States will respond to local aspirations and preferences voiced by parents who would like their children to possess language communication skills that can facilitate intrastate as well as global mobility. Keeping this in mind, the NPE 2016 (draft) recommends that as long as the States ensure that the MT or the regional language forms the basis of primary education up to Class V (a fact underscored by the earlier two policies) the choice of the second (at primary level) and third language (at secondary level) should be left to individual States to decide (MHRD, 2016) [27]. By doing this, the concept of social and national integration is slowly taken away from the classrooms and it involves systematic elimination of modern Indian languages including Hindi from the classrooms, English might be the only linguistic link in India in future. In other words, a major shift from the ideals of India that has been nurtured and respected all through.

While State training institutes used the broad framework provided by NCERT, the problem is, while imparting it gets diluted due to various infrastructural issues. Therefore, the need of the hour in the teacher education curriculum is to go with innovative techniques like content and language integrated learning methods. However, it is very important to incorporate modules that enhance the motivation of the teacher to update their understanding on the subject, as well as the language they handle in the classroom practices with in-service training and developing innovative techniques in their classroom practices, are very critical. While Language policy provides only the broad framework, it is the teachers who understand the challenges involved in practices so as to improve their proficiency and interest in the teaching of language as well as learning of language and content by the students. This process is an on-going area of research and development in education that the key stakeholders, the teachers, should spearhead.

However, as the influence of market forces started to dominate the labour market in a globalised world, English became the prominent language. And as and when the affordability of parents improved they chose English as the medium of education for their children. It is unlikely to have a reverse trend in the near future. Therefore, what India needs at present is to improve the language teaching maintaining the multilingual character of the society in general and classrooms in particular. Education/ language policies can only provide a larger framework, but the teachers and teacher trainers including the higher education in India should work in an integrated manner to address the issue of language proficiency of MT, and the international connection language primarily and provide avenues for those who interest in national language. If the unhealthy debate between MT and English as a medium of instruction continues, children especially the majority who depend on the government institutions will suffer in the process.

India is the first Asian country, and amongst the first in the world, where English Studies was established as an academic discipline in higher education (HE). Developments therein from the mid-nineteenth century onwards have often been significant for disciplinary pursuits elsewhere, especially as the study of English language and literature tried to accommodate diverse cultural contexts, and insofar as the postcolonial condition came to be regarded as a fulcrum for understanding past and current political dimensions of such study. Equally, debates about English Studies in HE provide a useful index of social developments in India after independence. Some developments and debates are presented with a view to assessing the current condition of English Studies in India and considers its future prospects, the discipline consists in whatever is regarded as the professional concern of HE English teachers and English departments. That could include any variety of English language teaching, linguistics.

References

1. Ghosh, Suresh Chandra. *History of Education in Modern India 1757-2012.* Orient Logman, New Delhi. 2013

2. Census of India 2001 cited in Agnihotri, (2007). (Agnihotri, R.K and Dewan, H.K (eds.). *Knowledge, Language, and Learning. Macmillan Publishers India.* New Delhi. 2010.) 79-88.

3. Singh, Shiv Sahay. "Language Survey Reveals Diversity." *The Hindu.* 22 July 2013. Retrieved 25 July 2017

4. Banerjee, Paula; Chaudhury, Sabyasachi Basu Ray; Das, Samir Kumar; Bishnu Adhikari (2005). *International Displacement in South Asia: The Relevance of the UN's Guiding Principles.* SAGE Publications. 145.

5. Gupta, Suman; Allen, Richard; Chattarji, Subarno and Chaudhuri, Supriya (2015). *Reconsidering English Studies in Indian Higher Education.* Routledge Research in Higher Education, Routledge, London.

6. [Benson, Carole. "The Quality Imperative: The Importance of Mother Tongue-Based Schooling for Educational Quality. *Background paper prepared for the Education for All Global Monitoring Report 2005.* UNESCO. 2004 Accessed http://unesdoc.unesco.org/images/0014/001466/146632e.pdf

7. Baker, P. *Jumping the Language Barrier: the "fifth skill", English Teaching Matters.* 2006.

8. http://www.melta.de/archive/meltanews/melta-news-2006-12.pdf

9. Cummins, J. *Language, Power, and Pedagogy. Bilingual Children in the Crossfire.* Clevedon, England: Multilingual Matters. 2000

10. Basu, B.D. History of Education in India – Under the Rule of the East India Company, Cosmo Publications, New Delhi, 1989.

11. Naik, J.P and Nurullah, Sayed; *A Student's History of Education in India* (1800-1973), Sixth Edition, Macmillian India Ltd, Madras, 1974.

22

Higher Education Statistics in India

Dr. Seema G. Hariramani

Abstract

Higher education means education beyond the level of post higher secondary education. Basically it refers to colleges and universities but in fact, higher educational institutions include professional schools in the field of Medicine, Law, Theology, Business, Music, and Art. It also includes other institutions like Teachers' Training Schools, Technological Institutions, moreover, institutions for the training of highly skilled specialists in the field of finance, economics, management, science, technology and culture of various types of higher levels are treated as Higher Educational Institutions. In short, it can be said that the courses offered after Higher Secondary School Education are a part of Higher Education.

Introduction

As per the report of MHRD, "Higher Education is defined as the education, which is obtained after completing 12 years of schooling or equivalent and is of the duration of at least nine months (full time) or after completing 10 years of schooling and is of the duration of at least 3 years. The education may be of the nature of General, Vocational, Professional or Technical education". India has a federal set-up and the Indian constitution places education as a concurrent responsibility of both the centre and state. While the centre coordinates and fixes standards in higher and technical education, school education is the responsibility of the state. Under the department of higher education, there are several regulatory bodies and research councils which are responsible for the higher education in India.

Regulatory Bodies

- University Grant Commission (UGC)
- All India Council for Technical Education (AICTE)
- Council of Architecture (COA)
- Research Councils:
- Indian Council of Historical Research (ICHR)
- Indian Council of Social Sciences Research (ICSSR)
- Indian Council of Philosophical Research (ICPR)
- National Council of Rural Institute (NCRI)
- A project of History of Indian Science Philosophy and Culture (PHISPC)

Background of Higher Education

The concept of higher education is not new. It has had long roots since ancient times. The concept had changed during the times of British Rule in India. The Education System during British Rule was designed to suit the Britishers. Since then there have been radical changes. In ancient times, Indian universities like Takshshila (Taxila), Nalanda were renowned institutions of higher learning, attracting students from the whole world. The universities of Vikramshila, Nalanda and Vallabhi were perhaps the most important universities of ancient India. During the colonial era, the rulers consciously did not use education for sustainable development. The first three universities were set up in 1857. Thirty years later the fourth was established and yet after another 29 years, the fifth and sixth university emerged in 1916. These universities were established on the pattern of the University of London, thus, they were basically affiliating, examining and regulating bodies. With the establishment of the British Raj in India, India got the Western Education. In the pre-independence period, there was very limited access to higher education. At that time the existing colleges engaged in teaching and learning were affiliated to these universities. For several decades, only colleges continued to offer the degree courses. It was only around the year 1920 that post-graduate teaching and research departments began to be established. From the year 1883 till the independence of India; the number of colleges and enrolment of students was found to be very low. The following table shows the picture of Higher Education in India from pre-independence to post-independence:

Table-1: Number of colleges and the intake of students

Year	1885	1928	1947	1961-62
Number of colleges	139	307	591	2,282
Enrolment of students	16,088	90,677	2,28,881	11,77,245

Source: http:/www.education.nic.in/cd50yrs/n/2j/3j/2j3j0201.htm p, 1 of 4 dated 31.08.2011.

HIGHER EDUCATION AFTER INDEPENDENCE

Inherited from the British Colonial Raj, India's modern educational system was in many ways similar to the British educational system. After Independence in 1947, Modern India began to focus on its Agriculture and Industries. It was after the second Five Year Plan, industrialisation strategy and a pool of talented human resources were required for fuelling economic development. Then the Focus shifted on building elite tertiary institutions along with strengthening the primary education. India's first Prime Minister, Shri Jawaharlal Nehru insisted on the foundation of elite technological training in engineering and management.

Since independence, the number of colleges, institutions, and universities has increased significantly. From 1950-51 to 2017-18, the number of universities has increased from 28 to 903, the number of colleges has grown from 578 to 39,050. During this period, enrolment in higher education has registered a steep increase from around 0.174 million to 36.642 million. The number of teachers has also gone up from around 24,000 in 1950-51 to 12,85,000 in 2017-18. It is evident from data that during this period, universities and colleges in the country have grown approximately 32 and 67.5 times respectively.

India occupies an important position in respect of Higher Education. India's position in the field of Higher Education system is 3rd after the United States and China. After independence, the number of Higher Educational Institutions and the number of students both have been increasing exponentially.

As of March 31, 2007, the country had 46 central universities, 614 state universities, 123 deemed to be universities (an institution other than a university, working at a very high standard in specific area of study, can be declared by the Government of India on the advice of University Grants Commission as an institution deemed to be university. Institutions deemed to be universities enjoy academic status and privileges of universities), and 101 institutions of national importance. Institutions of National Importance are established under the Institutes of Technology Act, 1961. Their main objective is to impart world-class training in engineering and technology, to conduct research in the relevant fields for the advancement of learning and dissemination of knowledge.

These institutes are also contributing significantly to education and research in basic sciences and humanities.

INDIAN HIGHER EDUCATION – STATISTICS (CENSUS 2011)

Literacy Rates (%)

- Male – 82.14
- Female – 65.46
- Both – 74.04%

Highest Literacy rate – Kerala: 93.91%

Lowest Literacy rate –Bihar: 63.82%

Universities and Colleges

- Universities in India – 523
- Total Colleges – 33, 023

Enrolment by Gender Higher Education

- Male – 99.26 Million (58.5%)
- Female – 70.49 Million (41.5%)
- Total – 16. 97 Million

Enrolment by Stages – Higher Education

- Undergraduate – 86.11%
- Postgraduate – 12.07%
- Diploma/ Certificate – 1.01%
- Research – 0.81%

Faculty-wise Enrolment

- Faculty of Arts – 36.39%

- Science – 18.42%
- Commerce/Management – 17.11%
- Other Professional Faculties – 28%
  - Engineering/Technology – 16.86%
  - Medical Courses – 3.85%
  - Agricultural and Veterinary Courses – 0.55%
  - Veterinary Science – 0.16%

(Source: UGC Annual Report 2010-11)

The growth trends in higher education may be seen in the table-2 given below:

Table – 2: All-India Growth of Institutions, Enrolment and Teaching Faculty at Higher Education Level, 1950-51 to 2017-18

Year	Universities*	Colleges	Stand Alone	Enrolment@ ('000)	Faculty@ ('000)
1950-	28	578	_	174	24
1960-	45	1,819	_	557	62
1970-71	93	3,227	_	1956	190
1980-	123	4,738	_	2752	244
1990-	184	5,748	_	4925	271
2000-01	266	11,146	_	8399	395
2010-	621	32974	11095	27500	766
2017-18	903	39050	10011	36642	1285

Notes: * Universities include Central, State and deemed to be universities as also institutions of national importance established both by the central and state governments.@ Annual Reports of the UGC, various years and MHRD Report AISHE till 2017-18.

The decadal growth in the number of higher education institutions was much higher in the 1950s and 1960s, primarily because of the relatively small number of such institutions. The planned expansion of higher education began after independence. In the 1970s and 1980s, the growth of these institutions was relatively slow; it picked up the momentum after 1990 onwards. This happened because of the realisation on the part of the Government who realised that development is not possible without education. It was realised that Higher education occupies a special position in the education system of any country. It influences all important segments of all the national activities. It provides manpower for many areas like production and operations planning, science and medicine, management and technological development. It heavily influences the future of the nation through ideas and innovations. Rigorous steps were taken by the Government of India that increased the demand for higher education and the participation of the private sector, particularly in technical and professional education. There has been a greater focus in recent years on reforming higher education, by adopting the American semester system model and the use of credits and letter grades.

Table-3: Type of Universities

Sr. No.	Type of University	Number of Universities
1	Central University	45
2	Central Open University	01
3	Institution of National Importance	101
4	State Public University	351
5	Institution Under State Legislature Act	05
6	State Open University	14
7	State Private University	262
8	State Private Open University	01
9	Deemed University – Government	33
10	Deemed University – Government Aided	10
11	Deemed University – Private	80
	Total	**903**

(Source: MHRD Report AISHE till 2017-18)

It is to be noted here that higher education institutions are absent in Dadra and Nagar Haveli and Lakshadweep.

Table-4: Top 10 Districts having Maximum Number of Colleges

Sr. No.	District Name	Number of Colleges
1	Bangalore (Urban)	893
2	Jaipur	558
3	Hyderabad	472
4	Pune	442
5	Rangareddy	343
6	Nagpur	337
7	Allahabad	332
8	Mumbai	313
9	Guntur	303
10	Bhopal	270

(Source: MHRD Report AISHE till 2017-18)

Table-5: Number of College per Lakh Population (18-23 Years) and Average Enrolment per College

State/ UTs	No. of Colleges	College per lakh population	Average Enrolment per College
Andaman & Nicobar Islands	7	14	928
Andhra Pradesh	2624	48	493
Arunachal Pradesh	30	19	810
Assam	512	14	983
Bihar	770	7	1686
Chandigarh	25	13	2052
Chhattisgarh	741	24	550
Dadra and Nagar Haveli	8	13	690
Daman and Diu	9	15	336

Delhi	178	8	1531
Goa	56	32	640
Gujarat	2196	30	519
Haryana	964	30	611
Himachal Pradesh	327	45	553
Jammu and Kashmir	297	23	720
Jharkhand	309	8	1786
Karnataka	3593	51	416
Kerala	1306	44	554
Lakshadweep	0	0	0
Madhya Pradesh	2124	24	646
Maharashtra	4314	33	678
Manipur	87	26	1156
Meghalaya	60	18	1087
Mizoram	30	23	612
Nagaland	66	27	484
Odisha	1042	23	685
Puducherry	76	47	569
Punjab	1053	33	526
Rajasthan	2957	33	526
Sikkim	17	22	737
Tamil Nadu	2472	35	919
Telangana	2045	51	558
Tripura	52	12	1156
Uttar Pradesh	6922	28	816
Uttarakhand	440	37	621
West Bengal	1341	12	1170
All India	39050	28	698

(Source: MHRD Report AISHE till 2017-18)

Table 6: State-wise Enrolment at various levels

State/ UTs	Ph.D			M.Phil			Post Graduate		
	Male	Female	Total	Male	Female	Total	Male	Female	Total
1	2	3	4	5	6	7	8	9	10
Andaman and Nicobar Islands	42	26	68	_	_	_	730	771	1501
Andhra Pradesh	4007	2282	6289	555	342	897	120479	98817	219296
Arunachal Pradesh	397	247	644	43	67	110	4333	3358	7691
Assam	2633	1704	4337	129	224	353	39907	48393	88299
Bihar	1902	954	2856	-	-	-	70534	54605	125139
Chandigarh	472	415	887	168	67	235	9572	14184	23756
Chhattisgarh	740	425	1165	149	150	299	29365	34811	64176
Dadra and Nagar Haveli	-	_	_	_	_	_	126	198	324
Daman & Diu	-	-	-	-	-	-	-	-	-
Delhi	7580	7132	14712	1243	1380	2623	76741	76782	153524
Goa	71	41	112				2718	3528	6245
Gujarat	3256	1995	5261	306	291	597	62301	76475	138776
Haryana	1632	1696	3328	170	270	440	47613	82880	130494
Himachal Pradesh	906	794	1700	92	167	259	15003	17158	32161
Jammu and Kashmir	1235	1261	2496	119	123	242	37274	34486	71760
Jharkhand	1158	640	1798	79	125	204	31720	37448	69168
Karnataka	9103	5087	14190	189	338	527	96827	112435	209262
Kerala	2256	3655	5911	280	630	910	39873	80106	119979

Lakshadweep	_	_	_	_	_	_	4	33	37
Madhya Pradesh	2427	1558	3985	299	466	765	95923	110113	206036
Maharashtra	5365	3841	9206	1176	1245	2421	214430	231353	445783
Manipur	332	314	646		7	7	4467	3668	8135
Meghalaya	466	513	979	29	57	86	4535	4907	9441
Mizoram	347	296	643	71	75	146	2206	1852	4058
Nagaland	222	201	423	11	23	34	3538	2564	6102
Odisha	1671	1311	2982	404	676	1080	37153	36080	73233
Puducherry	522	254	776	13	53	66	11169	9434	20603
Punjab	3054	3823	6877	389	513	902	39504	78006	117509
Rajasthan	3925	4054	7979	173	182	355	106170	107051	213221
Sikkim	77 53	53	130	9	17	26	3760	3863	7623
Tamil Nadu	16267	13511	29778	4424	12755	17179	175012	263874	438886
Telangana	3252	1632	4884	454	340	794	91044	103754	194799
Tripura	75	44	119	-	-	-	6474	4734	11209
Uttar Pradesh	10069	5339	15408	350	510	860	281755	355718	637473
Uttarakhand	2419	1489	3908	11	5	16	32756	38386	71142
West Bengal	4690	2255	6945	952	724	1676	96056	91414	187470
All India	92570	68842	161412	12287	21822	34109	1891071	2223239	4114310

(Source: MHRD Report AISHE till 2017-18

Table 7: State-wise Enrolment at various levels

State/ UTs	Under Graduate			P G Diploma			Diploma		
	Male	Female	Total	Male	Female	Total	Male	Female	Total
2	12	13	14	15	16	17	18	19	20
Andaman & Nicobar Islands	3967	4170	8137	47	28	75	429	273	702
Andhra Pradesh	711831	578322	1290153	1596	1018	2614	100939	66275	167214
Arunachal Pradesh	18731	17734	36465	84	54	138	1202	663	1865
Assam	278600	277744	556344	1735	1627	3362	10223	7709	17932
Bihar	763699	570070	1333769	1926	845	2771	30361	13988	44349
Chandigarh	40221	33673	73893	533	639	1172	1571	1398	2969
Chhattisgarh	185435	199088	384523	18658	18485	37143	51571	33441	85012
Dadra and Nagar Haveli	2134	2628	4762	-	-	-	586	98	684
Daman & Diu	573	1061	1634	-	-	-	1235	221	1456
Delhi	452469	394715	847184	4815	3517	8332	17797	13228	31025
Goa	15656	20031	35687	118	81	199	5971	841	6812
Gujarat	642272	487400	1129672	3485	3341	6826	103277	38690	141967
Haryana	361144	332361	693505	1846	1200	3046	45449	20955	66404
Himachal Pradesh	102122	118598	220720	930	1180	2110	7949	8227	16176
Jammu and Kashmir	127725	139845	267570	1254	899	2153	7875	3716	11591
Jharkhand	294358	284420	578778	2753	1250	4003	21240	8345	29585
Karnataka	733767	769158	1502925	3283	2929	6212	122296	77766	200062

Kerala	397008	479224	876232	1283	905	2188	36299	30897	67196
Lakshadweep	112	403	515	-	-	-	-	-	-
Madhya Pradesh	790447	656610	1447057	27998	31271	59269	98060	55851	153911
Maharashtra	1831960	1482951	3314911	11566	8164	19730	194153	121758	315911
Manipur	45381	48526	93907	127	54	181	964	810	1774
Meghalaya	34233	36156	70389	122	112	234	890	1482	2372
Mizoram	12348	10079	22427	20	12	32	613	1140	1753
Nagaland	17197	17467	34664	39	79	118	1041	1060	2101
Odisha	407713	385835	793548	2001	999	3000	93021	32578	125599
Puducherry	20536	25219	45756	63	58	121	3121	1355	4476
Punjab	345399	343378	688777	3306	4125	7431	81647	45198	126845
Rajasthan	836893	732447	1569340	7771	3782	11553	86431	22570	109001
Sikkim	8697	10304	19002	16	18	34	906	966	1872
Tamil Nadu	1189690	1302087	2491777	9594	8245	17839	321101	66605	387706
Telangana	555992	523346	1079338	2786	1913	4699	78198	49810	128008
Tripura	37026	32829	69856	143	104	247	5851	3293	9144
Uttar Pradesh	2785330	2661439	5446769	11691	7930	19621	178531	82016	260547
Uttarakhand	159415	160459	319874	1285	920	2205	25849	9529	35378
West Bengal	842222	824266	1666488	3979	2626	6605	101570	46965	148535
All India	15052304	13964046	29016349	126853	108410	235263	1838217	869717	2707934

(Source: MHRD Report AISHE till 2017-18)

Table-8: State-wise Enrolment at various levels

State/ UTs	Certificate			Integrated			Grand Total		
	Male	Female	Total	Male	Female	Total	Male	Female	Total
2	21	22	23	24	25	26	27	28	29
Andaman and Nicobar Islands	-	-	-	26	91	117	5241	5359	10600
Andhra Pradesh	258	529	787	7132	2900	10032	946798	750484	1697282
Arunachal Pradesh	246	79	325	177	49	226	25213	22251	47464
Assam	1082	1353	2435	2630	2651	5281	336939	341405	678344
Bihar	2336	1075	3411	1512	788	2300	872270	642325	1514595
Chandigarh	464	262	726	1058	1133	2191	54059	51771	105829
Chhattisgarh	211	313	524	1014	1005	2019	28714	287718	574861
Dadra and Nagar Haveli	-	-	-	4	2	6	2850	2926	5776
Daman & Diu	-	-	-	-	-	-	1808	1282	3090
Delhi	2317	1544	3861	2126	1019	3145	565089	499317	1064406
Goa	12	-	12	198	376	574	24743	24898	49641
Gujarat	5599	10162	15761	7115	7290	14405	827611	625644	1453255
Haryana	1241	1833	3074	8294	4858	13152	467389	446054	913443
Himachal Pradesh	572	851	1423	762	397	1159	128336	147372	275708

Jammu and Kashmir	8	3	11	1532	1875	3407	177022	1822208	359230
Jharkhand	471	1070	1541	2316	1329	3645	354095	334627	688722
Karnataka	2049	1637	3686	3879	3112	6991	971393	972463	1943856
Kerala	926	5163	6089	2252	2159	4411	480178	602739	1082917
Lakshadweep	-	-	-	-	-	-	116	436	552
Madhya Pradesh	2147	2332	4479	6118	3859	9977	1023418	862060	1885479
Maharashtra	6352	5499	11851	6076	5868	11944	2271078	1860679	4131757
Manipur	-	30	30	-	-	-	51271	53409	104680
Meghalaya	113	141	254	40	27	67	40428	43394	83822
Mizoram	190	143	333	66	37	103	15861	13634	29495
Nagaland	55	45	100	15	-	15	22118	21439	43557
Odisha	4153	5594	9747	3459	3128	6587	549575	466202	1015777
Puducherry	14	12	26	656	581	1237	36094	36967	73061
Punjab	391	893	1284	5416	4495	9911	479106	480430	959536
Rajasthan	5667	6016	11683	7480	5592	13072	1054511	881693	1936204
Sikkim	6	14	20	117	177	294	13588	15413	29000
Tamil Nadu	13852	26641	40493	9375	7912	17287	1739315	1701630	3440945
Telangana	661	1174	1835	2945	2005	4950	735333	683974	1419307
Tripura	114	108	222	563	322	885	50247	41435	91681

Uttar Pradesh	20258	22560	42818	20331	11549	31880	3308314	3147061	6455375
Uttarakhand	235	99	334	2638	1655	4293	224608	212543	437150
West Bengal	4962	3086	8048	7089	3125	10214	1061520	974461	2035981
All India	76962	100261	177223	114411	81366	195777	19204675	17437703	36642378

(Source: MHRD Report AISHE till 2017-18)

FACT SHEET OF HIGHER EDUCATION STATISTICS OF INDIA 2017-18 (SOURCE MHRD – GOI – AISHE REPORT 2017-18)

- Out of 903 Universities above, 343 Universities are managed privately and more than 78% of colleges are run without any aid from central or state government.
- 75.47% of the Stand Alone Institutions are mainly run by the Private sector.
- 357 Universities are in rural areas.
- 15 Universities are exclusively for women, state of Rajasthan leading with 4 such Universities.
- There are 110 Universities which offer education through Dual mode; regular mode as well as distance mode also. State of Tamil Nadu leads with 16 such Universities followed by Andhra Pradesh and Karnataka.
- There are 285 affiliating Universities with 39,050 colleges. Among them, 15 such Universities have 500 or more colleges.
- There are 10 Language Universities, 13 Sanskrit Universities, 22 Law Universities, 58 Medical Universities, 70 Agriculture & Allied Universities, 126 Technical Universities, 500 General Universities, and rest 83 Universities are of other Categories.
- Chhatrapati Sahuji Maharaj Kanpur University of Kanpur has the maximum number of colleges i.e. 931.
- The Population under the age group of 18 to 23 Years, as per the AISHE DATA OF MHRD in the year 2017-

18 is 14,18,29,528 which was 14,03,17,069 during the year 2010-11.

- Out of the total enrolment, 79.19% students are enrolled for undergraduate courses, 11.23% are enrolled for postgraduate courses, 7.39% students enrolled for Diploma courses, 0.48% for Certificate Courses and 0.53% for PG Diploma courses.
- As far as State-wise enrolment is concerned Maharashtra tops followed by Tamilnadu and Delhi.
- Average Enrolment per college in India during 2010-11was 700; which is more or less same during the year 2017-18 i.e. 698.
- College per lakh population during 2010-11was 23; which is 28 during the year 2017-18.
- Out of the total colleges, only 3.6% Colleges run the Ph.D. programme and 36.7% Colleges run Post Graduate Programmes.
- 33.75% of Colleges run the only a single programme, out of which 83% are privately managed. Among these privately managed colleges, 55.1% of colleges run B.Ed. Courses only.
- 78% of Colleges are privately managed i.e. without any aid from central or state government. Maximum of them fall in the states of Andhra Pradesh, Telangana, and Tamil Nadu.
- 18.5% of the Colleges in India are having enrolment less than 100 students and only 3.6% of Colleges have enrolment more than 3000 students during the year 2017-18.

- Total enrolment in higher education has been estimated to be 36.6 million students with 19.2 million boys and 17.4 million girls. Girls constitute 47.6% of the total enrolment of the students.
- Gross Enrolment Ratio (GER) in Higher which is calculated for 18-23 years of age group education in India is 25.8%. GER for the male population is 26.3% and for females, it is 25.4%. For Scheduled Castes, it is 21.8% and for Scheduled Tribes, it is 15.9% as compared to the national GER of 25.8%.
- Of the total enrolment of students; distance mode constitutes 11%, of which 41.9% are female students.
- Of the total enrolment of students, less than 0.5% of students are enrolled for the Ph.D. program. The maximum Ph.D. enrolments are from Science stream followed by Engineering and Technology.
- At Undergraduate level the highest number (36.4%) of students are enrolled in Arts/Humanities/Social Sciences courses followed by Science (17.1%), Engineering & Technology (14.1%) and Commerce (14.1%). Maximum number of Students is enrolled in the B.A. programme followed by B.Sc. and B.Com. Programmes.
- At Post, Graduate level maximum students are enrolled for M.A. followed by M.Sc. and M.B.A.
- Out of nearly 188 programs, 81.2% of the total students enrolled in higher education; enrol themselves in the ten programs only.
- Only Medical Science stream showed a different picture with a higher number of female students, wherein out

of total 10.99 lakh students, female students are 6.7 lakh. In all other courses and streams, male students overpowered the female students.

- Maximum students who enrol for Ph.D. after doing PG courses are for Agriculture and Allied (21.1%), followed by Engineering and Technology courses (20.07%), Science (6.9%), Medical science (4.9%) and Social Science (2.45%).
- The total number of foreign students enrolled in higher education during the year 2017-18 is 46,144. These foreign students come from 166 different countries from across the globe. The top 10 countries constitute 63.4% of the total foreign students enrolled. The highest share of foreign students come from the neighbouring countries of which Nepal is 24.9% of the total, followed by, Afghanistan (9.5%), Sudan (4.8%), Bhutan constitutes (4.3%) and Nigeria (4.0%).
- The total number of teachers as per the AISHE data 2017-18 are 12,84,755, out of which about 58.0% are male teachers and 42.0% are female teachers. At all-India level, there are merely 72 female teachers per 100 male teachers. Pupil-Teacher Ratio (PTR) in Universities and Colleges is 30 if regular mode enrolment is considered whereas PTR for Universities and its Constituent Units is 20 for regular mode.
- The share of female students is lowest in Institutions of National Importance followed by State Private Open Universities and Deemed University (Government).
- Fourteen states and union territories have much higher levels of access to higher education compared to the national average (28) in terms of the number of

institutions available per 1,00,000 population in the age group 18-23 in 2017-18. While Telangana and Karnataka have around 51 and Bihar has the lowest level of access with only around 7 institutions per 100,000 population in 2017-18 (MHRD 2017-18).

CONCLUSION

It has been seen the sea change in higher education post-independence. Indian Government realised during the second five-year plan after independence that without education development of any country is not possible. Since then the Government took initiatives to increase the level of higher education in India but due to certain reasons, it could not achieve much. It is after 1990 only; rigorous steps have been taken by the Government. Many schemes, programs, and initiatives have been taken and launched to increase the numbers and quality of higher education. Various schemes like "Udaan" for girl students, launching of a mission Pandit Madan Mohan Malviya, Unnat Bharat Abhiyan, Rashtriya Avishkar Abhiyan, Global Initiative of Academic Networks (GIAN), National Mission in Education through Information & Communication Technology (NMEICT), National Mission on Teachers & Teaching (NMTT), Rashtriya Uchcha Shiksha Abhiyan (RUSA), National Education Policy (1986-92), Sarv Shiksha Abhiyaan, National Institute Ranking Framework (NIRF), Higher Education Statistics and Public Information System, Digital India and many more. Many private institutions have been given permission to open up the schools, colleges or Universities. Several open and distance education programs are started. Several types of scholarship schemes are offered to increase the Gross Enrolment Rate. Several awards and rewards systems have been introduced. Different types of financial aids are given to students for higher education. Today India is at the 3rd position as far as the higher education system is concerned. Days are not far away when India will top the world.

REFERENCES

Information retrieved from official websites:

- http://www2.deloitte.com/content/dam/Deloitte/in/Documents/IMO/in-imo-annual- status-of-higher-education-2014-noexp.pdf
- aishe.nic.in/aishe/viewDocument.action?documentId=204
- Choudhary, Sujit Kumar. "Higher Education in India: a Socio-Historical Journey from Ancient Period to 2006-07." The Journal of Educational Enquiry 8.1 (2009).
- https://data.gov.in/dataset-group-name/higher-education-statistics
- https://www.dreducation.com/.../indian-universities-colleges-latest-data-statistics-heera
- Education, Deloitte. "Indian Higher Education Sector: Opportunities Aplenty, Growth Unlimited." New Delhi (2012).
- GoI, M. H. R. D. "National Policy on Education 2016." Report of the Committee for Evolution of the New Education Policy. New Delhi: Ministry of Human Resource Development (MHRD) (2016).
- http://gujarat-education.gov.in/education/alluniversity.htm http://www.highereducationinindia.com/universities
- http://www.indiaonlinepages.com/population/india-current-population.html

- Maity, Amit Kumar, and Sanglap Maity. "Evolution of higher education in India." Evolution 1.10 (2016).
- http://www.mhrd.gov.in
- http://mhrd.gov.in/sites/upload_files/mhrd/files/statistics /ESAG-2018.pdf
- http://mhrd.gov.in/statist
- MHRD, Department of Higher Education, 2011 Planning, Monitoring and Statistic Bureau Pilot Report All India Survey Higher Education.
- www.mospi.gov.in/statistical-year-book-india/2016/198
- www.mospi.gov.in/sites/default/files/publication_reports/s arvekshna_102.pdf
- https://www.ojs.unisa.edu.au/index.php/EDEQ/article/vi ew/484
- PWC report on "India-Higher education system: Opportunities for Private Participation, 2012.
- Sharma, Sahil, and Purnendu Sharma. "Indian Higher Education System: Challenges And Suggestions." Electronic Journal for Inclusive Education 3.4 (2015): 6.
- shodhganga.inflibnet.ac.in/bitstream/10603/66829/10/10_ chapter%203.pdf
- https://www.ugc.ac.in/page/Annual-Report.aspx
- https://www.ugc.ac.in/pdfnews/9764381_Complete-AR-2016-17-English.pdf

23

Education 4.0: Need for Innovation in Higher Education

Dr. Renji George Amballoor

Abstract

The higher education sector is slowly inching towards Education 4.0. Disruptive technologies are challenging the traditional educational system. To catch up with the recipe of the gig economy and for tapping our demographic dividend, we need to usher in an innovation revolution. The mushrooming bottlenecks and challenges in the system need to be addressed for making the innovation ecosystem sustainable. The paper identifies the stakeholder preparedness and collaboration for the higher education sector to take off into the era of Education 4.0.

Keywords: Education 4.0, Innovation, Higher Education, Disruptive Technology, Demographic Dividend

Introduction

The 21st century higher education sector in India has witnessed both quantitative and qualitative expansion. The neo-liberal policies have resulted in the entry of the private sector in higher education.

India is one of the fastest growing economies in the world. There is a strong correlation between economic growth and growth in the tertiary enrolment ratio even in economies with low levels of per-capita gross domestic product (Everitt, 2014). In its forward march, the economy needs to create higher education opportunities for first-time learners. This assumes significance with 65% of the current population below 35 years of age (Census, 2011). The demographic sweet spot reinforces the urgent need for optimizing this dividend. Skilling the youth for making them industry ready and employable requires a big push of innovation in higher education.

NEED FOR INNOVATION

We are living in an incredible period where the echoes of Education 4.0 are becoming louder and clear. Under the new system, education needs to have a profile which includes personalised learning to suit the competency of students, flexible schedules, multiple entries and exit points, lifelong learning, knowledge enhancement at one's own pace (EY, 2017), etc. Social media, machine learning, analytics, mobile, virtual reality, cloud computing, etc. have become the part and parcel of the new education system. The ripples of disruptive innovation (Christensen, 1997) can be also felt with the mushrooming of Massive Open Online Course (MOOC), emergence of new pedagogies, increased visibility of concepts like course and programme outcome, competency mapping, increased acceptance of work integrated learning (WIL), collaborative and multidisciplinary research, campus start-ups, incubation and accelerators, eagerness to earn top slots at NIRF and QS ranking, etc. In order to assimilate and win over the disruptive innovation, the stakeholders including the government, academic leadership, management, teachers, students, and society needs awareness building to understand their role, roadmap and challenges. This can be a resounding success only if an ecosystem can be created for enhancing the ease of introducing the innovation index in higher education.

Indian institutions and universities habitually fail to secure a large number of ranks and positions within the elite 200 clubs of best institutions. According to the Quacquarelli Symonds (QS) World University Rankings-2019, only IIT Mumbai featured in the 200 clubs out of 1000 institutions ranked by the agency (Research Matters, 2018). Similarly, THE World University Ranking-2018 did not have any institutions from India in its first 200 ranks (Business Standard, 2018).

The luxury to ignore the disruptive and incredible innovation bandwagon of Education 4.0 is over. The higher education stakeholders need to discuss and debate about the evolving technology. The new phenomena need to be understood, clarified through FAQ's, adapted and optimally utilised in order to extract the maximum benefit. There are going to be challenged in its implementation. The runway of higher education needs to clear off the obstacles for its technological take-off.

FACING THE CHALLENGES

Many times, innovation is stunted in higher education due to the absence of academic leadership both at the college and university level. The present system of selecting the academic leadership through the academic performance indicators (API) mechanism is biased inappropriately in favour of publications and research. The real world experiences show that there is no positive correlation between publication/research quotient and leadership acumen. Lack of managerial expose is a great bane in bringing innovation to higher education. Once the leadership lacks the stamina for innovation, the vicious circle spreads to teachers and to students, eventually, status quo becomes the guiding principle of the institution. This, in turn, will fasten the roller coaster drive into doom. On the other hand, leadership should have exposure to management strategies for constraint optimisation. The leadership needs vision and positive attitude towards accepting, managing and reviewing change and innovation.

Our affiliation system is another stumbling block for skyrocketing innovations on our campuses. The affiliation process looks only at the fulfilment of the age-old standards and not the innovative practices of the institutions. It fails to incorporate personalised and customised learning with flexible schedules. For instance, there are examples of young institutions which religiously provide internship opportunities beyond their syllabi that fails to have any impact during the affiliation process.

When we examine institutions with high NAAC score / NIRF ranking, it is very clear that these institutions scrupulously examine the evaluation criteria, find the gaps and put in efforts to bridge the gap through innovative measures. The lack of innovative ecosystem prevents out of box thinking resulting in low scores/ ranks. Our institutions and the academic leadership can aim at quality enhancement measures and in this process, higher score/rank can be a by-product.

The ease of adapting and incorporating technological changes among the teaching fraternity has to be improved. This cannot be achieved overnight through an office order or circular. The transition from chalk and board to virtual boards has to be slow and sustainable. Before embarking on such a venture, the teaching community has to be taken into confidence about the limitations of missing the bus. Their suspicions and doubts have to be bowled out with innovative strategies. Elaborate capacity building measures on a continuous basis need to be chalked out. Once the teachers get comfortable with technology, the classroom situation can be more interesting and interactive. Numerous analytical tools coupled with data science can be used to evaluate a course and learning outcomes. The datasets so generated have tremendous value as it reflects the real world situation. When the teacher can wear different thinking hats, the features of the technology can be extracted and used more optimally.

The role of the teacher in the new paradigm will be that of a facilitator and not merely that of an instructor. The teachers have to be enlightened with the happenings around them and the craze to be living long learner has to be infused in them. MOOC's provide an ecosystem for knowledge enhancement.

A major concern among industry stalwarts and students is that the existing curriculums are obsolete. Teacher-industry linkages have to be incorporated to make the curriculum relevant again. Teachers should be encouraged to take up industrial internships to understand the latest happening in the industry and economy. Collaborative research and partnerships can provide exposure for inventions and innovations.

The social media engrossed student communes have to be made innovation ready. Using technology as a catalyst, the creativity and scientific temper of the students have to be ignited. The student should be able to choose courses based on outcomes and competency quotient. Every higher education institutions have to incorporate work integrated learning (WIL) into their curriculum and prepare the students for the same. The nature of classroom learning has to undergo a drastic change to ensure that the students do not come to class merely for fulfilling the 75% attendance criteria.

The threshold levels of soft skill know-how, critical thinking expertise, problem-solving proficiency etc. have to be advanced. This cannot be achieved by conventional strategies. Innovative mechanisms and processes need to be put in place for creating freshly minted students tangent with the new technological ideologies. Students need to be mentored, incubated and accelerated for inducing start-up culture in our campuses. Student-centric learning, learning by doing, application-oriented question paper, studying beyond textbook, exchange programmes, etc. have to be incorporated. Like some progressive western universities, at the end of the course, students can be challenged to put into practice what they have learned for the last few years.

The choice-based credit system (CBCS) being implemented in undergraduate colleges should become more realistic. Students need to be encouraged to study courses across their disciplines, teachers to be magnanimous to respect the choice of students and the college administration liberal to offer as many courses as possible. At many institutions, in the name of workload, space and manpower constraints, only selective choices are available to students.

In the present gig economy, permanent full-time employment is a mirage. Gig economy is characterised by short term, project-based or contract employment. Students need to be trained to be a part of the new workforce. They need to exhibit a high level of positive attitude, motivation, creativity, cognitive skills, etc. The traditional approach to education may not serve the purpose, hence the need for an innovative perspective.

The employment in the organised sector is not keeping pace with the long labour market queue. The conventional education has created an intimate love for white and blue collar jobs. In the present globalised economy, it is difficult to even for *Paul the Octopus* to identify such jobs due to unimpressive economic growth rates, trade war, *Trumponomics*, politically dictated economic reforms, etc. The demographic dividend can be tapped by persuading students into start-ups. The start-up ecosystem cannot emerge from thin air into our non-professional degree colleges. We require teachers who can arrange a festival of ideas for students to think about start-ups and who can implant the idea that failure is a stepping stone to success. The teacher has to find time beyond the University specified curriculum to nurse and mentor their ideas into start-ups. Local industry captains can be roped into academic institutions for providing sector-specific mentoring as a part of the corporate social responsibility.

Involving the industry in specific curriculum development and its delivery will be path-breaking innovation in our higher education. The industry can formulate and run courses along with educational institutions to ensure that the final output has the required competency, soft skills, and exposure. For example, *Udacity*, the online educational platform for its self-driving car engineering nano-degree assigned its students with industry mentors (Jisc, 2018). The real challenge is to convince the teachers to accept the change and not to consider it as an encroachment on their domain area.

In the process of reaching the goal of Education 4.0, the higher education institutions have to initiate cutting edge collaborative cross-country multi-disciplinary research. Such research endeavours require visionary leadership and proactive teachers who can be compatible with cross-cultural dynamics. Innovative funding mechanisms like crowd source, venture capital, philanthropy, etc. have to be explored for funding research of huge magnitude. All these should matcrialise into more patents from the undergraduate education system

The emotional competency of the undergraduates needs to be scaled up to reduce the proportion of depression, anxiety, and suicide among them. The present education system gives too much emphasis on the cognitive domain at the cost of emotional well-being. The innovation induced Education 4.0 will be punctured if emotional calibre and happiness quotient of students are not given their due importance. The challenge for the educational sector is to build into curriculum standards like sense of purpose, ethical values, empathy, creativity, emotional intelligence, people management, etc.

With the emerging trends, every institution can have dedicated workstation to fiddle with technology and equipment's, manage dissection and repairs of various devices, gymnastics with ideation tools, developing *jugaad* techniques, assembling and reengineering experiments, etc. Such activities will instil confidence in the students to inflate their survival footprint in the real world dynamics.

The space craft of education has to reach the destination at the earliest. Only an innovative leadership can leapfrog the institutions into greater accomplishments. With the growth of digital spectrum, only innovative curriculum can attract and retain students from far and wide. The teaching community has to be baptised into the emerging technology. The stakeholders have to put in a joint effort for reaching the goal of Education 4.0.

REFERENCES

1. Christensen C M. (1977). *The Innovator's Dilemma: When New Technologies Cause Great Firm to Fall.* Boston; Harvard Business School Press.

2. Everitt, Richard. (2014). *Understanding India: The Future of Higher Education and Opportunities for International Cooperation* retrieved from https://www.british council.org/ sites/default/files /understand ingindia _ report.pdf on 5th October, 2018.

3. *Census of India.* (2011). Age Structure. Retrieved from www.censusindia. gov. in on 8th November, 2017.

4. https://researchmatters.in/news/qs-world-university-rankings-2019 announced-feature-24-indian-universities-among-top-1000-world retrieved on 29th October, 2018

5. https://www.business-standard.com/article/current-affairs/the-world-university-rankings-2018-no-indian-institute-in-top-200-117090501136_1.html retrieved on 1st November, 2018.

6. Earnest Young (EY). (2017). *Leapfrogging to Education 4.0*: Students at the Core retrieved from https://www.ey.com/Publication/vwLUAssets /ey-leap-forgging/ $File/ey-lea -forgging.pdf on 6th January, 2018.

7. https://www.jisc.ac.uk/blog/the-potential-of-education-4-is-huge-the-uk-must-take-the-lead-now- retrieved on 12th September, 2018/

8. Al-Atabi, Mushtak. (2018). *Education 4.0:* A New Paradigm of Innovation https:// www.youtube.co /watch?v=afzzsV2bKZI retrieved on 3th October,2018.

Contributors

1. **Dr. Gurudutta P. Japee**, Associate Professor, S.D. School of Commerce, Gujarat University.
2. **Dr. Preeti Oza**, Department of English, St. Andrew's College, University of Mumbai.
3. **Dr. Rupal S. Patel**, Associate Professor, Department of English, Umiya Arts and Commerce College for Girls, Ahmedabad.
4. **Dr. Manish B. Raval**, Assistant Professor, SDRB Mahila Home Science, Lt. M.J. Kundaliya English Medium Mahila Commerce College, Rajkot.
5. **Dr. Ashish B. Gorvadiya**, Supervisor Instructor (Employability Skills) Industrial Training Institute, Rajkot.
6. **Dr. Swati Saxena**, Shri Chimanbhai Patel Institute of Management & Research, Ahmedabad.
7. **Dr. Vani Ramesh**, Certified CSR Professional, Bangalore.
8. **Dr. Vishal C. Jaunky**, Certified CSR Professional, Bangalore.
9. **Dr. Lila Simon**, HoD (Department of Management), The Bhopal School of Social Science, Bhopal.
10. **Dr. Sai Madhavi D.**, Associate Professor, CSE Department, Rao Bahadur Y Mahabaleswarappa Engg. College, Ballari, Karnataka.

11. **Dr. Mala Sharma**, Principal, Government Arts College, Mandal, Ahmedabad.
12. **Dr. Krupa B. Bhatt**, Faculty of Commerce (SMPIC), GLS University, Ahmedabad.
13. **Dr. Rushiraj Upadhyay**, Assistant Professor, Department of Sociology, Bhakt Kavi Narsinh Mehta University, Junagadh.
14. **Dr. Kamal. H. Kharecha**, Associate Professor, Department of Accountancy, Tolani Commerce College, Adipur.
15. **Dr. Satyajeet S. Deshpande**, Associate Professor, L.J. Institute of Commerce, Ahmedabad.
16. **Dr. S.S.Sodha**, Associate Professor, S.D. School of Commerce, Gujarat University.
17. **Dr. Nimesh P. Bhojak**, Assistant Professor, Department of Hospital Management, Hemchandracharya North Gujarat University, Patan.
18. **Gargi Gohil**, Associate Professor, Umiya Arts College, Ahmedabad.
19. Dr. **Seema G. Hariramani**, Assistant Professor, Chimanbhai Patel Institute of Business Administration, Ahmedabad.
20. **Dr. Renji George Amballoor**, Deputy Director, Department of Higher Education, Goa.

Index

O

P

Q

R

S

T

U

V

W